The MyPyramid for Kids

Gone are the days of the food pyramid you came to know and love, but the new pyramid for kids is a fantastic resource, as it presents general guidelines for 2- to 8-year-olds. You can even get info tailored to your child's needs on www.MyPyramid.gov. **Note:** The food pyramid doesn't include guidelines for 0- to 2-year-olds because their needs change so much. See the corresponding chapters in this book for the specifics on those tiny tots.

Grains	Vegetables	Fruits	Milk	Meat & Beans
Eat 6 oz. every day	Eat 2½ cups every day	Eat 1½ cups every day	Get 2 cups every day	Eat 5 oz. every day

Foods to Avoid During Baby's First Year

When it comes to your developing child, all foods aren't created equal. Be sure to steer clear of these common problem foods (which often cause serious allergic and intolerance reactions) during the first year of your baby's life!

- Citrus fruit
- Cow's milk and milk products
- Eggs
- Honey
- Nuts
- Shellfish
- Strawberries
- Wheat

Helpful Foods for Common Ailments

When your child is sick, you should follow the advice of your doctor (of course). In addition to any medicine the doctor may prescribe, consider serving the following foods when your child (over age 1) isn't feeling well.

- **For a cold:** Chicken soup (the old standby)
- **For a fever:** Oatmeal and juices
- **For a sore throat:** Flavored gelatin and fruit smoothies
- **For a stomachache:** Bananas, rice, apples, and toast (dry), also known as the B.R.A.T. diet

For Dummies: Bestselling Book Series for Beginners

Staple Foods to Have on Hand

When you have a young child, grocery shopping isn't the easiest task. With that in mind, we've compiled a list of perishable and nonperishable foods you'll want to have on hand, so you can take care of the essentials in one fell swoop. **Warning:** Don't serve the foods with stars to kids under age 1. For two stars, wait until age 2.

Nonperishable foods:

- ❑ Broth, reduced sodium, chicken or beef
- ❑ Cheerios
- ❑ Cinnamon
- ❑ Flour, all purpose and whole wheat
- ❑ Fruit, dried (chewy fruits are best, such as dried apricots)
- ❑ Honey*
- ❑ Jelly or jam, low sugar
- ❑ Maple syrup
- ❑ Mustard, dry ground
- ❑ Nonstick cooking spray
- ❑ Nuts, assorted* (For peanuts, wait until age 2.)
- ❑ Oil, olive and vegetable
- ❑ Pasta, assorted
- ❑ Peanut butter**
- ❑ Pepper
- ❑ Pizza sauce
- ❑ Raisins
- ❑ Rice cakes
- ❑ Rice, brown
- ❑ Rolled oats
- ❑ Salt
- ❑ Sunflower seeds

Perishable foods:

- ❑ American cheese, slices
- ❑ Bread, whole wheat
- ❑ Butter, not margarine
- ❑ Cheddar and mozzarella cheese, shredded
- ❑ Eggs*
- ❑ English muffins
- ❑ Fruits, assorted and fresh
  - ❑ Apples
  - ❑ Avocados
  - ❑ Bananas
  - ❑ Pears
  - ❑ Strawberries*
  - ❑ Tomatoes
- ❑ Ketchup
- ❑ Mayonnaise, full fat
- ❑ Milk, whole*
- ❑ Mozzarella cheese sticks (string cheese)
- ❑ Parmesan cheese, grated
- ❑ Soy sauce
- ❑ Tortillas, wheat or flour
- ❑ Vegetables, assorted and fresh
  - ❑ Broccoli
  - ❑ Carrots
  - ❑ Lettuce
  - ❑ Squash
- ❑ Yogurt, full fat and varied flavors

For Dummies: Bestselling Book Series for Beginners

Baby & Toddler Meals

FOR

DUMMIES®

Baby & Toddler Meals

FOR

DUMMIES®

by Dawn Simmons and Curt Simmons, with Sallie Warren, MS, RD, LD

WILEY

Wiley Publishing, Inc.

Baby & Toddler Meals For Dummies®

Published by
Wiley Publishing, Inc.
111 River St.
Hoboken, NJ 07030-5774
www.wiley.com

For general information on our other products and services, please contact our Customer Care Department within the U.S. at 800-762-2974, outside the U.S. at 317-572-3993, or fax 317-572-4002.

For technical support, please visit www.wiley.com/techsupport.

Wiley also publishes its books in a variety of electronic formats. Some content that appears in print may not be available in electronic books.

Library of Congress Control Number: 2006920626

ISBN-13: 978-0-471-77384-9

ISBN-10: 0-471-77384-0

Manufactured in the United States of America

10 9 8 7 6 5 4 3 2 1

1O/QX/QU/QW/IN

WILEY

About the Authors

Dawn Simmons is a cooking instructor and caterer. The co-author of *Cooking For Crowds For Dummies* (Wiley), Dawn enjoys cooking for her children, family, and friends, and she's always on the lookout for a new recipe! You can contact Dawn at dawnfsimmons@hotmail.com.

Curt Simmons is a technology trainer and author of more than 50 general computing and networking books. Curt is the co-author of *Cooking For Crowds For Dummies* (Wiley), and he enjoys gardening and eating Dawn's cooking. You can contact Curt at curt_simmons@hotmail.com.

Sallie Warren, MS has been a Registered and Licensed Dietician for the past 20 years and is currently a consultant dietician for hospitals, assisted living centers, and long-term-care facilities. Sallie's work enables her to work with all ages of people concerning their nutritional needs, including new mothers, babies, and children.

Dedication

This book is for all new moms and dads and especially for Brad and Marty Bugg and their son, Seth.

Authors' Acknowledgments

We would like to thank Tracy Boggier for the idea and the green light to write this book. We owe a debt of gratitude to our editor, Kristin DeMint, who worked tirelessly to make this book better. We're also grateful to our technical editor, Sheri Ouellette, RD, and our recipe tester, Emily Nolan, who both checked all the details. Also thanks to Carrie Burchfield, our copy editor, for crossing all our *t*'s and dotting all our *i*'s. Finally, thanks to our agent, Margot Hutchison, for her support.

Publisher's Acknowledgments

We're proud of this book; please send us your comments through our Dummies online registration form located at www.dummies.com/register/.

Some of the people who helped bring this book to market include the following:

Acquisitions, Editorial, and Media Development

Project Editor: Kristin DeMint

Acquisitions Editor: Tracy Boggier

Copy Editor: Carrie A. Burchfield

Editorial Program Coordinator: Hanna K. Scott

Technical Editor: Sheri Ouellette, RD

Recipe Tester: Emily Nolan

Senior Editorial Manager: Jennifer Ehrlich

Editorial Assistant: Erin Calligan

Cover Photo: © T. J. Hine Photography

Cartoons: Rich Tennant
   (www.the5thwave.com)

Composition Services

Project Coordinator: Adrienne Martinez

Layout and Graphics: Lauren Goddard, Joyce Haughey, Stephanie D. Jumper, Julie Trippetti

Special Art: Elizabeth Kurtzman; Kathryn Born, M.A.

Photographer: © T. J. Hine Photography

Food Stylist: Lisa Bishop

Proofreaders: Christine Pingleton, Techbooks

Indexer: Techbooks

Publishing and Editorial for Consumer Dummies

Diane Graves Steele, Vice President and Publisher, Consumer Dummies

Joyce Pepple, Acquisitions Director, Consumer Dummies

Kristin A. Cocks, Product Development Director, Consumer Dummies

Michael Spring, Vice President and Publisher, Travel

Kelly Regan, Editorial Director, Travel

Publishing for Technology Dummies

Andy Cummings, Vice President and Publisher, Dummies Technology/General User

Composition Services

Gerry Fahey, Vice President of Production Services

Debbie Stailey, Director of Composition Services

Contents at a Glance

Recipes at a Glance

Foods for 2-Year-Olds

Foods for 3- to 5-Year-Olds

Foods to Get Your Child Involved

Foods for the Whole Family

Foods Fit for the Allergic and Intolerant

Foods to Entice a Picky Eater

Foods for When You're Away from Home

Table of Contents

Introduction

. . . .

As a parent, especially if you're reading this book, you want to do what's right for your kids. From training and teaching to fun and laughter, you want your home to be a safe haven and a place of health for your children. When it comes to creating the optimal environment for your youngsters, food is an inevitable part of the process. After all, you want your child to be healthy, and good health stems from good nutrition. With that in mind, we wrote *Baby & Toddler Meals For Dummies* just for you. After all, if you want to ensure the most wholesome nutrition for your "little you," so to speak, you need to know how and what is best to feed your young one.

Perhaps you've strolled the supermarket aisles, looking at all the baby food and toddler snacks, and you've wondered, "Is this stuff wholesome? Could I make it myself? Could I do it better?" Those are important questions to ask, and the answers are unequivocally, Yes! We tell you how in the pages that follow.

When you choose to make your child's meals on your own, you put yourself in the driver's seat of your child's nutrition. Not only will these homemade meals be nutritious for your child, but also you'll find that the work and care involved gives you a great sense of satisfaction in knowing that you're doing your best to bring your baby up healthy.

About This Book

We wrote this book so you can find the information you need quickly and easily. We don't ramble on about things that don't matter, and you don't have to read the entire book if you don't want to. In fact, you can read the book from cover to cover or simply jump around to the topics you want to find out more about at the moment. And best of all, we don't expect you to remember anything — we know you probably have a string on each finger to remind you of doctor appointments, daycare schedules, sports schedules, and on and on, so we organized this book in a logical, straightforward format so you can get the information you need quickly and easily.

Conventions Used in This Book

Before you use the recipes in this book, here are a few guidelines that'll help ensure your success:

✔ Before you start cooking, make sure that you read through the entire recipe. Doing so ensures that you have all the ingredients and cooking tools before you begin.

✔ Pepper means ground black pepper unless otherwise specified.

✔ If a recipe calls for mayonnaise, don't substitute salad dressing.

✔ All butter is unsalted.

✔ All eggs are large.

✔ All milk is whole.

✔ Flour is all-purpose unless otherwise specified.

✔ Sugar is granulated unless otherwise noted.

✔ All onions are yellow unless otherwise specified.

✔ All temperatures are Fahrenheit. (See the Metric Conversion Guide in Appendix A at the end of the book for information about converting temperatures to Celsius.)

In addition to the conventions we follow for the ingredients, we use a few other conventions to point out helpful info:

✔ We use *italics* to point out new terms that we define as well as terms or concepts that merit emphasis.

✔ We use **boldface** to highlight the keywords in a bulleted list or the action parts of numbered steps.

✔ We use `monofont` to point out Web addresses that you may want to check out for further information that we don't dive into here.

○ We use a tomato symbol like the one shown here to point out the vegetarian recipes. For the purposes of this book, we define *vegetarian* as including no meat — that means no seafood, no chicken broth, nada. (We don't include this symbol for drinks and desserts, though; those recipes are naturally okay for vegetarians.)

What You're Not to Read

Sidebars contain extra information, so you don't have to read 'em. However, they often explain some technique or issue in more detail, and you may find the information helpful.

We also won't threaten treachery if you don't read the text marked with a Technical Stuff icon — although we put our hearts and souls into providing every ounce of information you may want or need pertaining to this book's topic, some of the info just isn't read-or-die. So skip over these paragraphs if you want, but know that you may be missing some gold nuggets of additional info if you do.

Foolish Assumptions

As we wrote this book, we made a few assumptions about you:

- ✔ We assume you know a thing or two about cooking, but we don't assume you're a professional chef. In the pages of this book, you'll find real-life tips, suggestions, and recipes you can use right away, but we don't dwell on the basics of cooking.

- ✔ We assume you can get your hands on common, everyday items and ingredients. If you want to cook a recipe in this book, you'll be able to find the ingredients at your local supermarket or health-food store; you won't need to buy ingredients from exotic places.

- ✔ We assume you want to cook for your child in a practical, down-to-earth way and want to do your best. We think that's great, and we've written this book for you from that perspective.

- ✔ We assume that you need help pulling everything together. You may know a thing or two about feeding babies and children and may need a few recipes. But you also may need help understanding portion sizes and nutritional balance, and you need practical recipes you can whip up in a flash. Don't worry; you've come to the right place.

- ✔ We assume you're deeply concerned about being a good parent. You care so much about your child's well-being that you're convinced that cooking your tyke's meals is the best step toward raising a healthy child.

- ✔ We assume you're intelligent. After all, you bought this book!

How This Book Is Organized

Baby & Toddler Meals For Dummies is divided into seven parts, which we describe in this section. Each part contains appropriate chapters that as a whole cover everything you need to know about cooking baby and toddler meals. With this design, you can find the information you need without having to dig around.

Part I: Lovin' Spoonfuls: Feeding Your Baby and Toddler

In this part, you find some basic information about cooking for babies and toddlers. If you want to cook for your child but you don't really know where to start or what tools you need, this is the perfect place to start. In Chapter 1, we provide an overview of the many topics this book covers as well as a brief quiz to assess your nutritional know-all. We also point you in directions tailored to your needs. In Chapter 2, you find out what it means to raise a well-fed child — we're talking the whole shebang, from serving balanced meals to setting appropriate mealtimes to recognizing the most important vitamins and minerals for your child's health. In Chapter 3, we cover kitchen basics, including kitchen appliances you need, feeding and storage equipment to have on hand, advice on how to stock your pantry, and instructions on how to properly store and reheat food.

Part II: From Womb to Highchair: The First 12 Months

The first months of your baby's life are critical in terms of nutrition. In this part, we cut through the mystery of feeding babies and make things simple and straightforward. In Chapter 4, start figuring out the mystery of the milk diet, which your baby embraces during the first four months of life. In Chapter 5, begin feeding solid foods and find out what to start with. In Chapter 6, you explore foods for your crawler from ages 6 months to 1 year.

Part III: Big Changes Ahead: Feeding Your Toddler

Ah, the age of the toddler! A lot of things change around your house, and your toddler's eating needs and habits change, too. In Chapter 7, you find recipes that work with the exploring 12-to-18-month age. Discover advice and recipes in Chapter 8 that help you decide what to feed your growing tyke now that she's 18 months to 2 years old. Finally, in Chapter 9, you find toddler meals and advice for children 2 to 3 years old.

Part IV: Welcoming Your Child to the Big People's Table

So you've survived the days of infancy and early toddlerhood, and now it's time to pass along the important values of mealtime. As your child ages and starts to grasp concepts, Chapter 10 helps you set routines for your kids and gives you ideas for meals away from home. We think that Chapter 11 is a fun chapter because you get to cook with your little one. In Chapter 12, we supply several recipes that suit the entire family.

Part V: Fast Fixes for Mealtime Hurdles

No one likes to deal with food-related problems and challenges, but you're likely to run into some issues when you feed your kid. Relax — we have all the advice and recipes you'll need to jump these hurdles. In Chapter 13, you uncover the common food-related challenges, such as allergies, food intolerance, and reflux. In Chapter 14, you find out how to deal with your picky eater. In Chapter 15, we talk about eating away from home and avoiding the pitfalls of fast food.

Part VI: The Part of Tens

The Part of Tens is a helpful reference for choosing the homemade route, saving time, and introducing new foods. In Chapter 16, we explore why homemade meals are best. In Chapter 17, we try to help you save some time by cutting corners in the kitchen. Finally, if you have some anxiety about serving new food choices to your child, hit Chapter 18 for tips on how to introduce new items into meals.

Part VII: Appendixes

In the appendixes of this book, we give you even more help and tips to be successful in the kitchen and with home-cooked meals. Use Appendix A, the Metric Conversion Guide, to understand common abbreviations for cooking measurements and to figure out how to change the measurements in the recipes to metric sizes. Appendix B provides you with a space to record your child's food intake. This can be important when trying to gauge food allergies, intolerances, or even food variety in your child's diet. And for the beginner in you, if you want a whole week of meals already planned for you, check out Appendix C to get started.

Icons Used in This Book

We use icons throughout this book to call your attention to certain details and pieces of information that you may find helpful, funny, or just plain interesting. The icons, and the information that goes along with them, are also designed to save you time and avoid common problems, so be sure to check them out.

Paragraphs marked by this icon indicate extra information, advice, and tidbits to help make your cooking experiences easier or to provide you with an alternate way to do something.

This icon is used to call your attention to extra morsels of important information that you should store away in your noggin for further use.

This symbol alerts you to potential problems that you may experience in the kitchen. We do use this icon sparingly, but when we do, take note. The warning icon provides information that helps keep you and your youngster from harm's way.

If you're curious and have time to spare, check out the tidbits of info that this icon flags. Although the information attached to these icons isn't essential to your success as a parent or as a cook, you may find these nuggets helpful and interesting.

Where to Go from Here

It's time to embark on the journey of preparing your little one's meals. If you've never cooked a meal for your infant and you're just getting started, we recommend that you begin at the beginning, of course, with Part I. If you can't wait to check out the recipes, flip ahead to Parts II, III, IV, and V (depending on your child's age). If you want to find info on a particular topic, be sure to use the table of contents and index for extra help and direction. And if you just want to peruse the recipes before diving in, take a look at the "Recipes at a Glance" section, which falls right before this introduction. No matter where you start, you're already well on your way to increasing your cooking repertoire and providing your baby or toddler (not to mention your entire family) with a healthy lifestyle (or healthy food, anyway)!

Part I
Lovin' Spoonfuls: Feeding Your Baby and Toddler

"I'm not actually buying this stuff, I'm just using it to hide the fruit, legumes and greens until we get checked out."

In this part . . .

Feeding your child is one of the most important activities that you'll ever do as a parent. After all, food makes the body and brain grow in a healthy way, so each nutritional need is important. Don't worry, though; in this part, you discover the basics of baby and toddler meals. You find out about the joys and struggles of feeding, discover the basics of baby nutrition and how to introduce foods, and capture the tricks of the trade.

Chapter 1

Little Meals for Little Folks, from Applesauce to Zucchini

● ●

In This Chapter

▶ Getting schooled in the ways of baby and toddler meals

▶ Understanding the basics of feeding your child

▶ Facing the tough times: Common obstacles

▶ Putting your nutrition knowledge to the test

● ●

The glorious day finally arrives. You're a new parent, and when you look at this new bundle of joy in your arms, you're filled with a sense of wonder and amazement — this new child is actually yours! You've spent months preparing, anticipating, and studying to be the best parent possible.

Parenthood is an important journey, and you may be fretting over taking in every glorious moment of your baby's life. Don't worry; many parents feel the exact same way during the first few days of parenthood. You want to raise your child in the right way to grow up to be healthy. And yet, what you quickly find is that every day is a discovery — minute details reveal themselves every second (or so it seems). Many answers aren't found in a book or magazine.

One of those details is feeding — it's one of the issues you need to address. After all, you want the best for your baby, and as he grows, nutrition plays a large part in his overall health. As a new parent, do everything you can to give your child a healthy diet through the homemade meals laid out in this book. Use this resource as the means to accomplish your goals.

The authors of this book are all parents — we've been and are in your shoes. That's why we've written this book. Find out the answers to how you feed your infant through toddlerhood. What foods are best? Is homemade food truly better? How can you control portions and keep a balanced diet?

Understanding the Importance of First Meals

All firsts for your baby seem important. First steps, first words, and of course, that first smile. First meals are no different. They hold vital importance as your baby starts life outside of the womb and as her body grows. First meals, as life fuel, support your baby's mind, growth, and development. The human body is highly complex and comes with complex nutritional needs. Your baby's first meals must support these complex needs as your baby grows and develops.

But meals aren't simply about nutrition. Mealtime provides a strong time of bonding between Mom and Baby through breastfeeding, and between other members of the family and the baby through bottle feeding. (See Chapter 4 for information on breastfeeding and formula feeding.) As your baby grows and starts eating other foods, mealtime becomes a time of socialization and training. Your child collects more verbal skills, manners, listening skills, and general communication skills at the dinner table.

Why intuition isn't enough

No matter what you may think you know, your basic intuition about food may not be enough. Nutrition can be a complicated matter — children have different nutritional needs than adults. The typical wisdom you have about food may not be nutritionally sound, and although you may not spend much time thinking about your own nutrition, you certainly need to consider your child's.

If you really want to beef up your general nutrition knowledge, check with your local hospital or community center for classes taught by registered dieticians who can really help you get some fundamentals of nutrition under your belt.

For starters, take into account some basic nutritional facts about babies and children that every parent needs to know. Commit these morsels to memory as you feed your tyke:

- ✔ **Breast milk or formula is your baby's first drink.** Milk remains a vital part of your child's diet for several years, and children need the calcium, along with the vitamins, minerals, and fat that milk provides.

  Your child shouldn't have cow's milk until one year of age and should only be given full-fat cow's milk (read that: whole milk) or a cow's milk substitute (such as soy or goat's milk) at that point. See Chapter 4 to discover more about milk.

✔ **Foods need to be dense in calories, fat, and nutrition.** Because children don't eat as much as adults, their foods need to be more focused. We'll give you plenty of pointers to accomplish this goal throughout the book.

✔ **Babies don't have the ability to digest high fiber foods.** Although higher fiber foods are healthy for older children and adults, your baby needs less fiber. Also, most high fiber foods are low in calories, which is the opposite of the previous bullet.

✔ **Children need three square meals a day along with healthy snacks in-between.** Of course, babies 4 months old or younger need to be fed breast milk or formula on demand, but as your child begins eating solids and nears age 1, she needs to eat every few hours, and every meal and snack should be seen as a time to offer solid nutrition. Don't worry; we'll help you along the way!

Your child also needs a wide variety of vitamins and minerals for healthy growth that your instincts may not trigger. The following list highlights some of the major players, but we tell you everything you need to know about important vitamins and minerals in Chapter 2, including what foods you can find them in.

We begin with the vitamin superstars:

✔ **Vitamin A:** Aids the immune system; helps form some hormones and helps in cell reproduction; helps with the growth of bones, teeth, and healthy skin, hair, and mucus membranes

✔ **Vitamin B2 (also called riboflavin):** Aids in general growth and red cell production; helps with energy conversion from carbohydrates

✔ **Vitamin B12:** Helps the body's metabolism; aids in the formation of red blood cells; maintains the central nervous system

✔ **Vitamin C:** Acts as an antioxidant, which prevents the body from tissue damage by free radicals (which can cause cardiovascular disease and cancer); is an effective antiviral agent, meaning it helps your body defeat viruses you come into contact with

✔ **Vitamin E:** Helps with antioxidants and the creation of red blood cells

Continuing on, the big wigs in the mineral category are as follows:

✔ **Calcium:** Builds strong bones and teeth; helps nerve function and blood clotting when you're wounded

✔ **Iron:** Essential part of hemoglobin, which delivers oxygen to the body's muscles through the blood cells. Iron is what gives blood its red color and it's necessary for energy production.

   ✔ **Zinc:** Promotes cell reproduction, tissue growth, and wound healing; works with other body enzymes and helps the body use carbohydrates, protein, and fat; an important mineral for general health

   ✔ **Potassium:** Regulates fluids and mineral balance; helps maintain blood pressure

Why homemade foods are best

If you walk through your favorite grocery store, you'll find plenty of manufactured baby foods and products. You may look at the foods and prices and think, "Are these products nutritious, and is the price worth it? Is this the way to go? Is there a better method?"

Let us say this upfront: We aren't anti-prepackaged baby food. Each of us, as parents, has used it, and in many cases, prepackaged baby food provides a quick solution. If you must use prepackaged foods, the iron-fortified cereals and basic purees are all good choices. Yet, as a general rule, homemade food is simply better for the following reasons:

   ✔ **Freshness:** When you make your baby's food, you can use the freshest ingredients and prepare the food in a way that harbors the vitamins and minerals. Fresh is best.

   ✔ **Control:** With homemade foods, you're in complete control of what your baby eats and you have more flexibility with options.

   ✔ **Preservatives:** Well, the *lack* of preservatives to be exact. Home-cooked food avoids preservatives. Most store-bought baby foods are careful to eliminate excess preservatives and salt. Yet, homemade meals are always going to be preservative free *if* you use fresh ingredients.

   ✔ **Cost:** For $3, you can buy a whole squash or a package of green beans that feeds your baby for a week or more. To the contrary, you can feed your baby the prepackaged stuff for only two days with the same amount of dough! The reason for the price difference is that when you make your own food, you avoid all the materials and marketing costs that heighten the cost of store-bought food. Pocket your money and use it in other ways for your family, such as paying a sitter so you can have a night out with your partner!

   ✔ **Bonding:** You'll feel better about your role as a parent when you prepare food yourself. And the love that goes into your meals creates closeness to your child. That spoonful of love doesn't come prepackaged.

Need more convincing? See Chapter 16 where you'll find ten quick reasons why homemade baby food is best.

What mealtime teaches your child

Mealtime is about more than food; it enhances moments of bonding and sharing, especially as your baby turns into a toddler and begins interacting with the world around him. We assert that mealtime is one of the most important family times of the day. In fact, family mealtime is important enough that we've devoted an entire chapter to family meals; see Chapter 12 for an enlightening discussion and some hard-to-beat recipes (if we do say so ourselves).

So what can be learned from? Valuable lessons can be reinforced each day during meals, but here are a few of the most important:

- ✔ **Togetherness:** Family meals can be a great way for all members of the family to share their time and day together. These family bonding moments become a normal part of the routine and a healthy part of your family's.

- ✔ **Dexterity:** As your child begins to use a spoon and fork, she begins to manipulate and use tools and items.

- ✔ **Manners:** Use this time to teach "please" and "thank you" and phrasing for passing dinner dishes. Also use other table manners like excusing yourself from the table when finished. Many of these manners are taught by example. Make sure to explain table manners to your children for any social setting as well.

- ✔ **Balanced diet:** If you eat healthy meals together, your child begins understanding the importance of proper health and food from a young age. Your child witnesses his family eating in a healthy way, and he begins to understand which foods are healthy and which are occasional treats. What better place to gather these life skills than in your kitchen?!

- ✔ **Conversation:** As you watch your child grow and his language skills develop, you'll find that the family table is a great place to practice and reinforce conversation skills. Eating and visiting at the same time is an age-old practice, but make sure to pass on the tricks of the trade to your little ones. Such skills like not interrupting when others are talking and not screaming to get what you want can be emphasized at the dinner table. Your child also discovers new words about foods, utensils, and other objects in the kitchen. Mealtime is a powerful learning tool, so keep the conversation positive and upbeat!

Weaning Baby and Introducing New Foods

Breast milk is a starter food, but your baby can't drink it as his only source of nutrition forever! In fact, by the time your baby reaches 4 months old, he'll be almost ready for real food, but you have to start out simply — with a small amount of cereal — and transition gradually. And although your infant will eat different foods before his first birthday, breast milk remains an important part of his diet until at least that point.

Because your child isn't born eating a smorgasbord of food, you'll need to introduce new foods as he grows. Naturally, certain foods are better at certain ages than others, and you can find out more about what foods to introduce at what ages in the various age-related chapters in this book. To whet your appetite for all you'll discover in this book, though, the following list gives you a brief global look at feeding your child:

- **0–4 Months:** Feed breast milk or formula only, fed on demand.

- **4–6 Months:** Add small amounts of rice, oat, or barley cereal. If you begin serving cereal at 4 months, you may begin serving pureed veggies at 5 months and pureed fruits at 6 months.

- **6–8 Months:** Add pureed fruits and veggies, such as bananas, pears, applesauce, peaches, avocado, cooked carrots, squash, and sweet potatoes.

- **8–10 Months:** Continue with previous foods, and add

  - Small amounts of soft pasteurized cheese, yogurt, cottage cheese (but no cow's milk until age 1)

  - Cereals (wheat and mixed cereals)

  - Mashed (versus pureed) fruits and vegetables (such as bananas, peaches, pears, avocados, cooked carrots, squash, potatoes, sweet potatoes)

  - Finger foods (such as lightly toasted bagels, cut up; small pieces of ripe banana; well-cooked spiral pasta; teething crackers; low-sugar O-shaped cereal)

  - Small amounts of protein (such as pureed meats and poultry; tofu; well-cooked and mashed beans like lentils with soft skins, split peas, pintos, black beans)

  - Noncitrus juice (apple or pear)

- **10–12 Months:** At this stage, add

  - Fruit cut into cubes or strips, or mashed

  - Bite-size, soft-cooked vegetables (peas, carrots)

  - Combo foods (macaroni and cheese, casseroles)

- **12–18 Months:** Switch to whole milk. You can feed everything you've been feeding, but you can now feed these foods as well:

  - Honey

  - Any other dairy products

- Same food as family, mashed or chopped into bite-size pieces

- Other grains (whole-wheat bread, pasta, rice)

- New fruits: melon, papaya, apricot, grapefruit (citrus is now okay)

- New vegetables: broccoli and cauliflower — essentially any veggie is okay now

- Protein (eggs; cut-up or ground meat, poultry, boneless fish)

✔ **18–24 months:** Everything you've been feeding plus

- Other grains (whole-wheat crackers, pretzels, rice cakes, ready-to-eat cereals)

- Fruit (cooked, canned or fresh, cut up or sliced, or even dried)

- Fruit and vegetable juices

✔ **24 months and on:** Everything you've been feeding. At this stage, you can continue to introduce new foods as desired, including nuts and peanut butter. Be careful of choking hazards — make sure that items are cut in small bites and carefully continue to supervise mealtimes.

It can take ten or more attempts before children feel comfortable eating an unfamiliar food. So, don't give up or get discouraged.

Leaving the nipple and grabbing a spoon

As your child nears age 1, you may want to begin weaning him from formula and move him to cow's milk. Breastfed babies are typically breastfed a bit longer, depending on what works best for Baby and Mom. Remember, though, that you should only give your tot whole cow's milk or a cow's milk substitute until he's 3 or so. At that point, you can cut some of the fat and move to 2 percent milk.

Honey is for bumblebees, not babies

Perhaps you've heard that you never give honey to an infant, and indeed, if you look on honey containers at the supermarket, the labels tell you the same. Why? Honey may contain bacterial spores that produce the bacterium, *Clostridium botulinum.* This bacterium creates a toxin that can give your baby botulism, which makes your child sick and, in rare cases, affects the central nervous system, resulting in death. Honey is safe for older children and adults, but babies haven't yet developed the bacteria in their digestive tracts that can control the spores and prevent the production of the toxins. So, never give honey to a child under age 1 for any reason.

The transition from milk to solids is an exciting time for both the baby and the parent, but the progression is slow as molasses. Typically, the transition from milk to simple solids and then to more complex solids takes months, even years, to develop fully.

Your baby's first solid food should be rice cereal, typically during 4 to 6 months of age. Make the cereal watery, and your baby will eat only a few bites at a time. You can then slowly mix in other watery cereals, such as barley and oatmeal. In fact, you can make these cereals from scratch with little fuss, and we show you how in Chapter 5.

As your baby's appetite grows, you'll begin introducing pureed and watery veggies. We recommend yellow veggies, such as corn, potatoes, sweet potatoes, and the like. These veggies are bland and easy to digest but still pack that nutritious punch.

As your baby continues to grow, you'll also introduce basic and bland fruits, such as apple, pear, and banana. Find out more about feeding your 4- to 6-month-old in Chapter 5.

Moving from bland to beautiful, from purees to well-crafted dishes

As your child moves past the 6-month stage, you'll continue to see more changes in her eating needs and habits. Her digestive system gets stronger, and as she gets teeth, her food options expand greatly. You'll begin mixing in other veggies, fruits, and then meats, with progressively chunkier textures as Baby gets older, and on to combination meals that'll start to look more and more like real food instead of mush!

To help you navigate the changing needs of your child, you'll find a chapter addressing each age range with advice, tips, pitfalls, and of course, practical recipes to put to work in your kitchen (see Chapters 6 through 10).

Observing basic rules when feeding your tyke

So you have this hungry child and you need to feed him. What are the rules? What should you watch out for? What are the common difficulties?

Relax! Feeding your child takes a mix of common sense and some specific rules. We expand on the following topics throughout the book, but to get started, keep these issues in mind:

✔ **Your child's eating needs aren't like yours.** You may worry about things like calories and fat and try to eat foods with lower calorie and fat contents. Your baby's needs are the complete opposite. Because your youngster eats lower volume, she needs food that has

- Dense calories and good fat

- Low sugar

- High vitamins and minerals

- Low fiber (especially for children under 1)

You don't need to know countless rules, but remember that your child needs a dense calorie, higher fat diet for proper growth and brain development. Children aren't little adults, so don't get in the habit of thinking that way. Check out Chapter 2 to find out more about childhood nutrition.

✔ **Texture, appearance, and taste are more important than you may think.** Just because your child is young doesn't mean that his senses don't come into play when he eats. In fact, he's attracted to food by both sight and smell, just like you. In addition, texture is important for safety reasons — babies can choke easily, so you need to make sure that you're serving food at the right consistency at the right age. Naturally, we've provided you with a lot of information and a bunch of recipes. Check out Chapters 5 through 10.

✔ **Start with bite-size portions.** Offering your child just a teaspoon or so of a new food makes it feel less intimidating.

✔ **Team up favorite tastes with new ones.** Pick a food that your child likes and alternate bites between the new food and the favorite food.

✔ **Not all foods are created equal.** Some foods simply have more nutrition than others, and you should have an understanding of what foods provide a stronger source of nutrition. Don't worry; head to Chapter 2.

✔ **Not all foods should be given to children.** Some foods commonly provoke allergies in children, and some foods are simply dangerous. For example, honey contains botulism spores and should never be given to a child under the age of 1. Peanuts are a common allergen and shouldn't be given to children (including peanut butter) until after the age of 2. Shellfish is a common allergen for many people as well. Avoid it until your child is several years old. You can find out more about these issues in Chapter 13.

✔ **Be careful with juice.** Juice is a wholesome drink for your child, but make sure that you give only pure fruit juice that contains no added sugar (look for "100 percent juice" on the label). We recommend apple juice as a first juice because it's easy to digest. As a starter, it's best to dilute juice 50 percent with drinking water (tap water is fine). Too much juice can cause diarrhea until your child ages a bit and can handle its intensity.

✔ **Beware of choking hazards.** As your baby ages and becomes a more independent eater, he needs to be very careful of items that pose potential choking hazards. These items include whole grapes, hard candy, popcorn, hotdogs, peanut butter, and any larger items. Think small bites!

✔ **Water is a building block of life, but your baby gets all the water he needs from milk.** If you formula feed, the formula is mixed with water (regular tap water) as your child grows. After the age of 1, you can offer more water as a drink, but make sure that you continue feeding milk and juice. See Chapter 4 to find out more about milk.

✔ **Use common sense.** Use this book as a guide for when to serve what foods and how much, but be wary of well-meaning relatives and friends who're flippant about what your child can and should eat.

Facing and Hurdling Obstacles

In a perfect world, you'd never have any problems. Of course, none of us get to live in *that* world, and you may experience several common problems when feeding your baby. If you're armed with the right information (which this book provides), you can pinpoint a problem and handle it successfully. The following sections give you a quick introduction to the most common problems.

When Ricky is really picky

Fact #1: The majority of children go through some kind of picky eating phase.

Fact #2: This phase will make you want to run screaming down the street.

Some children seem to be born as picky eaters. Others seem to eat well and then suddenly go through a stage where they'll barely eat anything or eat the same food over and over. This spell can last a few months or even a few years.

Utilize these practical tactics to combat your picky eater, and in fact, you can find more tips and special recipes to help in Chapter 14. Here are a few quick tips to tuck in your hat:

✔ **Relax.** Realize that picky-eater syndrome is normal and more children than not go through some variation of this behavior. Although aggravating, realize that the behavior is normal, take a deep breath, or maybe two, and relax.

✔ **Vary it.** Don't give in to demands for the same foods over and over. Keep exposing him to new foods and don't let him dictate what he'll eat. Don't worry; your child won't starve.

✔ **Watch out for visual appeal.** Children are typically only interested in eating pleasant-looking food. Try to make food more visually appealing and stimulating.

✔ **Use a base.** If your child loves cheese, serve dishes that mix other items, such as veggies into the cheese.

✔ **Get your children involved in the kitchen.** Use cooking time as discovery time. Teach your little ones about different foods and let them help you prepare some items. This is a great way to break down the pickiness barrier because kids are more likely to try something they've helped create. Check out Chapter 11 for some recipes that just may get you started cooking together and increase your child's knowledge of foods and interest in eating them.

If Grace is intolerant (or allergic)

Children have immature body systems, including their digestive and immune systems. It isn't uncommon for kids to end up with some sort of food allergy or intolerance, but most children outgrow these issues with time. Food intolerance affects the digestive system, while an allergy affects the immune system. Intolerances are more common than allergies.

A food intolerance or allergy reveals itself with a few telltale symptoms:

✔ Allergy symptoms:

- General irritability

- Problems breathing

- Rashes, especially around the face or neck

- Sneezing, wheezing, and a runny nose

✔ Intolerance symptoms:

- Bloating

- Digestive problems

- General irritability

- Vomiting

You'll notice these symptoms typically within 30 minutes of eating the offending foods if the food is intolerance. In the case of an allergy, the symptoms may appear within a few minutes, but can take several hours to appear.

In most cases, food intolerance or allergies are annoyances (for both you and your child), and you simply need to avoid feeding those foods to your kid or adjust serving size in cases of intolerance. Some foods, however, such as peanuts and shellfish, can lead to a swelling of the throat, preventing proper breathing and anaphylactic shock. *Anaphylactic shock* is a life-threatening reaction characterized by a swelling of the throat tissue and lowered blood pressure. So, it's important not to take intolerance or allergic problems lightly. Naturally, a pediatrician can be an invaluable resource if your child's having these problems, and also check out Chapter 13 for more information on the most common allergies and intolerances as well as a handful of recipes that steer kids clear of trigger foods.

If Charlie is on the chubby side

In most cases, children won't end up chubby. The main contributing factors to overweight children are the consumption of highly processed, high-fat foods (instead of a well-balanced diet), and the lack of physical activity. In rare cases, medical conditions cause a child to be chubby, and you should work with your pediatrician, but in most cases, it's simply an issue of eating poorly and living lazily.

It's important to note that all babies and young children look chubby — this is a normal part of your baby's development. But as your child grows to around age 2, you'll notice that she loses this baby fat and starts to thin out.

If you feel that your child eats too much and is gaining weight, check with your pediatrician who may have some specific suggestions for the situation. Also, check out Chapter 2, where we discuss in detail the basics of proper nutrition. Armed with the right information, you can make changes to your child's diet and activity level that'll likely take care of the chubby problem.

When Father Time gives you a squeeze

You have all the time in the world and are never in a rush. Yeah, right! When you find that world, please let us know, so we can join you.

In many cases, parents want to cook meals for their children, but they rely on prepackaged foods in a fix. We understand, because our lives are hectic, too. With two parents working full time, raising two kids isn't easy! However, with a few tricks up your sleeve, you can keep your nutrition goals even when time isn't on your side. (For more great tips, flip to Chapter 17, near the end of the book.)

- ✔ **Get organized.** Get a calendar and try to plan out your week's meals in advance. This way, you'll know what needs to be cooked and when, and you'll avoid a lot of confusion.

- ✔ **Cook several meals at once.** Try cooking a couple of different recipes at the same time and storing the portions in the freezer. When you don't have time to cook later, pull out your freezer portions for a quick, healthy meal. Throughout this book, we note the recipes that'll freeze well.

✔ **Prepare snacks for the road.** Eating out is a major culprit of poor nutrition, but you can survive this problem by taking healthy food along. It's not as hard as you may think, and in Chapter 15, you'll find plenty of on-the-go recipes to get you started.

What Do You Know? A Nutritional Test

How much do you know about childhood nutrition? Take this simple test to find out. The following 15 questions test your knowledge of childhood feeding issues. If you find that you struggle to get the right answers, don't worry. That's why you have this book! (The answers are at the end of this chapter with references to other chapters in this book for more complete information.)

The questions

1. **At what age should a baby start drinking cow's milk?**

   A. 6 months

   B. 1 year

   C. 18 months

   D. 2 years

2. **Which food poses a common, but potentially dangerous, allergy for young children?**

   A. Apples

   B. Bananas

   C. Nuts

   D. Lettuce

3. **Which food presents a botulism danger in children under 1 year old and should be avoided?**

   A. Pears

   B. Honey

   C. Beef

   D. Cauliflower

4. **What is the fluid a newborn sucks from the mother's breasts before actual breast milk comes in?**

    A. Colostrum

    B. Antibody

    C. Sweet milk

    D. Vitamins

5. **What is the first solid food that you should offer to your child?**

    A. Chicken

    B. Veggies

    C. Fruit

    D. Rice cereal

6. **In terms of serving *first* veggies, which veggie isn't a good choice?**

    A. Sweet potato

    B. Squash

    C. Corn

    D. Broccoli

7. **Which is a common symptom of a food allergy?**

    A. Rashes

    B. Headaches

    C. Aching joints

    D. Fatigue

8. **Which food isn't a part of the B. R. A. T. diet for sick children?**

    A. Bananas

    B. Rice

    C. Apples

    D. Tomatoes

9. **What number of calories does the USDA recommend that the average 2-year-old consume per day?**

    A. 500

    B. 1,000

    C. 1,500

    D. 2,000

10. **According to the USDA, what food group should have the most servings per day for a 2-year-old?**

    A. Grains

    B. Milk

    C. Veggies

    D. Fruit

11. **Which food helps build strong bones and teeth?**

    A. Zucchini

    B. Sweet potatoes

    C. Whole wheat

    D. Milk

12. **Which of the following options isn't a benefit of breastfeeding?**

    A. Tailor-made nutrition

    B. Important vitamins and minerals

    C. Additional antibodies for your baby

    D. None of the above

13. **When you start feeding your baby purees, which food group should be served first?**

    A. Meat

    B. Fruits

    C. Veggies

    D. Nuts

14. **Which food is considered a dense source of calories, fat, and vitamins and is recommended for babies?**

    A. Corn

    B. Potato

    C. Carrot

    D. Avocado

15. **What eating problem in children can lead to Esophagitis?**

    A. Reflux

    B. Allergies

    C. Lactose intolerance

    D. Diabetes

The answers

1. **B**

   A baby should transition to cow's milk at 1 year of age. See Chapter 4.

2. **C**

   Nuts are a common allergen and should be avoided until after 2 years of age, when they can be slowly introduced into the diet. See Chapter 2.

3. **B**

   Honey should never be given to infants (under 1-year-old) because of the danger of botulism. See Chapter 2.

4. **A**

   Colostrum is a fluid that contains antibodies and basic nutrition for the newborn. See Chapter 4.

5. **D**

   Babies should start with a rice cereal. See Chapter 5.

6. **D**

   Broccoli is hard to digest and not a good choice for a *first* veggie. See Chapter 5.

7. **A**

   Rashes are a common sign of a food allergy. See Chapter 13.

8. **D**

   Tomatoes aren't a part of the B. R. A. T. diet. Instead, toast is the final food. See Chapter 1.

9. **B**

   The USDA recommends 1,000 calories for a 2-year-old with moderate activity. See Chapter 2.

10. **A**

    Your child needs more servings of grains than foods from any other group. See Chapter 2.

11. **D**

    Milk and other dairy products help build strong bones and teeth. See Chapter 4.

12. **D**

    Breastfeeding is best for your baby. All the answers are positive benefits! See Chapter 4.

13. C

Pureed veggies should be served before any other foods. See Chapter 5.

14. D

Avocados — the perfect food for a baby — are very rich and easy to digest. See Chapter 2.

15. A

Reflux, in severe cases, can lead to Esophagitis and esophageal cancer. See Chapter 13.

Chapter 2

Raising a Well-Fed Child

. . . .

In This Chapter

▶ Studying the USDA's MyPyramid for Kids

▶ Exploring vitamins and minerals

▶ Implementing a well-rounded diet for vegetarians

▶ Being prepared for wacky eating habits

. . . .

*R*aising a well-fed child may bewilder you. You probably receive conflicting advice from family and friends every day, and deciphering who's right and who's wrong can be hard. And even the Internet, masking as your all-knowing best friend, may steer you along a bumpy path. So you're still left with looming questions: What foods should my child eat and how much of which food group? Don't worry; we're here to help!

Raising a well-fed child isn't as complicated as it may seem. Armed with the right information, you can ensure proper nutrition for your baby without becoming a worry-wart or stressing yourself out. In this chapter, the mystery of raising a well-fed child is crushed. You discover some tips and skills to put to work right away as you plan meals and feed your child.

Exploring the USDA Food Pyramid

You're probably at least vaguely familiar with the USDA Food Guide Pyramid. The Food Guide Pyramid has served as a standard of good nutrition for years. However, with recent updates and revisions, the name of the pyramid has become "MyPyramid." The new pyramid encompasses nutrition and exercise and encourages

✔ Making smart choices from every food group

✔ Finding a balance between food and physical activity

✔ Getting the most nutrition out of your calories

Now, you may not realize that the USDA has also developed a food pyramid just for children, now known as "MyPyramid for Kids." (Check out www.my pyramid.gov, too.)

Because their bodies develop and grow at such a rapid rate, children have diverse nutritional requirements. These needs aren't radically different from older children or even adults, but the food pyramid you're used to seeing is modified slightly for youngsters, meaning that you don't have to overhaul your understanding of good nutrition completely.

To build a foundation for your nutritional knowledge, take a look at MyPyramid for Kids in Figure 2-1. (Access a downloadable, printable version of this food pyramid at www.teamnutrition.usda.gov.)

	Grains	Vegetables	Fruits	Milk	Meat & Beans
Figure 2-1: The USDA's MyPyramid for Kids.	Eat 6 oz. every day	Eat 2½ cups every day	Eat 1½ cups every day	Get 2 cups every day	Eat 5 oz. every day

Source: www.MyPyramid.gov

The first concept to understand the latest food pyramid is that it isn't age specific. Rather, it's meant to serve as a general guide. Follow MyPyramid for Kids for children ages 2 through 8. Children younger than 2 still generally follow the pyramid, but they need more servings of milk and dairy products than the pyramid recommends. Also, MyPyramid for Kids proposes lowfat milk products for kids ages 2 to 8, but keep in mind that children from 1 to 2 years old still need full-fat milk. To find out more about your child's milk needs, be sure to check out the age-specific chapters in Parts II through IV.

When looking at Figure 2-1, notice that MyPyramid for Kids divides into five food groups with a different amount for the daily need for each category. The pyramid simply gives you a graphical representation of the importance of each food group in your child's diet. For children ages 2 to 8, the USDA recommends the following general daily needs of each food group:

- ✔ **Grains:** 6 ounces per day. At least half of this suggested portion should be whole grains, and in truth, consider serving mostly whole grains — they're simply more nutritious.

- ✔ **Vegetables:** 2½ cups a day. Strive for a mixture of veggies to get the proper balance of vitamins and minerals. Naturally, your child may eat a bit less or more based on her age.

- ✔ **Fruit:** 1½ cups per day. Again, strive for a mixture of different kinds of fruits.

- ✔ **Milk:** 2 cups per day. You can substitute other milk products, such as cheese and yogurt, which count for milk servings.

- ✔ **Meat and beans:** 5 ounces per day. Strive for lean beef, chicken, and fish prepared by baking, broiling, or grilling. Fried meats are usually more delicious, but they aren't as healthy due to the fat content, so limit fried food.

Tailoring serving sizes to age

Because the USDA's MyPyramid for Kids is for a big age range (see the preceding section), the daily recommendations vary among that group. The USDA provides a Web site where you can enter your child's age, gender, and activity level and get instant feedback on what foods and how much of each food group to serve your kid (go to www.mypyramid.gov). To guide you in the right direction, in each age-related chapter, we tell you how much food a child in that age range, with a moderate activity level, needs from each food group.

As if the daily recommendation issue isn't confusing enough, the food pyramid differs a bit for males and females. Here are some examples:

✔ At age 3, male children require a bit more food in some categories than females. However, this advice is flexible, so don't worry about the distinction.

✔ The food pyramid recommends 3 ounces of grains for girls and 5 ounces for boys. However, we suggest between 3 and 5 ounces for either sex, depending on your child's size, eating needs, and activity level (and to cover our tails with the USDA).

Breaking down the pyramid: The five food groups

As you look at the five basic food categories, you wonder what foods belong in each group and what foods should be staple foods in your child's diet. That's a good question, and we have the answers for you in the following sections.

Grains

When you think of grains, you probably think of bread first. Rightly so. Bread is a major food in this group. As you feed your child grains, make sure that you feed more whole grains than other processed grains. Whole grains are healthier.

Keep these foods in the grain group in mind:

✔ Barley

✔ Brown rice

✔ Oat flour (substitute for all-purpose white flour)

✔ Oatmeal

✔ Whole-wheat bread

✔ Whole-wheat pasta

✔ Wild rice

Vegetables

The vegetable category naturally includes all vegetables. However, all vegetables aren't created equal. As such, keep the following suggestions in mind when you feed vegetables to your child:

✔ **Feed more potassium-rich foods.** Include beets, kidney beans, lentils, soybeans, spinach, split peas, sweet potatoes, tomatoes, white beans, white potatoes, and winter squash.

- ✔ **Strive for 1½ cups of dark green veggies a week.** Try out broccoli, collard greens, kale, mustard greens, romaine lettuce, spinach, turnip greens, and watercress.

  Vegetables that are darker in color are more nutrient rich than those that aren't. So, keep the veggies dark to supply your tot with plenty of nutrition!

- ✔ **Plan for 1 cup of orange veggies a week.** Alternate among acorn squash, butternut squash, carrots, hubbard squash, pumpkin, and sweet potatoes.

- ✔ **Serve 1 cup of dry beans and peas per week.** Include black beans, black-eyed peas, garbanzo beans, kidney beans, lentils, lima beans, navy beans, pinto beans, soybeans, split peas, tofu, and white beans.

- ✔ **Feed 2½ cups of starchy veggies per week.** Serve corn, green peas, lima beans, and potatoes.

- ✔ **Dish up 4½ cups of other veggies per week.** Take your pick from artichokes, asparagus, bean sprouts, Brussels sprouts, cabbage, cauliflower, celery, cucumbers, eggplant, green or red bell peppers, iceberg lettuce, mushrooms, okra, onions, parsnips, tomato juice, pure vegetable juice, turnips, wax beans, and zucchini.

Fruit

Fruit, aside from being sweet and delicious, provides a lot of nutrition for your child. Serving a variety of fruits exposes your child to different kinds of fruits, and hopefully she ends up eating a variety. Feed more fruits with higher potassium levels, such as apricots, bananas, cantaloupe, honeydew melon, peaches, prunes, and oranges. Potassium helps regulate blood pressure, which pumps the blood to your muscles, thus keeping the muscles in working order.

Watch out for imitation fruit juices or fruit snacks. These products often have little actual fruit and contain more sugar. When you serve fruit juices, insist on juices that are made with 100 percent real fruit with no sugar added.

Milk

The milk category includes whole milk, cheese, and yogurt. Your child can fulfill her milk intake for the day not only by drinking milk but also by eating cheese and yogurt. American or cheddar cheeses are always good options for kids because of their mild flavors. Many recipes in this book call for yogurt because it's healthier and helps bump up your child's calcium intake.

Children ages 1 to 2 need full-fat milk. See the age-specific chapters in Parts II and III to find out more about milk.

The fat about oils

Oils are a natural part of any diet, and they're necessary for good health because of the fatty acids they contain. As a general rule, each day your child needs about four teaspoons of oil — choose from canola, corn, cottonseed, olive, safflower, soybean, and sunflower. All of these oils are unsaturated and derive from plants.

Some foods are naturally high in oil, such as nuts, olives, fish, and avocados. You don't have to be concerned about measuring oils in your child's daily diet, but make sure that you feed the foods that are high in oils as a consistent part of the diet.

Meat and beans

This category includes meat and beans as well as nuts. Nuts are listed in the meat and beans category because of their higher protein and natural fat levels.

Keep the following tips in mind as you feed these products:

- ✔ **Serve fish instead.** Replace a serving or two of protein each week with fish. Salmon and trout are good choices because they contain healthy fatty acids.

- ✔ **Choose lean beef.** Remember to trim all meats of visible fats.

- ✔ **Grill, bake, or broil beef and chicken.** Avoid fried meats.

- ✔ **Choose beans or peas as a side dish.** You can also make main dishes with beans and lentils.

- ✔ **Add nuts into meals.** Almonds, pecans, cashews, and walnuts are all our favorite choices. However, your child shouldn't eat nuts, including peanuts or peanut butter, until after 2 years of age due to common allergy problems. (See Chapter 13 for more on childhood allergies.)

Providing a Good Foundation

As you're thinking about feeding your child, it's important to understand that your child's brain needs a lot of power — just like yours. Interestingly enough, the brain only takes up about 4 percent of your body weight, but it burns 20 percent of your body's energy, even when you're at rest. Also, the brain doesn't store glucose well, so you need to "feed" your child's brain (and yours) regularly so it functions at its best.

In the mornings, your body's glucose is at an all-time low because you haven't eaten anything all night. You've heard that breakfast is the most important meal of the day, and we couldn't agree more. Breakfast replaces the body's already low blood-sugar levels and gives you energy to face the day.

So write this statement on a bunch of sticky notes and spread them throughout the house, chant it daily for 30 minutes, or do whatever you need to do to remember it: *Don't skip breakfast!* You may have developed that habit yourself, but it really is a bad habit for both children and adults. If you have this bad habit, it will probably rub off on your children, so now is the time to make breakfast a priority in your home.

Putting Vitamins and Minerals to Work

Vitamins and minerals are natural substances that a body needs for good health. If your children eat a healthy, varied diet, they'll get the nutrition they need. Still, a lot of confusion surrounds vitamins and minerals, and children need the same vitamins and minerals that adults do.

To cut through the confusion, Tables 2-1 and 2-2 are here to help. Here's what they tell you:

  ✔ The basics of the most important vitamins and minerals

  ✔ What these vitamins and minerals do in your body

  ✔ Which foods provide rich sources of vitamins and minerals

Use Tables 2-1 and 2-2 for quick references when you have questions about vitamins and minerals.

About water-soluble vitamins

You may have heard the term *water soluble vitamins.* When you eat foods that have water-soluble vitamins, the vitamins don't get stored as much in your body. Instead, they travel through your bloodstream. And whatever your body doesn't use comes out when you urinate.

So these kinds of vitamins need to be replaced often because they don't stay in your body. This collection of vitamins includes

  ✔ Folic acid (B9)

  ✔ Niacin (B5)

  ✔ Pyridoxine (B6)

  ✔ Riboflavin (B2)

  ✔ Thiamin (B1)

  ✔ Vitamin B12

  ✔ Vitamin C

Table 2-1	All You Need to Know about Vitamins	
Vitamin	**What It Does**	**Foods You Can Find It In**
A	Aids the immune system, helps form some hormones; assists cell reproduction; helps with growth of bones, teeth, healthy skin, hair, and mucus membranes; promotes vision	Almonds, apricots, asparagus, avocados, broccoli, cantaloupe, carrots, chestnuts, eggs, green bell pepper, hazelnuts, kale, milk, oranges, peas, pecans, pine nuts, pistachios, pumpkin seeds, spinach, squash, sunflower seeds, sweet potatoes, tomatoes
B1 (thiamine)	Helps in converting carbohydrates into energy; maintains a healthy functioning heart, muscles, and nervous system	Avocados, dairy products, grains, peas, watermelon
B2 (riboflavin)	Aids in general growth and red cell production; helps with energy conversion from carbohydrates	Artichokes, asparagus, avocados, broccoli, Brussels sprouts, cayenne, currants, dairy products, dandelion greens, eggs, kelp, kiwi, lima beans, meat, mushrooms, navy beans, parsley, peas, pumpkins, rose hips, sage, spinach, sweet potatoes, watercress, whole-grain breads
B5 (niacin)	Assists digestive system; helps healthy skin and nerves; converts food to energy	Almonds, artichoke, asparagus, avocado, bananas, beef, broccoli, cantaloupe, carrots, chestnuts, corn, diary, eggs, green bell pepper, kale, kiwi, lima beans, liver, mushrooms, peaches, peanuts, peas, pine nuts, potatoes, squash, strawberries, sweet potatoes, tomatoes, watermelon
B6 (pyridoxine)	Helps create antibodies; aids in nerve function and formation of red blood cells	Avocados, bananas, carrots, garbanzo beans, lima beans, meat, oatmeal, peanuts, peas, potatoes, soybeans, tomatoes, walnuts, watermelon, whole grains

Vitamin	What It Does	Foods You Can Find It In
B9 (folic acid)	Helps produce red blood cells; supports the nervous system	Almonds, artichokes, asparagus, avocado, bananas, blackberries, brazil nuts, broccoli, brown rice, cantaloupe, carrots, cashews, cheese, chestnuts, corn, fortified cereals, green bell pepper, hazelnuts, kale, kiwi, lamb, legumes, lentils, lima beans, liver, macadamia nuts, onions, organ meats, peanuts, peas, pecans, pine nuts, pistachios, pork, potatoes, poultry, pumpkin seeds, spinach, squash, strawberries, sunflower seeds, sweet potato, tomatoes, turnip greens, walnuts
B12	Helps metabolism and the formation of red blood cells; maintains the central nervous system	Dairy, eggs, meat
C	Serves as an antioxidant, which prevents the body from tissue damage by free radicals (which can cause cardiovascular disease and cancer); serves as an effective antiviral agent	Apples, artichokes, asparagus, avocados, bananas, blackberries, broccoli, cantaloupe, carrots, cauliflower, corn, cucumber, grapes, green bell pepper, kale, kiwi, lemons, lima beans, limes, mushrooms, onions, oranges, peaches, peas, potatoes, spinach, squash, strawberries, sweet potatoes, tomatoes, watermelon
D	Helps in the growth of healthy bones and teeth	Butter, egg yolk, fatty fish, liver, milk, mushrooms. Milk is fortified with vitamin D. Children get all the vitamin D they need from milk.
E	Serves as an antioxidant; helps with the creation of red blood cells	Almonds, apples, bananas, blackberries, brazil nuts, grains, kiwi, meats, peanuts, pine nuts, sunflower seeds, vegetables
K	Helps with blood clotting; regulates calcium levels in the blood	Broccoli, cashews, chestnuts, green veggies, hazelnuts, kale, pine nuts, spinach

The amazing but aggravating avocado

If you study Table 2-1, you may notice that one food keeps popping up: the avocado. Avocados are vitamin dense and easy to digest, so they're a perfect food for babies and children. In fact, as you glance at recipes in this book, you may see many recipes that contain avocados. Considering its vitamin content, ease of digestion, and even healthy oils, the avocado is perhaps one of the most perfect foods for babies, children, and even adults! However, avocados can be difficult to pick at the supermarket and they can be a real pain to work with. Here are a few helpful tips to keep your avocados from sending you to the loony bin:

✔ **Choose firm, but pliable fruit.** That's right — avocados are a fruit, and like a banana, they turn soft after they're ripe. So your first clue to a ripe avocado is firmness. Avocados that are too hard aren't ripe, and ones that are too soft are overripe.

✔ **Look for an even unblemished texture.** Avoid bruises, soft spots, and hollows between the flesh and skin. Shake the avocado to test it. If the pit is loose, don't buy it!

✔ **Ripen your avocados at home.** Simply place the fruit in a brown paper bag and store it at room temperature out of sunlight for three to five days. Put a banana in the bag with the avocado and it will ripen more quickly.

✔ **Prevent darkening.** The flesh of the avocado quickly begins to darken when exposed to the air, so it's important to work quickly with the "meat" after the avocado is cut. Add a lemon wedge to it — the acid in the lemon will slow down the darkening process. Also, keeping the pit of the avocado with the avocado insides slows down darkening as well.

✔ **Slice the avocado.** Slice the avocado lengthwise all the way around to the pit. Then gently twist each side in the opposite direction to separate halves. The pit should remain in one side. Slip a large spoon in between the skin and the meat and scoop out the flesh or peel and slice. Wrap it tightly to store it in the refrigerator for one to two days.

Table 2-2	All You Need to Know about Minerals	
Mineral	*What It Does*	*Foods You Can Find It In*
Calcium	Builds strong bones and teeth; helps nerve function; coagulates blood when you're wounded	Broccoli, dairy products, fish, kale, oranges, tofu
Chloride	Regulates fluids in body cells; aids in digestion	Table salt
Chromium	Helps insulin levels	Meats, nuts, and whole grains

Mineral	What It Does	Foods You Can Find It In
Copper	Helps hemoglobin levels; helps convert food to energy	Nuts, organ meats (liver), seafood, seeds
Fluoride	Helps with strong teeth and bones	Salmon, tea
Iodine	Helps regulate the body's energy use	Saltwater fish
Iron	Essential part of hemoglobin	Legumes, meats, nuts, seafood, seeds
Magnesium	Helps regulate energy production and nerve cells; helps maintain teeth and the immune system	Green veggies, legumes, nuts, whole-grain breads
Manganese	Part of the many enzymes in the body	Kale, pineapple, strawberries, whole grains
Molybdenum	Works with riboflavin to put iron into hemoglobin for red blood cells	Breads, grain products, legumes, milk
Phosphorus	Helps produce energy and regulate metabolism; a major component found in teeth and bones	Breads, legumes, meats, nuts
Potassium	Regulates fluids and mineral balance; helps maintain blood pressure; assists in muscle contraction	Apricots, avocados, bananas, cantaloupe, dried fruits, fish, grains, grapefruit, honeydew, kiwi, meats, milk, oranges, potatoes, prunes, strawberries, tomatoes
Selenium	Works with vitamin E to protect cells	Grains, organ meats (liver), seafood, seeds
Sodium	Regulates body fluids, blood pressure, and nerves; assists in muscle contraction	Processed foods, table salt
Zinc	Promotes cell reproduction, tissue growth, and wound healing; works with other body enzymes and helps the body use carbohydrates, protein, and fat	Legumes, liver, meats, seafood, soybeans, whole grains

Measuring calcium intake

Children need milk, but how much is a good amount to ensure that your child gets the necessary calcium, and what other foods are good choices for children who don't like milk? Generally, follow these guidelines:

✔ Ages 1 to 3 years: About 500mg of calcium each day (about two 8-ounce glasses of milk)

✔ Ages 4 to 8 years: About 800mg of calcium each day (about three 8-ounce glasses of milk)

✔ Ages 9 to 18 years: About 1,300mg of calcium each day (about four 8-ounce glasses of milk)

So how do you know how much calcium certain foods contain? The following table gives you some hints.

Food	Serving	Calcium
Broccoli (cooked)	½ cup	35mg
Cheddar cheese	1½ ounces	300mg
Medium orange	1	40–50mg
Milk	1 cup	300mg
Oatmeal	1 cup	100mg
Orange juice	1 cup	350mg
Soy or rice milk	1 cup	300mg
Sweet potatoes	½ cup	44mg
White beans	½ cup	113mg
Yogurt	8 ounces	300mg

Going Green: The Well-Rounded Vegetarian Diet

You may opt for a vegetarian diet and wonder whether that same diet is healthy for your child. Naturally, vegetarian diets differ — some include seafood, some don't, some allow dairy products, some don't, and so on, with an infinite number of nuances thanks to a lot of different people. Generally, lacto-ovo-vegetarians include milk, milk products, and eggs in their diets but exclude all meat and meat products. Lactovegetarians include milk and milk products, but exclude eggs and all meat. Vegans are *pure* vegetarians (also called strict vegetarians and total vegetarians) in that they exclude all animal-derived food. In the end, the kind of diet parents follow typically determines the diet the child follows.

At a basic level, a vegetarian diet avoids all meat and sometimes animal products, opting instead for a diet of only vegetables, fruits, grains, and nuts. Challenges exist in an adult vegetarian diet, and you have the same obstacles with a child's diet, but namely in the areas of protein and milk, which young children must have for proper nutrition.

Pediatricians argue among themselves concerning the safety of a vegan diet with children. Naturally, vegetarian diets that permit dairy are easier to manage because you can derive more calories, calcium, and protein from products such as milk, cheese, and yogurt. Those diets that allow eggs also have more flexibility because eggs are high in protein, and you won't have to look hard for other sources of protein. A strict vegan diet has some greater challenges, such as the following:

- ✔ Vegan diets tend to be lower calorie and higher fiber diets — both of which aren't good for young children due to their eating habits and immature digestive track. Because babies and children need more milk products and sufficient energy to support growth, provide a greater soy and tofu base to build the calories.

  The small quantity of food consumed by a child from a vegan diet at one sitting fails to provide enough energy from that quantity of food. A child's small stomach often becomes full before an adequate amount of food is eaten to meet nutrient and energy needs.

- ✔ Children need higher levels of fat for brain development. Fatty foods, such as whole milk, provide a necessity for children.

A vegan diet isn't ideal for children; therefore, follow a more balanced diet, such as MyPyramid for Kids discussed earlier in this chapter. If you feel strongly about raising your child on a vegan diet, at least allow all dairy products and also consult your physician.

If you choose to follow a vegan diet, pay more attention to the food balancing act and be highly organized with regard to the following issues:

- ✔ **Calcium:** Calcium is a mineral that's mostly present in your child's bones. A calcium-rich diet helps meet daily requirements for the development of strong bones and teeth in children. Calcium thrives in many foods: broccoli, sweet potatoes, great northern and navy beans, and leafy greens. You can also provide calcium through soymilk or orange juice that is fortified with extra calcium.

✔ **Calories:** Ensure that your child receives enough calories each day (refer to the charts in this chapter). In general, if your child eats a well-balanced and varied vegetarian diet, gains weight, and has plenty of energy, he's probably getting enough calories.

✔ **Iron:** In general, the absorption of iron from meat, chicken, and fish is higher — around 15 to 30 percent — than other sources, such as fruits and veggies, which have absorption rates of only about 5 percent. Although some vegetables and fruits contain iron, that iron is usually not absorbed as readily as the iron from meats. You may need to give your child iron substitutes to make sure that he's getting enough.

✔ **Protein:** Make sure that your child gets enough protein and amino acids by serving a balance of grains, legumes, nuts, seeds, vegetables, and fruits.

✔ **Vitamin B12:** This vitamin is found only in animal-derived foods, so your child may need to take supplements or eat vitamin B12-fortified foods such as soymilk, fortified cereals, meat substitutes, and nutritional yeast.

✔ **Vitamin D:** Most children don't have problems with vitamin D deficiency because the human body makes vitamin D when exposed to sunlight. This vitamin is present in fortified milk, egg yolks, and fish.

✔ **Zinc:** Your child may need to take supplements or eat foods that are fortified with zinc to get enough of this mineral. The best sources of zinc are meat and yogurt. Zinc is also found in whole grains, brown rice, legumes, and spinach.

Don't use the Internet as your main source of information. A strict vegetarian diet is challenging and requires planning and knowledge. Many claims on the World Wide Web are wrong and simply push a vegetarian agenda.

The B. R. A. T. diet for a sick toddler

When your toddler is sick, always check with your healthcare professional for advice, but remember to increase your child's fluid intake and offer foods that naturally help with the problem. One special diet for an upset stomach is the B. R. A. T. diet. Doctors have recommended this diet for years. Take a look:

✔ **Bananas:** Bananas reduce stomach acidity and keep your child's potassium level in check. Potassium helps regulate the body's blood pressure.

✔ **Rice:** Rice is a quick source of carbs and protein and it helps when a child has diarrhea. It's easy to digest and provides energy.

✔ **Apples or Applesauce:** Apples are easily digestible (important for already aggravated tummies) and provide a good source of sugar and vitamins, which provide energy for your ailing youngster.

✔ **Toast:** Serve dry toast. It helps provide carbs and often settles the stomach.

Seek the advice and help of a registered dietician so you can make certain that your child gets a well-rounded, healthy diet that promotes growth and development. A pediatrician can also point you in the right direction concerning resources to help. For further reading, check out *Being Vegetarian For Dummies* and *Vegetarian Cooking For Dummies,* both by Suzanne Havala (Wiley).

Knowing What to Expect of Your Child's Eating Habits

Children aren't adults. Sure, you knew that, but unfortunately, many parents stress themselves out because they don't keep in mind that children don't naturally eat on an organized schedule — a conditioned routine taught to you by your parents and society. But train your child to eat meals and healthy snacks on an organized schedule to avoid grazing. However, do realize that children often eat a lot one day and not the next. This behavior is normal and simply a part of your child's development.

So, what pattern will your child likely follow? You can break down childhood eating into three primary stages: 0 to 12 months, 12 to 18 months, and 18 months to 5 years. Table 2-3 gives you an overview of how your child may behave in terms of feeding.

Table 2-3	Eating Habits by Age
Age	*Eating Habit*
0–12 months	Babies depend on breast milk or formula and slowly grow into eating mashed baby foods and then to solids. Milk requirements change during the first year. (Check out Chapters 4 through 6.)
12–18 months	Your child eats five meals a day, with a constant source of milk. Move from pureed baby food to solids. Provide small portions at planned times with snacks between meals at consistent times. Don't be surprised if your child is hungrier at some meals and not at others. Don't let your child graze throughout the day or he may not come to mealtime ready to eat.
18 months–5 years	Your child slowly grows into eating three primary meals a day with snacks between meals. Your child eats more at times than others (totally normal behavior). Never force your child to eat if she's not hungry or interested. Introduce new foods and dishes during these years and strive to provide healthy snacks.

Growth spurts and humongous appetites

When your child enters a strong growth stage, he often tanks up for several days or even weeks in a row and then backs off the food after the quick growth stage passes. Use these opportunities to feed more calorie-dense and calcium-rich foods to support growing bones. Our 4-year-old follows this pattern, and we keep cheese sticks and yogurt on hand, along with fresh fruit. In fact, during a growing spurt is a perfect opportunity to introduce new foods and recipes because your growing child is naturally more hungry and interested in food.

Chapter 3

Tools and Tricks of the Trade: Kitchen Basics

*T*he first (and perhaps most important) step in cooking baby and toddler meals is simple preparation. You need additional items in your kitchen, and you need to get organized before cooking. You may want to skip over this chapter and get to the fun stuff — recipes! — but preparing the recipes in this book requires that you stop first and get ready.

This chapter explores gearing up for your child's first meals. You find out about your pantry needs, basic on-hand equipment, and storing and heating food. The kitchen basics in this chapter are simple and practical. You receive tips that help you get organized and keep your sanity. Put the information to work, and your kitchen is ready for meals in no time!

Getting the Right Equipment

You probably heard someone in your family at some point say, "Always use the right tool for the right job." When it comes to feeding babies and toddlers, we couldn't agree more. With the right tools and equipment on hand, preparing meals for your child is easier and more rewarding simply because you save time and aggravation. That's why we're devoting a few pages to equipment.

Preparation and storage equipment

Start out with the basics. Because you make healthy and tasty meals in your kitchen, be aware of the few equipment must-haves.

Basic stuff you probably already have

You need typical items used in the kitchen: bowls, spoons, a can opener, and so on. Aside from the standard equipment options explored here, a few additional items may make your life a bit easier. You can find the following recommended tools at most retail, department, or superstores:

✔ **Cutting board:** Use a standard cutting board for an array of different cooking chores. Be aware that debate occurs over which kind of cutting board is safer for your health: wood or plastic. Theories state that wood cutting boards harbor more germs. However, whether you choose wood or plastic, the key is simply washing the board with soap after each use and allowing it to air dry. You may want to use two cutting boards, one for meats and one for vegetables. However, with careful washing, you don't have to worry about cross-contamination.

General concern exists in the scientific community that antibacterial soap is really just making bacteria more resistant to antibodies, which we really need for treating illnesses and such. So, the advice across the board is to avoid using antibacterial soap for this reason. These soaps and such not only kill good bacteria but also could lead to resistant strains of bacteria that we can't treat and manage with antibodies.

✔ **Knives:** Special knives aren't needed to cook for your child. However, a general kitchen knife set is handy, and a paring knife or peeler to peel fruit is essential.

✔ **Measuring cups and spoons:** A set of measuring cups and measuring spoons enables you to measure both liquid and dry ingredients.

✔ **Mixing bowls:** You may already own a collection of mixing bowls, but if you don't (or if you need new ones), now is the time to head to the store. You mix a lot as you prepare meals, so an assortment of sizes of mixing bowls comes in handy. Glass, plastic, or metal works well. Make sure that no matter what bowls you choose, you purchase ones that are durable.

✔ **Rubber spatula:** A spatula makes scooping baby food out of a food processor a lot easier. Of course, you can use a normal dinner spoon, but the spatula does a much better job of removing excess food from the sides of the processor or mixer, leaving little food to be wasted.

✔ **Saucepans and skillets:** Aluminum pans are coated with Teflon and tend to flake their coating over time, and aluminum should never come in contact with the food because of possible food contamination. So if you own older saucepans and skillets, which are commonly aluminum, consider replacing them.

A good set of stainless steel saucepans and skillets will serve you well. You won't have to worry about flaking and aluminum contact with your food. Shoot for a midline collection. You don't need the most expensive, but avoid the really cheap pans as well because they don't withstand prolonged use.

Food processors, blenders, or hand grinders

You're going to do a lot of cutting and processing in order to make foods edible for a young mouth and stomach. Make the experience easier by using a food processor for chopping and processing (unless you train for body building competitions and want to mash the food by hand; in that case, you should be reading *Weight Training For Dummies,* too).

A standard food processor tends to be flatter and more elongated than a blender. Figure 3-1 shows you a sketch of a typical food processor. In truth, any food processor works well for the tasks performed in the kitchen. But you do have a few options:

- ✔ **Standard food processor:** The processed foods for your baby or toddler are easily handled by a standard food processor — likely costing around $20 — but you may want one with more bells and whistles. Keep in mind that if you're buying a food processor to make baby food but not for other family needs, a basic model does everything you need. If you're looking at several processors at a department store, choose a midrange model.

- ✔ **Baby-food processor:** You're likely to find a processor advertised online as a specific product for making baby food. These processors are often small (which is nice because they save counter space), and you may enjoy using a food processor especially for baby foods. However, a standard food processor gives you more flexibility, especially when making more than baby food. If the idea of having a food processor solely dedicated to baby food sounds great, and you have the money in your budget, visit www.onestepahead.com. Baby-food processors usually sell for under $30.

- ✔ **Bells-and-whistles processor:** The higher priced models have more processing modes and related electronic features. For $50, you can get almost anything you want, within reason, for single-family use.

Now for the burning question: Can you use a blender instead of a food processor? Yes. However, we don't recommend it. Generally speaking, a blender blends liquid products. A food processor, instead, is designed to process a variety of foods. If you use a blender, you may get irregular results and find yourself frustrated — depending on the kind of food you're trying to make. This frustration may come into play even if you're making smoothies because many shakes and smoothies start with fresh fruit and need extra processing to break down the food thoroughly. Save yourself the headache and buy a food processor.

Figure 3-1:
A standard
food
processor is
handy for
pureeing.

food processor

Strainers

Strainers are used to sift food contents, most often in order to separate liquids from solids. You may have some kind of strainer in your kitchen, although it may technically be called a colander, which is a bowl shape and is used for draining liquid from foods such as pasta.

A strainer typically has very small holes so you can more effectively remove liquid without losing any food. You can find plastic models, but we recommend a wire mesh strainer for preparing your child's meals because they're more durable and tend to give you finer straining quality.

A *wire mesh strainer* (shown in Figure 3-2) is a simple strainer made from wire that forms a mesh (probably didn't need to spell that one out, did we?). You can use the wire strainer to mash food quickly by hand (use the back of a large spoon and press the food down through the strainer). You can also use the strainer to remove food from the liquid you're cooking it in.

Don't forget to have a bowl to catch the strained liquid if you're using the liquid in some other part of your cooking.

Strainers come in different *gauges,* or wire strength, and a medium gauge strainer works well. Keep your strainer handy when traveling, or in a pinch, and you can quickly mash food without using a food processor.

Electric mixer

For preparing meals, the basic mixer is a helpful tool. Unless you want your meal preparation to be a personal bicep workout, it's a good idea to have an electric mixer — regardless of whether it's a hand mixer or a stand mixer, you're still avoiding the hassle of moving your arm around in circles a billion times.

Figure 3-2:
A wire mesh strainer is a versatile tool.

WIRE MESH STRAINER

If you don't have an electric mixer, you can buy a simple, hand-held version for around $15. Shop around at discount stores or garage sales for a cheap model. Don't spend extra money unless you want additional features, such as extra mixing speeds. All you need is a mixer that has at least a low and high speed.

Steamer

Steamers cook and soften vegetables, but more of the nutrients stay in the vegetables when compared with boiling or frying. A stand-alone model (meaning an electric unit, as opposed to the stovetop steamer) that steams food and even works as a double boiler starts at $75. The electric steamer is shown in Figure 3-3.

Figure 3-3:
Using a steamer is a healthier alternative to boiling or frying.

ELECTRIC STEAMER

However, you can save yourself the $75 and simply buy a stovetop steamer (shown in Figure 3-4). The manual version allows you to place the steamer over a boiling pot of water to steam vegetables and costs about $10.

Figure 3-4:
You can use a stovetop steamer if you don't want to go electric.

steamer insert   collapsible steamer

Storage and microwaveable containers

One advantage of our modern world is refrigeration. After you've cooked your food and served it, you can store leftovers in the refrigerator or even the freezer for an extended period of time. When it comes to freezing or refrigerating leftovers, follow the helpful hints below:

- ✔ **Don't be prejudiced against containers of various sizes.** Have a variety of storage containers on hand of differing sizes (we recommend 10 to 15 containers). Some recipes in this book yield several servings that you can freeze and use at your convenience, and other meals make only one or two servings, so you don't waste a lot of storage space when you have different-sized containers to fit the foods.

  Break up the leftovers into individual serving sizes for freezing. In this case, have a good collection of smaller freezer containers. You can even purchase them with labels so you can write down the meal and the freeze date.

- ✔ **Gather a few ice cube trays.** Purchase larger ice cube trays and fill with soups, prepared baby cereal, smoothies, or any other liquid and place the trays in the freezer. Remove the frozen cubes, thaw, and serve them as you need them.

- ✔ **Let marketing copy be your guide.** Use only freezer containers that are sold as such. These containers withstand the rigors of freezing and protect your food from freezer burn. Use both hard containers (such as plastic containers) as well as high-quality freezer bags.

- ✔ **Look for reheatable containers.** In many cases, you'll take something directly from the freezer and want to reheat it. Easily transferable containers allow for multiuse and easier cleanup, because you don't have to dirty a separate bowl for reheating your leftovers. Durable plastic freezer containers can be a real timesaver because you can remove them from the freezer and place them directly in the microwave.

Feeding equipment

If you're expecting a new baby or one has just arrived, a number of items may come in handy within the next few months to make feeding your baby safer and easier. Naturally, if you walk into any baby store or even a baby section in a department store, you're bombarded with many different choices and brands of feeding equipment. The following sections give you a few pointers to keep in mind while you're shopping.

Stocking up on the essentials: Bowls, spoons, and forks

Feeding bowls, baby spoons, and baby forks come in different colors, sizes, and materials.

- **Bowls:** Bowls should be dishwasher safe, so you can clean them often and sanitize them in the dishwasher. Plastic bowls work best because they don't break. Don't use glassware around a baby or young child.

- **Spoons:** Feed a baby with only a rubber-covered spoon during the first year to prevent mouth injuries (babies commonly make jerky head movements, so the rubber-covered spoon prevents cuts in your baby's mouth).

- **Forks:** Your child can start using a rubber-covered fork at about 15 months of age but shouldn't use a real fork until well over 2 years old. Parent supervision during mealtime continues to be the most important aspect in preventing injuries from utensils as well as choking. Forks are dangerous — even though they're coated, your baby can still jab his mouth, lips, nose, and eyes. Play it safe and make sure that you supervise.

Reducing the spill factor with sippy cups

Sippy cups, spill-proof cups that enable babies to sip juice, milk, formula, or water without spilling, are invaluable to your kitchen repertoire after your baby is old enough to use the cups. Sippy cups, shown in Figure 3-5, have a flow-control valve that allows a child to sip a liquid from the cup, but when the child throws the cup down, nothing leaks out (keeping you from having to replace all your carpet around the time your baby turns 1).

Make sure that the sippy cup lid screws on tightly and that you can easily clean the cup. Check for a removable flow-control mechanism inside the cup's lid. This feature allows for more thorough cleaning of all the cup's parts.

Getting baby comfy in a highchair

Many different brands and models of highchairs are marketed each year. Each type of chair looks different and comes with a variety of options to suit the needs of your child (and you too). Shopping for a highchair can be difficult because of marketing ploys, and you may not understand exactly what you need.

SIPPY CUPS

Figure 3-5:
Sippy cups
make cup
drinking
easier.

Here are some tips that help you cut through the marketing lingo and figure out which highchair is high in quality and safety:

✔ **Check the chair's credentials.** Before you become enamored with a particular highchair, make sure that the chair meets the Juvenile Products Manufacturers Association (JPMA) standards. This association provides voluntary safety standards that all reputable highchair manufacturers follow. Inspect the chair for a safety rating and information (look on the tags and stickers attached to the chair). You can also check out the highchair manufacturer's Web site for more details. Check out the JPMA's Web site at www.jpma.org/consumer/index.html for more information or to see if your highchair meets the standards.

✔ **Consider the design.** Work with the chair in the store for a moment and see that it's easy to adjust the height. Also, many chairs recline, which makes feeding a young baby starting on cereal easier because of the extra head support (see Figure 3-6). Work with the mechanisms and imagine yourself juggling a baby and other kitchen demands. Is the chair easy to work with or complicated and problematic?

✔ **Make sure that the chair is stable.** A secure highchair has a low center of gravity and a wide base so the chair doesn't turn over. Grab the chair and shake it around a bit to see that the chair feels stable and sturdy.

✔ **Consider cleanup time.** Highchairs get messy, so when you're looking at chairs, try to imagine cleaning them. If the chair has excessive cracks and crevices that you have to clean out, you may want to consider another model. Also, check the seat and padding — make sure that it can be easily scrubbed clean. We think that plastic chairs are easier to clean than wood (and just as flexible). Fabric highchair covers should be machine washable and dryable.

Figure 3-6:
A reclining highchair makes feeding easier.

✔ **Look for locking wheels.** If the highchair has wheels, make sure that the wheels have a locking mechanism that is easy to lock and unlock. Locking wheels prevent the highchair from rolling around, or if you have other kids, the locking mechanism prevents your children from pushing around your baby in the chair and possibly causing injury. Locking wheels can also prevent a roller derby from breaking out in your kitchen.

✔ **Make sure that folding highchairs completely fold up for easy storage.** Try to fold and unfold the chair a few times while you're in the store. Make sure that the locking mechanism works well, so the chair can't fold up with a child in it.

✔ **Look for seat belts.** All highchairs should have a seat belt, preferably one that has a five-point shoulder harness. Don't buy a model that only has one simple belt. Also, check the belts for comfort and durability, and make sure that you can easily clean them (and believe us, the belts get really dirty!).

Look for highchair models with removable, machine-washable belts, because cleanup is much easier than having to scrub the belts by hand. You'll be sending thank-you letters for this tip when your little one pukes in his highchair.

✔ **Check out the food tray.** The food tray needs to be smooth, practical, and not include items that could hurt a baby's fingers. Rough-surface trays can trap food and germs. Tray rims help contain food, and dish-washer-safe trays eliminate extra cleanup time!

Stocking Your Pantry

Have you ever had that sinking sensation that you don't have food in your house, but you don't know what to buy when you get to the grocery store? This feeling is common, and as you get ready to prepare your meals, you need the right ingredients readily available in your pantry. Keep in mind that you can't keep everything you need on-hand at all times (without running out of room and breaking your grocery budget), but you'll want to keep some staple items in the cupboard.

First, follow a few simple steps when surveying your pantry:

- **Throw out old food and make room for new.** Rid yourself of that box of mac & cheese you bought when you were in college as well as the cans of vegetables that look like antiques.

- **Take inventory and find out exactly what you have.** Organize your pantry by food groups and even create a shopping list, so you'll be super-organized and prepared for cooking.

- **Throw away or donate items that you know you'll never eat.** Check the expiration date on food items you no longer want. If the food is still edible, donate the stuff you don't want to a food pantry, local shelter, or other charity in your area. Throw out the items that have expired. You probably don't want to eat it, and neither does anyone else.

Because the first few months of life primarily consist of breast milk or formula, don't worry about stocking your pantry until your baby begins to eat infant cereal. Even then, your baby eats small amounts, so don't buy a truckload of cereals at a wholesale store, because you'll want to make your own in most cases. At this stage in your baby's life, your pantry is primarily reserved for bottles, lids, rubber nipples, and so on, especially if you're formula feeding your baby. Because many babies begin eating cereal at around the 4-month mark, you'll need to have your food processor purchased and ready if you plan on making your own cereal. Discover more about cereal feeding in Chapter 5.

The more you integrate a healthy way of eating into your own lifestyle, your toddler meals begin to overlap with items you eat as well. Additionally, the recipes in this book tend to call for some staple items that you need to keep around. **Note:** The items indicated with a star aren't needed until the child is at least 1. Two stars indicate that you should wait until she's 2.

- Broth, reduced sodium, chicken or beef
- Cheerios (a quick food for hungry babies)

- ✔ Cinnamon
- ✔ Flour, all purpose
- ✔ Flour, whole wheat
- ✔ Fruit, dried
- ✔ Honey*
- ✔ Jelly or jam, low sugar
- ✔ Maple syrup
- ✔ Mustard, dry ground
- ✔ Nonstick cooking spray
- ✔ Nuts, assorted**
- ✔ Olive oil
- ✔ Pasta, assorted
- ✔ Peanut butter**
- ✔ Pepper
- ✔ Pizza sauce
- ✔ Raisins
- ✔ Rice cakes
- ✔ Rice, brown
- ✔ Rolled oats
- ✔ Salt
- ✔ Sunflower seeds

You'll also need some items that are perishable (cheese, for example) and semi-perishable (such as fruits and vegetables). Naturally, you need to do a bit of planning to ensure that you'll use the following items before they expire:

- ✔ American cheese, slices
- ✔ Bread, whole-wheat
- ✔ Butter, not margarine
- ✔ Cheddar cheese, shredded
- ✔ Eggs
- ✔ English muffins

- ✔ Fruits, assorted and fresh (strawberries are for children age 1 and up)
- ✔ Ketchup
- ✔ Mayonnaise, full fat
- ✔ Milk, whole (for children age 1 or older)
- ✔ Mozzarella cheese sticks (string cheese)
- ✔ Mozzarella cheese, shredded
- ✔ Parmesan cheese, grated
- ✔ Soy sauce
- ✔ Tortillas, wheat or flour
- ✔ Vegetables, assorted and fresh
- ✔ Yogurt, full fat and varied flavors

Going all natural: The organic diet

If you're into organic food options, or at least you want to be more so with your child, keep in mind that your pantry items don't change from the suggestions mentioned above, but add the task of shopping at a health-food store that offers organic produce and supplies.

If you haven't been living an organic life, but you're interested, it's important to understand what *organic* really means in order to get into the organic groove. Generally speaking, organic means *natural* food — food coming from plants and animals that have been grown without the use of synthetic fertilizers, pesticides, antibiotics, growth hormones, and feed additives (additives given to the animals in their food). Read more about the U.S. standards for organic food at www.ams.usda.gov/nop/Consumers/brochure.html.

The USDA doesn't make any claim that organic foods are better for you or more nutritious. Of course, it stands to reason that minimal chemicals and additives are always best. Yet, finding organic food (the label indicates organic items and carries a USDA organic seal of approval) can be difficult and more expensive. Many organic items don't have a long shelf life, which is another issue to consider. Still, you may want to use as many organic items as the availability and your budget allow because they're more natural.

Depending on where you live, finding an organic store or organic section within your grocery store may not be a problem, but if you're not near an organic store, shop online for several options. Try www.greenmarket.com and wellnessgrocer.com.

Selecting Good Produce

Old wives' tales abound about selecting good produce. How do you know if something is ripe, too ripe, under ripe? The conventional wisdom can be a bit maddening, but put these simple tips into place to help you select the best produce every time. Table 3-1 gives you the skinny on selecting produce.

Table 3-1	Selecting Produce
Produce	*Selection Method*
Apples	No bruising or mushy, soft skin. Firm — best test is taste.
Apricots	Color should be uniform.
Avocados	Brown skin with pale green tint. Soft (not mushy) to the squeeze if using immediately; ripens uncut at home. If squashy, they're over ripe.
Berries (any kind)	Smell for a sweet aroma. Check underside of carton to make sure it isn't berry stained or moldy.
Broccoli	Completely green with no yellowing; should smell sweet, not like cabbage.
Cantaloupes	Tan skin (not green). Smell sweet at stem end. Shouldn't hear seeds rattling when shaken.
Carrots	Bright green tops, crisp, deep orange color.
Cauliflower	Tightly packed florets without discoloration.
Citrus	Should feel heavy.
Corn	Fresh silk with unwilted leaves. Kernels should be plump, filled out.
Cucumbers	Firm skins, not limp or shriveled. English have smooth skin; Japanese have wrinkled skin.
Eggplant	Shiny skin with firm, even texture. Small to medium are younger and sweeter.
Green Beans	Crisp and bright.
Greens, Chard, Kale, Mustard	Rich, dark leaves with no yellowing.
Honeydews	Creamy yellow skin. Smell sweet at stem end. Shouldn't hear seeds rattling when shaken.

(continued)

Table 3-1 *(continued)*

Produce	*Selection Method*
Nectarines	Flesh gives slightly to pressure. Avoid fruit with green tinge.
Onions	Sweet summer onions should be firm.
Pears	Color and texture vary; best when firm with some give at stem end.
Plums	Uniform color and some spring when pressed.
Potatoes	Avoid sprouts. Small have better flavor.
Spinach	Bright green leaves (flat or crinkled).
Strawberries	Full red berries with some shine. No trace of mold.
Summer Squash	Not too scratched or limp; look for juice coming out of stem to tell if truly fresh.
Sweet Potatoes	Firm, smooth skin with no soft spots.
Tomatoes	Firm but not hard, aromatic, full red color. Cracking on skin doesn't matter.
Watermelons	Firm with a green (not yellowish) skin. Shouldn't hear seeds rattling when shaken.

As a general rule, if your child is younger than 1, try to pull away the first layer of a vegetable or the peeling of a fruit before using it, because infants aren't able to chew through the peel. Doing so removes any lingering pesticide residue and bacteria. After your child reaches the 1-year mark, you can leave the peel on — it contains most if not all of the nutrients — but be sure to wash the produce thoroughly.

Storing Food Safely in the Fridge

As you make meals for your youngster, you want to reduce the amount of work and time necessary for this noble task. After all, if you're creating purees and other dishes that require some processing, you want to prepare more than one meal at the time. After all that work, store the additional meals in a healthy, convenient, and practical way.

Sure, you've been storing food in the refrigerator for a long time, and you're an old pro at leftovers, but now you're thinking about your child's meals and wondering if the way you store food is good enough. Having a bit more concern

✔ **Place the frozen item in the fridge to thaw.** If you're not in a big hurry, the food naturally thaws out in a few hours without you having to baby-sit it.

✔ **You don't need to thaw frozen vegetables.** If you want to cook frozen vegetables, you don't need to thaw them first. Just proceed with cooking, and the produce quickly warms up to right temperature.

Food is safe when frozen, but as soon as you thaw the food, any present bacteria can resurrect and multiply. Don't leave thawing food at room temperature for more than two hours. Thaw and cook immediately!

Feeling Hot (But Not Too Hot): Heating and Reheating

Heating and reheating questions tend to be common as parents prepare meals. How hot is hot enough? What about reheating? What about using the microwave?

Follow the standard heating rules that apply to any food. These basic rules for heating food for older children or adults also apply to babies and toddlers:

✔ **Reheat all previously cooked food to an internal temperature of 165 degrees or above.** You may also want to have a meat thermometer for checking the internal temps of different meats.

✔ **Remove packaging before you heat the food.** If you're using prepackaged baby food, put the food in a different container before heating.

✔ **Heat the food to a suitable feeding temperature.** Prepackaged baby food is already cooked and canned, so all you need to do is warm it up.

Concerning temperature, your baby prefers warm meals (after all, she's had warm breast milk or formula). So serve the food warm but not hot. Simply put, taste the food to see that the temperature is just right. Lukewarm temperatures are typically good for babies.

✔ **Heat baby food in increments of 10 seconds on a high or medium setting.** Baby food tends to heat quickly, so gradually heating food saves you the time later standing in front of the freezer waiting for the food to cool down. Also, always stir microwaved foods well and taste them to avoid hot spots from uneven microwave heating. Never heat prepared formula bottles or breast milk in a microwave.

✔ **Cool overheated food in the freezer.** If you're heating baby food and it gets too hot, you can quickly cool it by placing it in the freezer for 30 seconds, stirring and retesting it before serving. Continue this process until the food reaches the desired temperature.

✔ **Add water to dried-out food.** Depending on what you're reheating, you may notice that the previously frozen item is a bit dry. Solve this problem by adding a little water to keep the food from scorching.

✔ **Make sure that you use microwave-safe dishes.** One way to test dishes for microwave safety includes putting a cup of water in the dish in question and microwaving it for one minute. If the water is cool and the dish is hot at the end of the minute, the dish isn't safe for microwave use.

✔ **Throw out food that's been microwaved too much.** Because food tends to get tough and difficult to eat the more it's reheated, your child may not eat continuously heated food. Do your baby a favor and toss those crusty leftovers.

✔ **Don't microwave fresh produce.** Research shows that microwaving fresh produce kills antioxidants that are naturally found in the produce.

Exercising Kitchen Caution

One significant source of food contamination occurs in the kitchen area simply because counters, dishes, and utensils don't get cleaned properly. The idea of putting bacteria in our mouths is a little scary. Because you're making food for your kids, you don't want to take the risk of spreading bacteria.

Just because a surface or dish looks clean doesn't mean that it *is* clean in terms of bacteria. So, here are a few tips to consider as you clean your kitchen:

✔ **Sterilize dishes and utensils.** Use a pot of boiling water and boil the times for ten minutes.

✔ **Use your dishwasher as a sterilizer.** Most dishwashers heat water to at least 140 degrees Fahrenheit, and this temperature is perfect for killing bacteria and sterilizing your cooking tools. Check your dishwasher's owner manual for water regulations.

✔ **Hand wash dishes or utensils with dish soap.** Scrub surfaces with a clean sponge or other cleaning pad.

✔ **Wash the bottle nipples separately.** If you fill the sink with dishes from dinner and throw the nipples in as well, the grease and oils from the other dishes are difficult to wash from rubber nipples (and deep inside bottles for that matter).

When you wash baby items, allow them to air dry rather than towel dry. Towels can harbor harmful bacteria, which you're rubbing onto the baby's bottles and nipples.

✔ **Clean all counter areas with soap.** Simply wiping away food and grime with a wet rag or sponge doesn't do the trick.

Use disposable disinfecting wipes that come in handy dispensing containers and a variety of scents. The bleach in the wipes kills germs as you scrub the counter. These wipes are also handy for cleaning and sanitizing highchairs.

In addition to basic kitchen cleanliness tips, practice food hygiene with raw eggs, meat, and fish. These common foods harbor bacteria and salmonella (in the case of raw eggs), so handling them requires care. Follow the guidelines below when handling raw eggs, fish, and meat:

✔ Make sure that you wash your hands with soap before and after contact with these foods.

✔ Never handle another food item after preparation without first washing your hands thoroughly with soap.

✔ Keep raw items in the refrigerator until you're ready to cook. Leaving this kind of food out at room temperature enhances the risk of bacterial growth. If you forget to refrigerate eggs, fish, or meat, throw them away.

✔ Thoroughly cook the raw foods. Children don't have the built-up immune system of adults, so they're particularly at risk for food bacteria. No runny eggs or rare meats for children — ever!

✔ Wash utensils, bowls, cutting boards, and counter areas with soap and water immediately after using them with these raw foods. Many people cross-contaminate another food because they forget to disinfect their kitchen gear with soap.

✔ Cook recipes containing eggs to at least 160 degrees in order to kill bacteria.

✔ Concerning eggs, meats, and fish, when in doubt, throw it out.

Part II

From Womb to Highchair: The First 12 Months

The 5th Wave   By Rich Tennant

"I steam and puree all her meals myself. Every 6th day I introduce a new food. This week I'm introducing brown."

In this part . . .

The first 12 months of your baby's life are full of growth and change — for both of you. You'll be amazed at the differences. In the same way, the nutritional needs of your baby change a lot during the first year, but these changes don't have to be overwhelming. In this part, that first mysterious year becomes a little simpler and clearer. Discover the basics of nutrition: demystifying breast milk and formula, serving solid foods, and nourishing your 6- to 12-month-old. Armed with the information in this part, you'll be able to easily take care of your baby's needs during her time of rapid growth and change.

Chapter 4

Welcome to the World, Baby! The First Four Months

You've arrived home with your bundle of joy and all is well in the world. But in all the changes and adjustments, the questions of eating schedules and what to feed come up. Is the baby eating enough? Too much? What's better — breast milk or formula? These looming questions can be complicated, but don't worry. This quick chapter helps you sort out the doubt and get your feet on solid ground again as we guide you through your baby's eating needs and habits during the first four months. If you have further questions, check out *Breastfeeding For Dummies,* by Sharon Perkins, RN, and Carol Vannais, RN (Wiley), for more in-depth information about breastfeeding. Also consult your healthcare provider and/or a lactation consultant, because many questions and concerns that are particular to different individuals can't be addressed by books.

Your Baby's Favorite Drink

Milk, milk, milk — the word at the core of your baby vocabulary for years to come. As newborns, babies' only food source is milk because they don't have mature digestive systems, and in fact, it takes some time for a baby to develop a more mature digestive system that can handle the demands of real food (not to mention that "real" food presents a choking hazard for your infant). As your baby grows, he begins eating other foods but still depends on milk. Later on, your toddler still needs a diet that contains milk in order to get the necessary calcium and nutrition. In short, it's all about the milk.

Milk contains proteins, fats, lactose, and various vitamins and minerals. The mammary glands of all mature female mammals produce milk after the females have given birth, and breast milk meets all the baby's needs for nourishment during the first four to six months.

That said, we enter the first topic of baby-food discussion — the choice between breast milk and formula.

Breast milk or formula?

The 20th century, for all its advances, uniquely made life much easier but much more complicated at the same time. For the thousands of years before this time, every new mother breastfed her baby or at least hired someone to do it. If a baby didn't breastfeed, the baby didn't survive.

Yet, in the 20th century, doctors and other healthcare professionals began saying that synthetic formula was, in fact, better. However, over the past several years, researchers and doctors have returned to breastfeeding, saying that Mother Nature knows best after all and that we simply can't copy breast milk and manufacture it. In fact, the World Health Organization and the American Academy of Pediatrics both agree that breastfeeding is best.

In the following sections, we help you iron out the benefits and potential obstacles of breastfeeding, as well as the drawbacks to formula feeding and the positive aspects of going that route.

Benefiting from breastfeeding

We, your authors, wholeheartedly agree with doctors when it comes to breastfeeding — hands down, it provides the best nutrition you can give to your baby. And of course, we'd never make that claim without giving you several reasons why — read this section for the plethora of supporting facts.

Sheer goodness from Day One: Colostrum

Before a baby's birth, the mother's breasts begin preparing for the ever-important task of breastfeeding. In fact, the mother's breasts first produce specifically formulated liquid called *colostrum* — a thick, yellow liquid that doesn't even look like milk. Colostrum is the first milk the baby needs and benefits your newborn in many ways:

- **Antibodies:** Antibodies help build your baby's immune system and are present in high concentrations in colostrum.

- **Nutrition:** Colostrum, containing the necessary fat, protein, and carbohydrates, is concentrated nutrition for your newborn.

✔ **Laxatives:** Colostrum lubricates your baby's digestive system to help him have his first bowel movement. It also gets your baby's digestive system ready for the breast milk that will come in two to five days following delivery.

After a few days, a week, or even a bit longer, the mother's breasts begin producing what you would think of as "breast milk" in place of colostrum. The liquid becomes thinner and whiter in color, but it's still chock full of nutrition for your baby.

The many great pros of breast milk

In terms of value, why is choosing to feed your baby breast milk worth it to you and your new baby? Consider the ingredients of breastmilk:

✔ Over 100 ingredients — including digestive enzymes, minerals, vitamins, and hormones — that can't be reproduced with formula.

✔ Special proteins that are designed to strengthen your baby's immature digestive system

✔ High carbohydrate levels and large amounts of *lactose,* a necessary sugar that impacts general growth and brain development

✔ Fatty acids such as DHA and ARA that enhance nervous system development, oligosaccharides (for healthy intestines), and growth-promoting hormones

Check out these other benefits:

✔ Breast milk is formulated for your baby. It changes as she grows (just like colostrum), giving her what she needs in terms of nutrition and calories.

✔ Breast milk is always ready — no mixing or heating.

✔ Children who are breastfed have fewer ear infections, colic, constipation, diarrhea, and trips to the doctor than formula-fed babies do. Researchers thought that this distinction was caused by the position of feeding, but recent studies say that it is the additional antibodies found in breast milk that makes the difference.

✔ Breastfeeding encourages a natural bond between a mother and her baby.

✔ Breast milk is free!

Facing the challenges of breastfeeding

Breast milk is the natural means to feed a new baby, so it should naturally be the right choice and the easy choice. Right? Not necessarily. For certain, breastfeeding boasts important benefits, but we do understand that it doesn't work for everyone — some women have trouble breastfeeding. Perhaps the milk supply just isn't there, or women have problems with blocked ducts. Regardless, understand that successful breastfeeding is dependent on several factors — some that breastfeeding women can control and some that they can't.

Check out the following typical challenges when it comes to breastfeeding your newborn:

- **General problems:** Many women experience a number of general breastfeeding problems and struggles, including milk letdown, nipple soreness, nipple cracking, frustration with breastfeeding, and general anxiety. These problems are common and can be addressed, but they often add much stress to a new mother. Check out *Breastfeeding For Dummies* (Wiley) for more information about these problems.

- **Working women:** The obstacles here aren't insurmountable! Yes, breastfeeding is more complicated and time consuming when mothers go back to work, but it can be done. Moms who's strictly feeding breast milk want to pump fresh milk daily before leaving for work. This milk can be used throughout the day to feed with a bottle while the breastfeeding mother is away. Breast milk also freezes well.

- **Privacy:** When new mothers are out and about, breastfeeding can be difficult for conservative moms who like privacy. Mom may want to bring a blanket along so that she can cover herself when breastfeeding in public.

- **A carefully monitored diet:** Simply put, mothers need to watch what they eat. Consumed nutrients pass from the mother to the infant through breastfeeding. Because this sharing occurs, certain foods that moms enjoy, such as chocolate, may give babies digestive problems. Some food groups may take a trial-and-error period to see how they affect a particular infant. Generally, breastfeeding women should avoid strong or acidic foods as well as caffeine and alcohol. See "Tackling food intolerance," later in this chapter, for more detailed information.

- **Health problems:** If a mother has a pre-existing health problem, she can still breastfeed. However, breastfeeding puts an extra demand on the mother's body, so the mother needs to take extra care of herself. Talk to a doctor about health conditions and concerns about breastfeeding.

In light of these obstacles, it's important to remember that breastfeeding is overwhelmingly the best choice for the baby. So, it's important to consider the obstacles and determine a plan of with a doctor if any of the problems seem insurmountable.

Discovering the good and bad in formula

Baby formula came on the scene in the late 1930s and was a necessary item for a time of war when so many women were working. Afterwards, formula manufacturers continued to promote formula's importance and many benefits.

But is formula good? Formula is better now than it ever has been. Companies know more about the composition of breast milk and are better able to copy it than ever before. The simple reality, though, is that breast milk is far better for your infant, and compelling *nutritional* reasons to choose formula over breast milk don't exist. In fact, most companies that produce formula tell parents upfront that breast milk is best.

With that said, we don't want to freak new parents out if they've chosen formula for their infant, whether by necessity or preference. So take heart — formula does have outside benefits:

- **Flexibility:** Hands down, probably the greatest benefit of formula is flexibility — enabling parents to feed their baby anywhere without the mother having to arrange for privacy. And the breastfeeding woman isn't the only person who can feed the infant.

- **Ease:** Breastfeeding is often difficult and challenging at first. Many women have problems with milk coming down as well as cracked and sore nipples. In this light, formula feeding is easier and usually involves fewer complications (see "Facing the challenges of breastfeeding," earlier in this chapter).

- **Portion control:** With formula feeding, you can see how much your baby eats, and you know whether he's eaten enough. With breastfeeding, you have to make sure that your baby is wetting enough diapers, which is your evidence of enough food. This isn't a major breastfeeding obstacle, but with formula, you simply have a measurement of how much your baby has eaten.

Formula feeding has negative aspects, too. Here are the most compelling cons that have to do with choosing formula over breast milk:

- **Nutrition:** Hands down, breast milk is better. Your baby survives and thrives on formula, but breast milk just has more components that lead to a healthy baby.

- **Slow digestion:** Formula can be slower for your baby to digest, and researchers say that this factor is actually negative because it's harder on the baby's digestive system.

- **Possible allergies:** Because formula is made from cow's milk, your baby may have an allergic reaction to it. Soy formula is an acceptable alternative, but your baby will still have to feel the discomfort of the allergy before you know the culprit.

- **Cost:** Because breast milk comes from the mother's body, it's free. Formula is expensive. During the first year of the newborn's life, expect the formula expense alone to run around $1,500. That's a lot of milk money!

Gauging the Amount Based on the Feeding Method

Regardless of whether your family decides that breastfeeding or formula feeding is best, you still need to make sure that your baby is getting enough milk. This need is often stressful for new parents. After all, babies aren't very good at saying, "Hey, I'm hungry." So in this section, we provide some specific tricks and tactics that you can put in place that help you make sure that your new baby is getting what she needs in terms of nutrition.

You can't overfeed a baby — she'll stop eating when she's had enough — but you can *underfeed.* The best rule of thumb of feeding is to let your infant eat until she's no longer interested. This method keeps your baby full, and you won't have to worry if your little darling is getting enough.

Measuring milk when baby's latched on

Because a breastfeeding mother can't see or measure the amount of milk the baby is taking in (unless Mommy pumps, of course), you need to know how to gauge amounts if you go this route. Not to worry, though, there are ways you can get around this issue.

The following bulleted list shows you what to look for to ensure that your baby is eating enough during the first four months of her life.

- ✔ **0 to 3 days old:** Because it's new to both Baby and Mom, your baby (and you, if you're Mommy) may have problems nursing during this time, so don't fret if you do. Remember to stay calm and patient and ask for help. Here's what to expect:

   - The baby breastfeeds during this time but is receiving colostrum instead of milk. Colostrum is nutritional, and its production is normal (see the section "Sheer goodness from Day One: Colostrum," earlier in this chapter, for more on colostrum).

   - Baby's first bowel movements (called *meconium*) will be dark green to black in color.

- ✔ **3 days to 4 weeks old:** The diaper is the best gauge to tell if your baby is eating enough at this stage, so keep a journal each day. Here's what to look for:

   - After the colostrum passes and the breasts start producing milk, expect your baby to have five to six wet diapers during a 24-hour period.

- Your baby passes three to five yellow stools per day. The stools darken after a few more days.

- The baby is satisfied when feeding (in fact, he may have trouble staying awake).

- Mommy's breasts seem softer after feeding and not as full.

✔ **1 to 2 months old:** At this stage, your baby eats more regularly.

- A common pattern of eating every few hours starts to form — typically 10 to 12 feedings every 24 hours.

- Continue to keep a close eye on the number of wet diapers per day (five to six in 24 hours).

- Your hungry baby becomes upset before feeding, including crying with clenched fingers. As he feeds, he relaxes and seems satisfied. Tickle your baby on the chin to keep him from falling asleep during feeding.

- Feeding lasts for about eight minutes on each breast, but let the baby determine when he's full. Never breastfeed by the clock!

✔ **2 to 4 months old:** Your baby continues on a regular eating pattern at this age.

- Expect him to gain weight at a pace of roughly 4 to 8 ounces per week.

- Stools are reduced and Baby may even go several days without passing a stool. Breast milk is tailor-made for your baby, so when he feeds, he absorbs most of the nutrition, so there's little waste.

Counting fluid ounces: The bottle method

One of the advantages of formula is that you always know how much your baby is drinking. You won't have to worry about checking the number of wet diapers each day (although checking isn't always a bad idea). Likewise, you can see how much Baby is drinking if you pump breast milk into a bottle. Because most moms who do so generally alternate between breast and bottle, you won't need to gauge the amount, because the total measured ounces per day are only part of the equation. For that reason, we devote this section to measuring formula.

In order to keep track of how much formula your 0- to 4-month-old should drink, refer to Table 4-1.

"Hey you, I'm hungry!"

It would be so much easier if your baby could simply tell you what she needs. Yet, until your baby turns into a toddler and develops language skills, you need to depend on baby talk, which is basically body language that tells you about your baby's hunger. Keep these common behaviors and issues in mind:

✔ Watch for sucking or chewing on hands.

✔ Notice when your baby is opening his mouth and trying to find the breast when you hold him.

✔ Feed your baby at the first signs of hunger. If you wait, he'll become more upset and will often have difficulty calming down enough to latch on. Your baby will cry loudly and arch his back, even when you try to feed. You'll need to talk and sing to your baby and try to get him to calm down enough to eat.

✔ As your baby eats, you'll notice that his body relaxes and he becomes calm. After eating, your baby is likely to fall asleep from satisfaction!

Table 4-1	Measuring Formula for Your Infant	
Age	*Number of Bottles Daily*	*Ounces of Formula Per Bottle*
0–1 month	8–12	2 ounces, gradually moving toward 3
2 months	8–12	3–4 ounces
3 months	5–8	4–6 ounces
4 months	6–8	5–6 ounces, gradually moving toward 7

Never put an infant to bed with a bottle or expect him to hold the bottle for feeding, even if he's able to do so. Hold him when you feed to avoid choking and unnecessary ear infections from fluid getting in the ear canal.

Detecting Early Digestive Problems and Intolerances

It's not unusual for babies from 0 to 4 months old to have digestive problems and possibly intolerances, especially to formula. These kinds of problems are rare in breastfed babies.

Keep in mind that a new baby's digestive system is immature, so time has to work out these issues. As we say time and again throughout this book, if you have concerns about how your baby is eating, be sure to mention them to your healthcare professional.

So, how can you know if your baby is having digestive problems and intolerances? And what can you do? The following information points you in the right direction.

Tackling food intolerance

You often hear the term *food allergy* thrown around when talking about young babies, but in truth, a baby is much more likely to suffer from food *intolerance,* which affects the digestive track (see Chapter 13 for a thorough discussion of the two terms). Because of food intolerances, some babies have a difficult time drinking formula because it's made from cow's milk, which is harder to digest than breast milk. If you think that your baby has an issue with regular formula, talk to your pediatrician about switching to a soy formula. How can you tell? The two most common signs are

- ✔ Digestive problems, characterized by diarrhea and excessive gas
- ✔ Crying excessively, especially after eating

If you're breastfeeding and your baby seems intolerant to your milk, *you* may be eating something that causes the digestive issue (don't forget that everything you eat is passed through you to your baby through breastfeeding). Watch your intake carefully and try to remove the following items from your diet (or at least consume them in moderation):

- ✔ **Acidic foods:** Avoid acidic fruit and foods with excessive peppers or spices.
- ✔ **Caffeine:** This category includes not only coffee but also tea and soft drinks.
- ✔ **Chocolate:** This rich treat is often too much for your baby to handle.
- ✔ **Dairy:** Diary has proteins that can build up your baby's intestinal track and create painful gas. Remove the dairy and see if things improve.
- ✔ **Gassy foods:** Broccoli, beans, and other high-fiber foods can pass the "gassy" effect onto your baby.
- ✔ **Spicy foods:** You may love your lasagne with the extra spicy sausage, but your baby will pay for it later.

If you're breastfeeding and anticipate a food binge on any of the previous items, pump several servings of breast milk *before* eating the food. That way your baby doesn't suffer the consequences.

Comforting colic

You'll hear the word *colic* quite a bit during the first two months of your baby's life. Colic is generally defined as crying spells that last more than two hours. Colic has been typically blamed on the baby's immature digestive system. However, recent research suggests that colic is really about the baby's immature nervous system, which prevents him from being able to filter out noise and distractions within the environment. This noise overloads your baby's nervous system until the nerves have more time to mature. If you have a colicky baby, try these helpful tricks:

✔ Turn on white noise: a vacuum, a fan, or static from the television. Sometimes the drone of these noises seems to calm a baby.

✔ Take the baby outside (assuming the weather is good). The sudden change of scenery and sound often helps the baby calm down.

✔ If you're breastfeeding, try eliminating all dairy products from your diet. A simple case of bad gas may be the culprit (see the preceding section for more on foods that cause digestive problems).

Combating reflux

All babies spit up and vomit; however, some babies seem to have a terrible time with it on a regular basis (which makes everything in your house and car have a nice sour milk smell). Spitting up and vomiting tend to reduce over time, but if your baby has *reflux* (technically called gastroesophageal reflux disease), you'll need some medical help. Note that breastfed babies usually don't have reflux, and the condition has a tendency to be overdiagnosed in all infants. If your baby seems to spit up after every feeding, you should at least mention it to your baby's pediatrician. The good news: Most babies outgrow reflux. (Check out Chapter 13 for more in-depth information.)

Reflux occurs when the ring of muscle around the stomach doesn't close properly. Stomach acid leaks back into the esophagus and causes heartburn, leading to a very irritated baby.

Nursing or feeding your baby in a more upright position and sitting her up for 30 minutes after feeding often alleviates immediate reflux issues.

Chapter 5

Enter Solid Foods: 4 to 6 Months

Up until now, your baby's primary nutrition has been breast milk or formula and will continue to be for some time. After your baby passes the 4-month mark (or shortly thereafter), you need to begin introducing solid foods. The initial solids that you feed your baby provide additional nutrition and bulk to your baby's diet. Of course, this transition takes quite a bit of time, so you need to feed go-between foods — not really solids, but not really liquids, but instead a mixture of the two (meaning we're not talking steak — think mush).

Most 4- to 6-month-olds are ready to begin eating solid foods, and in this chapter, we address your questions and give you some healthy, homemade options for welcoming your baby to the world of solids.

Moving Your Baby to Solid Foods

Naturally, you may get a lot of conflicting advice, such as Aunt Wanda's persistent instructions to start feeding your baby table food at 2 months old, but the age actually differs. You may wonder when you should begin introducing solid foods and what you should serve. Healthcare professionals overwhelmingly recommend that your baby's first food be rice cereal, which you can start serving around your baby's fourth month (if you're exclusively breast-feeding, you can wait until your child is six months of age).

Rice cereal contains a starting nutritional base of carbohydrates, and like other infant cereals, is fortified with iron, which is important for your baby's brain development. Additionally, rice cereal is easy to digest, which is very important during these early months.

As your baby adjusts to the new taste and texture of rice cereal, slowly introduce other cereals (such as barley and oatmeal after several weeks of rice cereal) and basic veggie purees. It's okay to begin feeding some fruit purees before your baby reaches her seventh month, but you may find that your child starts to love the sweet taste of the fruit and won't want anything else. With that addiction in mind, we recommend the cereal and basic veggie purees in this chapter, and try to hold off on the fruit until the latter part of the sixth month (you can find plenty of fruit puree recipes in Chapter 6).

So what do you feed, how much, and when? These important questions are answered in the following sections.

Knowing when to start

What are the signs that your baby is ready to begin eating cereal? Watch for these three signs:

- ✔ Your baby puts things in his mouth.
- ✔ Your baby can easily hold his head up on his own.
- ✔ Your baby seems interested in food when someone else is eating.

If you're saying "Yes, yes, yes" to the preceding bullets, then your baby can begin rice cereal during month four. However, what if your baby doesn't have these signs? In this case, wait a bit longer while your infant grows and develops.

The fourth month is just an average benchmark and doesn't mean that there's a problem if your baby isn't quite ready for solids. Naturally, if you have questions or concerns about your baby's development, you should check with your pediatrician. If your baby was born prematurely, he may develop more slowly, so check with your baby's doctor instead of spending time worrying and biting your nails.

If your baby seems to have all the readiness signs, but she only seems to push the cereal back out of her mouth instead of swallowing any, she may have a normal *tongue-thrust reflex*. This thrusting reflex is a normal condition that helps a baby to nurse.

Test your infant's reflex by touching your baby's lips with a spoon or your finger. If her tongue comes out of her mouth every time, she still has the reflex. Wait a week or so and try again. She'll outgrow this reflex in time and begin swallowing as you feed her.

Don't think that if your baby pushes the spoon out of her mouth on the first try that you should give up. Infants only know about suckling and have to learn to use the tongue to move solids from the front to the back of the mouth. This process takes time, and your first few tries of feeding cereal may end with most of the food down the front of your baby's bib, so don't get discouraged.

Introducing solids: Month 4

When you're ready to introduce cereal, you're likely to have some questions, such as when to feed your baby, how much, and how often. These questions are all important, and we show you what to do in this section.

When to feed

As you introduce rice cereal, you'll only feed the cereal once a day. You can choose whenever is best for your schedule; however, consider feeding rice cereal along with the final bottle or breastfeeding of the evening. Many advantages to this technique will start popping up:

- The cereal naturally helps your baby start to sleep longer.
  - Cereal is denser.
  - Dense foods keep your baby fuller longer.
- Solids help slowly decrease the number of bottle or breast feedings.
  - Night feedings decrease first.
  - You get more uninterrupted sleep.

How much to feed

Generally, you begin with only a tablespoon of cereal mixed with formula or breast milk until the mixture is very thin. Then you simply feed your baby small bites on a baby spoon. When you start trying purees, 2 tablespoons is plenty during the 4-month starting range.

Keep in mind that your baby has to discover how to eat solid foods — all your baby has known is liquid, so mastering this process takes some time.

How to feed a 4-month-old

Open mouth, insert food, chew, and swallow. It sounds simple enough —
maybe for older kids and adults. But remember that your baby has to discover how to chew and swallow. After all, swallowing liquids is a lot different
than swallowing solids. Your baby won't naturally eat cereal without some
practice.

As you're getting ready to feed your baby, follow these few steps to get on the
right track:

1. **Gather your props.**

   Decide where — such as a car seat or bouncy seat — you're going to
   feed your baby for the first time.

   - Make sure that your baby is inclined.

   - Don't place your infant in a highchair because he can't fully sup-
     port the weight of his head.

   - Think of the angle of a baby car seat, and you'll be in good shape.

2. **Make sure that the spoon and bowl are sterilized.**

   Sterilization eliminates germs found on feeding equipment and keeps
   your baby healthy.

3. **Get a good large bib and a towel.**

   Feeding can be a messy job!

4. **Mix the cereal and serve it at room temperature.**

   Make sure to taste the cereal for proper temperature before serving.
   Place a spoonful of the cereal against your lips. If the cereal is too hot for
   your lips, it's definitely too hot for your baby's sensitive mouth.

5. **Place a small bit of cereal (about ¼ spoonful) in your baby's mouth.**

   Allow your baby to open his mouth for the spoon just as he would a
   bottle nipple or the breast. Don't force the spoon into your baby's
   mouth. Touch the spoon to his lips and he should open his mouth.

   Your baby may push most of the food back out of his mouth and try to
   suck on the spoon. These behaviors are normal. Repeat this process
   several times and then call it a day.

6. **Repeat the whole process the next day.**

   Don't get discouraged. Soon enough, your child understands how to
   swallow the cereal, and he'll like it and want more.

Don't try to feed cereal to your baby when he's full, but make sure that he's not famished either! If he's full, he won't have any interest in trying a new cereal. If he's starving, he'll just get aggravated because he wants the bottle or breast, and he wants it *now!* Some parents find it helpful to alternate the bottle or breast between bites of cereal to help the baby stay interested. After your baby gets more practice with the new food and you offer it at a specific time of day, he'll get used to the routine.

As you get ready to feed your 4-month-old, keep a few safety tips in mind at all times:

- **Use a baby spoon.** They're covered with rubber to protect your child's gums and they're small enough to fit in your baby's mouth. Never use a regular adult-size spoon to feed a baby.

- **Feed your baby in an upright eating position.** Sitting up helps your baby's swallowing reflex and prevents the choking hazard that naturally comes if your baby is lying down after eating.

- **Don't feed cereal from a bottle.** Grandma may suggest feeding this way by cutting larger holes in the nipple of the bottle to feed solids. But using this feeding method presents a choking hazard because your baby may get too much cereal in her mouth at once.

  Feed cereal only with a spoon. (And if you see Grandma with a pair of scissors at your house, check your bottle nipples for extra holes and hide them where she'll never think to look.)

- **Don't rush.** This process is a lot for your baby to take in, so take your time. Rushing also presents a choking possibility because of too much food in the baby's mouth.

- **Don't keep uneaten portions of cereal or other purees.** The saliva from your baby's mouth will get into the puree as you scoop each bite of cereal. Bacteria can grow in the cereal. Whatever isn't eaten from the bowl that you're using to feed should go directly in the trash or garbage disposal.

  Storing portions of cereal or puree in single servings — like freezing them in ice cube trays with lids — helps reduce waste. You'll use only what you need at the time of feeding and have less to throw out if your baby doesn't eat all his food.

Enter cereal variety and veggies: Month 5

As your baby rapidly grows, you're still feeding rice cereal but as you move into month five, and if your baby is doing well eating the cereal, shake things up a bit and begin adding other cereal options and a few veggies. As an excited parent who wants to cook for your baby, you can start putting some of your pureeing skills to work.

Keep an eye out for any food allergies that may crop up. Because you need to watch out for food allergies, introduce a new food only every week or so (you should wait at least five days), and then watch and make sure that your baby doesn't have a reaction to that food. Look for the following symptoms that may indicate a food allergy:

- ✔ Excessive crankiness
- ✔ Diarrhea
- ✔ Excessive bloating
- ✔ Gas
- ✔ Rash around the mouth

If you expect an allergy, remove the last food you tried, and don't give it again for a few weeks. (Head over to Chapter 13 for an in-depth discussion about food allergies and intolerances, and use the food log in Appendix B to keep track of all the new foods you introduce to your youngster and how she reacts to them.)

When and what to feed

Continue with the early evening feeding as you've been doing, but add a lunch or late morning time to your schedule. This added feeding spaces out the meals adequately. When you try a new food, introduce it only during the lunch meal. This method gives you adequate time to watch your baby and make sure that he can tolerate the new food.

Don't get overly excited about your baby's newfound love of solid foods. Your baby isn't ready for any kind of chunky baby food. Stick with the plain veggie purees and cereals in this chapter. Start with orange and yellow veggies and then move on to green veggies after a few weeks. These foods are all your baby needs at this point.

If your baby seems to reject a veggie (some have a stronger taste than others), consider mixing the vegetable with a bit of the cereal. Your baby recognizes the texture of the cereal and then adjusts to the new taste combination.

Resist the urge to start feeding your baby items from the dinner table — no sweets, no soda, or anything like that. You can have more problems with pinpointing food allergies this way, and your child may want sweet foods instead of veggies. Also, never give your baby honey. Honey may contain spores that cause botulism. It's safe after your baby turns 1 year old, but never give it before then.

Relishing the highchair while you cook

The highchair is a great tool to help you with your little one when you create meals. You can put your baby in his highchair, recline the seat a bit for extra head support, and pull the chair up close to you as you work (but away from the stove). This process helps you keep an eye on your baby and gives you a chance to interact as you cook. Explain the steps of cooking as you go along. Show your tyke the tomato, for example. Let him feel it, smell it, and explain the color. After all, children are never too young to start learning.

How much to feed

Keep in mind that your little one may eat more or less at each meal and eating isn't an exact science. As she moves through month 5, her appetite continues to grow, but don't get in the habit of trying to measure food exactly and expecting your baby to eat all of every food you feed her. Your baby will grow to a few teaspoons of different foods at each feeding, but this process takes time. As long as your baby is gaining weight and seems happy, don't overthink the amount. Your baby lets you know when she's hungry and if she wants more.

On with the veggie introductions: Month 6

At the age of 6 months, most babies become more interested in other foods. However, we should say up-front that children develop at their own pace, so don't think that six months is a marker for certain behavior — more or less time may need to be devoted to your child's eating habits, so don't let this stress you out.

Continuing with more of the same . . . and then some

During the sixth month, you'll simply continue what you started in month 5.

- ✔ Continue adding new foods — about one new food every week or so — from the recipes in this chapter, always being mindful of food allergy symptoms.

- ✔ Give your baby some cereal in the morning, a lunch consisting of veggie purees, and a dinner with more veggies and some additional cereal.

- ✔ Offer your child only pureed veggies. Although fruit is tempting, your child may decide that fruit is more interesting and automatically start rejecting vegetables.

- ✔ Continue making your baby's cereal with formula or breast milk. Your baby shouldn't have cow's milk until she's 1. See Chapter 4 for more information on milk.

Your baby is likely to eat several tablespoons of food per meal at this point, and you can gauge how much she wants based on her response. Don't expect your baby to be on autopilot; she'll eat more at some meals and less at others.

As solids are continuing to be fed, you may be wondering, "How much formula or breast milk should my baby have each day?" As a general rule, feed 4 to 5 servings a day, totally 24 to 32 ounces. With this amount of milk and the new solids you're adding, your baby should be happy and growing at a rapid rate.

You should still offer the breast and bottle on demand at this point, because your baby may go through rapid growth spurts, requiring more calories and energy. Naturally, a feeding schedule will develop, but if your baby is hungry, feed her!

Adding juice to the repertoire

Now is a good time to start introducing your baby to apple or pear juice. Both of these juices are healthy and mild, making them easy to digest. Many combo juices — such as orange-pineapple juice — are on the market, but your baby doesn't need these. In fact, children shouldn't have any citrus fruit at this age because these types of juices are too harsh for your little one's digestive system.

As you're thinking about introducing juice, don't forget about water. As a newborn, your baby gets all the water he needs from breast milk or formula. But as he grows and starts eating solids, give him water periodically in his bottle. Just like in your diet, water is important to keep him hydrated (and to keep him from drinking too much juice, which has a lot of sugar).

At 6 months old, your child needs the extra nutrition and vitamin C that apple or pear juice provides. In fact, we recommend that you buy *pure juice* for children less than one year of age because it's fortified with vitamin C. You can also buy infant juice at the store. Serve 4 ounces each day and your child gets all the vitamin C he needs — it's like a healthy booster shot.

Pure juice doesn't mean homemade juice in this case. Juice made at home with a juicer doesn't contain enough vitamin C for your infant. Stick to store-bought juice with the label that says "fortified with vitamin C."

When you first start serving juice to your munchkin, dilute the juice with water. Two ounces of juice to 2 ounces of water is a good start. If you start off with straight juice, your baby will likely get a stomachache and diarrhea. Remember, his little digestive system is still adjusting to all these new foods.

Introduce the sippy cup (see Chapter 3 for more information about sippy cups) as you introduce juice. This initiation helps you wean your baby off the bottle a few months down the road.

Your Baby's First "Real" Food: Homemade Cereals

Even parents who're determined to prepare baby meals often start out with store bought cereal for one simple reason: It's well made and has additional vitamins and iron added, which your baby needs. We recommend a combination of store bought cereal and your own homemade varieties from the recipes you find in this chapter.

Wheat is the most common allergen of any grain, so it's best to leave wheat out of the diet until your baby is a bit older. In fact, allergens are exactly why you should avoid table foods because every little unplanned morsel may contain foods that have common allergy products. You'll often find wheat in such common items as:

- Many types of crackers
- Graham crackers
- Bran
- Cake flour
- Farina (bland-tasting flour or meal)
- Malt
- Semolina

Stick with the tried-and-true cereals in this chapter (they don't contain wheat products).

Freeze any of these cereals or purees in a covered ice cube tray for a month, and simply remove and thaw for use. However, freezing freshly made cereals often gives them a rubbery texture when you thaw them. Experiment with freezing, but in many cases, parents choose to simply grind the grains, store them in an airtight container, then simply make a new batch of cereal as needed.

 Rice Cereal

When your baby is ready, single-ingredient baby cereals (like rice cereal) make a perfect introduction because they're easy to digest and provide the iron your baby needs. Serve only rice cereal during the first few weeks of starting solids before adding anything else. This process gives your baby time to understand eating cereal and allows his digestive system time to adjust. Naturally, you can purchase dry rice cereal for infants at your local supermarket, but you can also make your own following this recipe. Brown rice has more nutrition than white, so use brown rice as the recipe suggests. This recipe makes two cups of cereal, which is much more than you need at one feeding, but you can freeze the rest for later use.

Preparation time: *20 minutes*

Yield: *2 cups*

¼ cup brown rice   1 cup water

1 In a food processor, grind the rice into a fine powder. Mix the rice and water in a small saucepan and bring the mixture to a boil.

2 Simmer for 10 minutes, whisking constantly.

3 Cool the mixture slightly and add 3 tablespoons of breast milk or mixed formula for a thin consistency. Add more breast milk or formula if the mixture is too thick. Serve warm — be sure to check the temperature.

 Barley Cereal

After your baby adjusts to rice cereal, barley cereal is a good addition to your food arsenal. Barley cereal, like brown rice, provides complex carbohydrates for energy but is also easy to digest. Here's a quick, homemade recipe. Because this recipe makes 2 cups, freeze the extra cereal for later use.

Preparation time: *20 minutes*

Yield: *2 cups*

¼ cup barley   1 cup water

1 In a food processor, grind the barley into a fine powder. Mix the barley and water in a small saucepan and bring the mixture to a boil.

2 Simmer for 10 minutes, whisking constantly.

3 Cool the mixture slightly and add 3 tablespoons of breast milk or mixed formula for a thin consistency, and add more breast milk or formula as needed. Serve warm — be sure to check the temperature.

 **Oatmeal Cereal**

Oatmeal cereal is also a good addition as your baby continues to move toward solids. Oatmeal's nutrition provides your baby with plenty of carbs. Keep in mind that you can freeze the extra and use it later.

Preparation time: *20 minutes*

Yield: *2 cups*

¼ cup rolled oats   ¾ cup water

1 In a food processor, grind the oats into a fine powder.

2 In a small saucepan, heat the water and add the oat powder, mixing constantly to reduce lumps. Bring the mixture to a boil. Simmer for 5 minutes, whisking constantly.

3 Cool the mixture slightly and add 3 tablespoons of breast milk or mixed formula for a thin consistency. Feel free to add more breast milk or formula if needed. Serve warm — be sure to check the temperature.

 **Mixed-Grain Cereal**

Try this mixed-grain cereal as an additional cereal to the single grains you've given your baby so far. Offer mixed cereal only after your baby has sampled all the single-grain cereals and you're sure that an allergic reaction doesn't exist. You can freeze the extra cereal that is left from this recipe for later use.

Preparation time: *25 minutes*

Yield: *2 cups*

2 tablespoons barley	*2 tablespoons rolled oats*
2 tablespoons rice	*1 cup water*

1 In a food processor, grind the grains into a fine powder. You may need to grind a bit longer to make sure that the rice grinds to a powder. Consider using a coffee grinder (if the grinder hasn't been previously used to grind coffee, nuts, or spices).

2 Mix the grains and water in a small saucepan and bring the mixture to a boil. Simmer for 15 minutes, whisking constantly.

3 Cool the mixture slightly and add 3 tablespoons of breast milk or mixed formula. This addition helps your baby adjust to the new texture and taste. Serve warm — be sure to check the temperature.

Solids Part 2: A Rainbow of Pureed Veggies

As your baby grows and adjusts to the texture of cereal, you can begin slowly adding some orange and yellow veggies (as well as a few green veggies) to your baby's diet. The veggie purees you'll find in this section are all easy to digest, so they're perfect for your baby's immature digestive system.

As you get ready to puree veggies, keep in mind that you want the puree to be thin. Even though your baby is eating cereal, she still needs time to adjust to other new foods as well.

○ *Summer Squash Puree*

Squash is a great food for 4- to 6-month-olds because squash is healthy and easy to digest. As a "yellow" veggie, it's perfect for your child, providing nutrition and easy digestion. You can freeze the leftovers in this recipe for later use.

Preparation time: *10 minutes*

Tools: *Steamer*

Yield: *¾ cup*

1 medium yellow squash	Water as needed

1 Peel the squash with a vegetable peeler or sharp paring knife. Cut the squash into small slices.

2 Steam the slices until completely tender, about 5 minutes.

3 Puree the squash by using a food processor, adding water as necessary to get a thin puree. Serve warm.

○ *Fresh Carrot Puree*

Carrots are another great food for 4- to 6-month-olds because they're chock-full of vitamins for your little tyke. Freeze the leftover puree for later use, too.

Preparation time: *10 minutes*

Yield: *½ cup*

1 medium carrot	Water as needed

1 Rinse the peeled carrot, cut it in half, and boil it for 5 minutes or until soft.

2 Cut the carrot in small pieces and then puree it in a food processor. Serve warm. If the puree seems a bit too dry, add a teaspoon of water.

○ Creamy Corn Puree

This recipe can be helpful if your child resists eating solids. The breast milk or formula makes the taste familiar to your infant. This addition helps your baby start to overcome the issue of texture because the taste is essentially the same. You'll have some leftover puree, so feel free to freeze it for later use.

Preparation time: *20 minutes*

Yield: *½ cup*

¼ cup frozen corn kernels   *¼ cup breast milk or formula*

1 Cook the corn according to the package directions and drain the water.

2 Puree the corn in a food processor until creamy.

3 Mix the puree with the breast milk or formula and serve warm.

○ Winter Squash Puree

Along with summer squash, you can also feed butternut or acorn squash as a puree. This type of squash takes a bit longer to prepare so we've given you a larger yield for your work, but it's a healthy food for your baby so it's well worth the effort. And, for added benefit, you can freeze the leftovers for later use.

Preparation time: *20 minutes*

Cooking time: *40 minutes*

Yield: *2 cups*

1 acorn or butternut squash   *Water as needed*

1 Preheat the oven to 400 degrees.

2 Cut the squash in half and scoop out all the seeds.

3 Put an inch of water in a baking pan and place the squash halves cut-side down in the pan. While baking, check the water and make sure that it stays at an inch.

4 Bake the squash for 40 minutes or until the skin puckers and the squash is soft.

5 Remove the pan from the oven, remove the squash from the pan, and let it cool for 10 to 15 minutes. Scoop out the squash meat. Puree the squash and add water as necessary to thin the puree. Serve warm.

 Potato Puree

As with the other purees, this one is easily digestible (thanks to the potato) and can be introduced — in pureed form — during the fourth month of life and up to 6 months. The leftovers are freezable for later use.

Preparation time: *50 minutes*

Yield: *2 cups*

1 potato	*Water or breast milk as needed*

1 Peel the potato and cook it in a saucepan of boiling water for 25 minutes or until soft. To speed up the process, cut the potato into cubes and cook them for 10 minutes or until soft.

2 Press the potato through a strainer to break it up and catch any hard lumps (which you discard) and then puree, adding water, breast milk, or formula to form a thin puree. Serve warm.

○ *Fresh Sweet Potato Puree*

Pure sweet potato and nothing else in this puree! Sweet potatoes are a nutrient-dense food. You can freeze the leftovers and use them later.

Preparation time: *15 minutes*

Yield: *1 cup*

1 medium sweet potato	*Water as needed*

1 Wash and scrub the sweet potato with cold water. Peel and quarter the sweet potato.

2 Bring a pot of water to a boil, and then place the sweet potato quarters in the boiling water. Return the water to boiling, reduce the heat to medium, and cover for 15 minutes until the potato is tender.

3 Puree the sweet potato until smooth and add a teaspoon of water if necessary for consistency. Serve warm.

Tip: *Because sweet potatoes have a different taste than other veggies, you can mix a bit of breast milk or formula with this puree, which can help it have a more familiar taste for your baby.*

○ *Oatmeal and Potato Puree*

You may find that blending veggies in with cereal makes feeding time easier. After all, your baby is already familiar with the texture of cereal, so mixing the two can help you introduce new veggies. This recipe makes more than you need in one feeding, so feel free to freeze the leftovers.

Preparation Time: *50 minutes*

Yield: *2 cups*

1 potato	*1 cup water*
¼ cup rolled oats	

1 Peel the potato and boil it in a saucepan of water for 25 minutes or until soft. You can also reduce cooking time by cutting the potato into cubes and boiling them for 10 minutes or until soft.

2 Press the potato through a strainer to catch any hard lumps, and discard the hard pieces.

3 In a food processor, puree the oatmeal into a fine powder. Heat the water and then mix the oatmeal and water in a medium saucepan and bring the mixture to a boil. Reduce the heat and simmer on medium heat for 10 minutes.

4 Add the potatoes and mix well. If you need to, remove the mixture from the heat and puree a bit more. Add water as necessary for a thin puree. Serve warm.

🍅 Green Bean Puree

This fresh green bean puree is a great addition to your baby's meals during the 4 to 6 month age range. Green beans are easy to digest and aren't overwhelming in taste like some veggies. You'll make more of this recipe than you need, so feel free to freeze the leftovers and use them later.

Preparation time: *10 minutes*

Tools: *Vegetable steamer*

Yield: *¾ cup*

1 cup green beans	*Water as needed*

1 Cut the tips off each end of fresh green beans and wash well. If you're using frozen green beans, cook the beans according to the package directions and proceed to Step 3.

2 Place the beans in a steamer and steam until tender, about 7 minutes.

3 Puree the beans in a food processor, adding water as necessary until the puree is thin. Serve warm.

 Mixed Greens Puree

This mixed greens recipe provides the perfect balance of green veggies. This recipe makes 2 cups of puree, which is more than the other recipes. However, because you're creating a mixture of greens, it's easier to puree a larger amount and freeze the leftovers for additional meals later.

Preparation time: *10 minutes*

Yield: *2 cups*

⅓ cup green beans	⅓ cup finely sliced zucchini
⅓ cup peas	1 cup water

1 In a small saucepan, place the veggies and add enough water just to cover the vegetables.

2 Cook the vegetables on medium heat until tender, reserving the water.

3 Puree the vegetables in a blender or food processor, adding the reserved water from the vegetables until the mixture is thin. Serve warm.

Chapter 6

Foods for Your Crawler: 6 to 12 Months

Your baby is now at least 6 months old and has turned into a wiggling, moving child. During these early days, your baby's diet changes, too. Milk continues to be your baby's main drink, but water also becomes an important source of hydration. You'll also notice that your child is becoming increasingly interested in what you're eating and drinking as well.

In this chapter, you find out about your baby's nutritional needs for 6 months up to 1 year of age and explore some healthy recipes you can start introducing into your baby's diet.

It's important to note, however, that we move from purees to chunkier foods in this chapter. This progression is natural as your baby grows, but you may find that some of the dishes in this chapter aren't appropriate for your 6- to 7-month-old because they require more chewing. If your baby isn't quite ready to move on at this age, continue serving him the purees we discuss in Chapter 5 until he's ready.

Wondering how you're supposed to know when Baby's ready? (We spill the beans in this chapter, so read on.) Of course, we guide you along the way as you introduce new foods to your infant, but just remember that moving from purees to chunky foods should be gradual, so hold your horses.

Moving On to Bigger and Better Foods

As your child moves toward the seventh and eighth months of life, you should see much improvement in his ability to eat solid foods. Most babies easily eat pureed veggies by the sixth month, so at this point they may be hungry for more. Your baby still needs pureed foods, but the foods become chunkier, in-between purees and full solids. At this point, you're likely to see baby teeth — another sign that your baby's body is getting ready for some changes nutritionally.

Feeding more than just veggies: Months 7 and 8

Hopefully by the time baby reaches the seventh month, she's eating a nice collection of basic veggies. As such, now is the time to start introducing a bigger variety of vegetables in addition to other food items and small amounts of finger foods. It's very important to watch out for foods that can be a choking hazard, so you need to make sure that bites of chunky food are small.

In the middle to that later part of the seventh month, you can introduce such items as

- ✔ **Additional veggies:** You introduced basic veggies during the 4- to 6-month range, but as your baby grows, you can introduce additional veggie purees and make them a bit chunkier as your baby develops.
- ✔ **Pureed soft fruits:** Make sure that the peel is removed and stick with foods that are less likely to cause your baby digestive problems, such as pears, bananas, apricots, apples, and other noncitrus fruits.
- ✔ **Soft bread:** Serve bread in small pieces with no crust. You can also serve small bites of crackers and graham crackers.
- ✔ **Chicken or beef:** Cut meat in small pieces.
- ✔ **Cooked pasta:** Serve pasta such as spirals, bowties, and so on — don't serve longer noodles because of the choking hazard. For 7-month-olds, even spirals and bowties will need to be cut up to avoid choking risks.

As your baby gets more and more interested in food, you'll be tempted to let her sample more than she should. Be careful what you experiment with because of unknown food allergies at this age and potential dangers of choking. Avoid such items as

- ✔ Candy
- ✔ Chips
- ✔ Grapes
- ✔ Large pieces of bread
- ✔ Popcorn
- ✔ Raisins
- ✔ Uncooked veggies

See Chapter 13 for a complete list of foods to watch out for when feeding your child.

So, what should the eating routine be during Baby's seventh month? Generally, your baby may

- ✔ Become less and less dependent on milk — probably three to five 8-ounce servings a day
- ✔ Eat cereal twice a day — early morning and evening are the best times
- ✔ Eat a combination of veggies, fruit, and meat at lunch and dinner, as well as additional fruit at breakfast
- ✔ Snack on little items, such as crackers, as desired

As your baby eats more solid food, avoid the temptation to introduce him to cow's milk — he isn't ready to go from breast milk or formula to cow's milk. At this age, cow's milk may cause an allergic reaction, and breast milk or formula still provide most of the nutrients your baby needs. However, you should start offering formula or breast milk, as well as water, to your baby in a sippy cup as well as the breast or bottle.

If you're having a lot of problems getting your child to eat, and he seems generally cranky, get his ears checked — ear problems can cause jaw pain, which may make your baby steer clear of eating. Naturally, your pediatrician can help you with any questions concerning eating behavior.

Expanding baby's palatal interests: Months 9 and 10

By the time your baby reaches the 9- to 10-month age, he'll probably have a couple of teeth, and he may start becoming more opinionated about what he's eating. You'll notice that your baby loves certain things and makes disgusted faces when you give him something else. This behavior is normal, and you can expect it to continue as your child grows.

During the 9- to 10-month period, your introduction of new veggies, fruits, and meats continues. Not a whole lot changes during this time, except you gradually make your baby's foods chunkier to help him get used to different textures, depending on his development and how many teeth he has. This process is slow, so don't get in a hurry.

Keep in mind that you must continue to avoid such potential allergy items such as cow's milk, eggs (although egg whites are okay), strawberries, nuts, and honey.

You'll also notice that Baby becomes more interested in feeding himself at this age. This sense of independence often comes as a surprise, but even at this young age, your baby wants to hold the spoon and starts trying to spoon food into his mouth. Although you'll have to assist, it's important to let your baby start practicing with the spoon as he shows interest. Your baby isn't only discovering how to feed himself but also gaining important dexterity skills as he handles the spoon.

Other than these restrictions, your baby starts to eat at least what appears to be a more grown-up diet with snacks and milk scattered throughout the day as well. Remember the following rules during this stage:

- ✔ **You can't overfeed your child at this age.** The trick is to let the child eat until she's full. Children stop eating when they've had enough, so don't worry about the amount of food — just be consistent in feeding healthy food to your child.

- ✔ **Don't assume that the choking hazard has passed.** Sure, your child is more skilled at handling food with his fingers and getting it in his mouth, but choking is always a risk. Keep small bites of food available.

- ✔ **Don't let food become a battleground.** Sometimes your child eats well and other times not. While this behavior is normal, you must maintain your child's good diet.

  - If your child doesn't eat dinner, don't give him a cookie instead.

  - Limit junk food — if you give in to demands for it, you're setting up an unhealthy eating pattern that's likely to get worse with age.

  - Expect that your child will eat only when he's hungry — never force him to eat.

  - Don't let eating become a discipline issue, because this behavior makes food become a reward and punishment system. Let eating be about eating — that's all.

Beginning to wean: Months 11 and 12

During the final two months of your child's first year, your helpless baby grows into a child that can crawl and stand. Your child understands and can probably say "no" and may be able to say "dada" and "mama" and understand the meaning of the words.

For the most part, what you serve your baby during these months is a continuation of what you've already been serving — you still introduce new veggies, fruits, and meats, giving your child more variety and even chunkier textures. The biggest change is that by the end of the 12th month, your pediatrician may suggest weaning your baby from breast milk or formula.

The American Academy of Pediatrics says that around the age of 12 months you should begin to wean your baby off formula. If you're breastfeeding, you may do so for longer, but you can expect breastfeeding to slow down, too.

Your baby may be resistant to breast and bottle weaning, or she may wean herself. It's important to note that this is a guideline and not a "must follow." All children are different and your baby may still want to nurse after her first birthday, even when she starts eating more foods. Instead of seeing weaning as a date on a calendar or an event, view the process as one that happens slowly as your baby begins to eat other foods around 6 months of age. The date-on-the-calendar approach usually gives you and your baby more stress.

We give you some tips on how to wean in Chapter 7, so if you're ready for that part, flip ahead.

Don't allow the weaning process to get out of hand; several dentists recommend bottle weaning at 1 year of age or soon after to prevent tooth decay and teeth spacing issues.

Losing the bottle, but not the milk

If your kid is still drinking from a bottle, start saying goodbye as he approaches 12 months old. (Say goodbye to the bottle, not your child!) In many cases, children wean themselves from the bottle and prefer to use a sippy cup. After all, a bottle requires more sucking work for less reward, and children quickly learn that.

But having a bottle, especially at certain times of the day (such as bedtime), can be comforting for your baby, so keep in mind that weaning is a process. If you're having problems weaning your child from the bottle, follow these steps for success:

1. **Begin by removing the bottle during certain periods of the day, such as lunchtime, and giving only a sippy cup.**

   You'll have to be firm, even if your child seems unhappy. Remember that this process is gradual, so don't force it all at once.

Keeping your child fit as a whistle

During the 6- to 12-month age range, your sedentary baby becomes a moving machine. As such, this time of a child's life is full of change and full of special needs. In terms of food, be sure to keep the following tips in mind:

✔ **Never use food as a reward, bribe, or punishment.** Food should be food and nothing more. If you start using food to get your child to behave or perform in a certain way, you're making food too much of a focus.

✔ **Milk isn't a traveling liquid.** When your child is at play, don't let her carry around a sippy cup of milk or juice continually. Juices are great for your child, but it doesn't have to be introduced into your child's diet every 10 minutes. Now is a good time to introduce drinking water, but still keep the liquid in the kitchen. Your child will indicate when she's thirsty.

2. **Continue to move more bottle feedings to the sippy cup over the next few weeks.**

    Replace snacktime feedings with the sippy cup.

3. **Save the final bottle feeding of the day for the last one to be removed.**

    With patience, firmness, and a bit of time, your child will make the switch over to the cup.

If your child sucks a pacifier, work on weaning from the breast or bottle first and worry about the pacifier later. Don't try to wean both at the same time, or everyone will end up in tears.

Simple but Satisfying Purees

When you first start feeding solids to your baby, begin with plain cereal (see Chapter 5). However, over the next couple of months, add pureed veggies and fruit and move on to bites of meat and combinations of foods. Naturally, it's always best to start out with the basics to give your child's digestive system time to develop, and in this section, you find some simple purees that you can put to work in your kitchen. They're all fresh, wholesome, and completely homemade!

The purees in this chapter build on the basic purees you begin with, which we discuss in Chapter 5. As you add the following purees, slowly begin to adjust the texture so that they aren't as thin as the purees you started with. Remember, though, that the taste of these new varied foods is different to your infant, so give her the opportunity to get used to them before you start increasing texture.

☞ *Avocado and Squash Puree*

Both avocados and squash are full of nutrition and easy to digest. This puree tastes great and contains plenty of *good* fat from the avocado. It's a healthy meal option for your little one. You can add this puree to your child's diet at 6 months.

Preparation time: *15 minutes*

Yield: *Two ½-cup servings*

½ medium yellow squash, peeled   *½ ripe avocado, peeled and pitted*

1 Cut the squash in bite-size rounds and boil it in water until tender (about 12 minutes).

2 Drain the squash and puree it with the avocado in a food processor until smooth. Serve warm.

☞ *Broccoli and Cauliflower Puree*

This puree is full of nutrition, but you need to wait until Baby is 9 months old to serve it, because both broccoli and cauliflower are denser and more difficult to digest than other vegetables. We recommend making this puree a bit chunky, so it has small chunks of broccoli and cauliflower in it.

Preparation time: *15 minutes*

Yield: *Two ½-cup servings*

½ cup small cauliflower florets   *½ cup small broccoli florets*

1 Place all the florets in a steamer and steam them for 10 minutes, or until tender. You can also boil them in a few inches of water in a saucepan with a lid if you don't have a steamer.

2 Drain the water from the vegetables and puree them in a food processor until blended but somewhat chunky. Serve warm.

Vary It! *You can mix this puree with others, such as the Sweet Potato Puree in Chapter 5, for a more interesting flavor.*

☺ Corn and Green Pea Puree

This puree combines easy-to-digest corn with green peas, making it a good combination meal for your baby. Because this one is great to introduce at the 6-month stage, keep the puree well blended and moderately thin.

Preparation Time: *15 minutes*

Yield: *One ¾-cup serving*

¼ green peas, frozen or canned	¼ cup whole kernel corn, frozen or canned

1 Cook the veggies according to the package directions.

2 When the veggies are tender, puree them together in a food processor, and add water as necessary for a moderately thin puree. Serve warm.

☺ Rice and Peach Puree

This recipe combines white rice with peaches for a yummy meal. For the best flavor, make sure that the peach you use is fully ripe, and to speed the preparation process, use minute rice. You can start serving this puree during Baby's sixth month and increase the chunkiness as your baby grows.

Preparation time: *30 minutes*

Yield: *Four ½-cup servings*

½ cup white rice	1 ripe peach, washed, peeled, pitted, and halved

1 Prepare the rice according to the package directions. You want the rice to be well done, almost mushy.

2 Puree the peach in a food processor, add the rice, and puree. The juice from the peach and the water from the rice is probably all you need for consistency, but you can add a little water if necessary. Serve warm.

☙ Banana Peach Puree

This pure-fruit dish will tantalize your child's taste buds with the sweetness of peaches and an old favorite — the banana. You can start this puree as early as 6 months of age — at that age, you want this puree to be slightly thin, but you can increase the consistency to pudding thickness as your child grows.

Preparation time: 5 minutes

Yield: One ¾-cup serving

1 medium, ripe banana, peeled   *1 medium, ripe peach, peeled and pitted*

Dice the banana and peach and puree them in a food processor. Add a bit of water for consistency if necessary. Serve.

Tip: Substitute kiwi, apples, pears, or avocado for the peach in this recipe.

☙ Pureed Apples and Pears

Here's a common apple and pear puree that you can serve as early as the 6-month stage. You can follow this basic recipe and amend it to include other fruit combinations as Baby grows, during which time you can also decrease the water and make the puree with a texture like pudding.

Preparation time: 20 minutes

Yield: One ¾-cup serving

¼ cup ripe apple, skinned and cut in small pieces

¼ cup ripe pear, skinned and cut in small pieces

1¼ cups water, divided

1 Mix the fruit and 1 cup of the water in a small saucepan and simmer until the fruit is soft (about 10 minutes).

2 Drain the fruit and place it in a food processor. Add the remaining water and puree until thin. Serve at room temperature.

⏱ Banana and Avocado Puree

Although the combination of banana and avocado may not sound appetizing to you, children often like it. Avocado has a rich taste that works well with the sweet taste of banana. It's also chock-full of vitamins, so it's a great puree to feed to your baby. As your child grows, decrease the water to make the puree a bit chunkier.

Preparation time: *10 minutes*

Yield: *One ¾-cup serving*

¼ cup peeled and mashed avocado   ¼ cup water

¼ ripe banana, mashed

Mix the mashed ingredients in a small bowl. If your mixture is lumpy, puree it in a food processor until creamy. Add the water and stir well, adding more water if needed.

⏱ Yogurt Banana Puree

Yogurt is a valuable health food for infants because it's a balanced source of protein, fats, carbohydrates, and minerals, and youngsters usually love its texture. Note that you should only use whole-fat, plain yogurt for this recipe, which works great for children 9 months old and up. As Baby grows, you can make it chunkier.

You can save the extra puree in your refrigerator for later use, but because bananas turn brown, the puree won't last longer than a day.

Preparation time: *5 minutes*

Yield: *Three ½-cup servings*

1 medium ripe banana, peeled   1 cup plain, full-fat yogurt

Cut the banana into small pieces, and then puree the yogurt and banana in a food processor. Serve slightly cool or at room temperature.

Vary It! *Substitute any other fruit for the banana in this recipe. Keep in mind that you should stick with fruits that are unlikely to give your baby a tummy ache, such as peaches, pears, avocados, and apples.*

☉ Dried Apricot Puree

Apricots are a good fruit for young babies because they're easy to digest. However, finding fresh apricots can be difficult depending on what time of year it is and where you live. As such, this recipe shows you how to use the dried variety instead. This puree is somewhat thick and chunky, so you shouldn't serve it until Baby's 9th month.

Preparation time: *5 minutes*

Yield: *Two ½-cup servings*

4 dried apricots	*4 tablespoons water*

1 Simmer the apricots in 4 cups of water for 15 minutes or until very tender.

2 Drain the fruit and put it in a food processor, along with 4 tablespoons of water. Puree finely. Add a bit more water to get a puree consistency, but keep in mind that this recipe will be a bit thicker and chunkier than other fruit purees. Because you're working with previously dried apricots, you may need to remove a few harder or larger pieces from the puree and then puree a bit more to get the right consistency. Serve at room temperature.

Vary It! *Consider mixing this fruit puree with baby cereal or with a bit of yogurt to make it more palatable for your baby. If fresh apricots are in season, you can simply peel and quarter them, remove the seeds, and puree.*

Basic veggie and fruit purees

You can essentially puree any veggie or fruit, but instead of giving you a recipe for each and every possibility, we provide a few tips about pureeing that will help with your preparation of all veggies and fruits.

For veggies, do the following:

1. **Wash and peel the veggie and boil it until it's soft.**

2. **Pureed the veggie in a food processor.**

   If you don't own a food processor, you can use a blender or hand mixer. See Chapter 3 for information on basic kitchen tools.

3. **Add a teaspoon of water (or more or less), depending on the veggie, to get the desired consistency.**

As a general rule, any basic puree should be thin but manageable with a spoon. For this reason, getting the right consistency can require a bit of water. As your child ages, add less water to make the puree thicker and gradually move your child toward chunkier foods.

Pureeing fruit is basically the same. Be sure to choose only ripe fruit.

1. **Cut the fruit into pieces or boil it if necessary to make it soft.**

2. **Puree to the desired consistency.**

   Add water as necessary.

The Best of Two Worlds: Combination Meals

As your baby reaches 6 months of age, her meal options become more complex and varied. Naturally, your child will like certain foods and have aversions to others. In this section, you find some healthy, homemade recipes that your baby is likely to enjoy (our kids loved them!). With pure, fresh ingredients, you'll feel good about serving these meals.

Keep in mind that when your wee one is 6 months old, you should puree these combination meals until they're thin, but as your baby grows, you can make them progressively chunkier. By 12 months, your baby will be able to eat some of these meals without you having to puree them at all.

Turkey and Peas

In this recipe, you have a couple of different options on how to prepare the meal. You can purchase the turkey and peas precooked (frozen), or you can start with fresh ingredients and do the cooking yourself. Follow the package directions for cooking the turkey breast if you take the uncooked route.

Preparation time: *20 minutes*

Yield: *Eight ½-cup servings*

10-ounce package frozen green peas

10 ounces skinless, boneless turkey breast, cooked

1 Follow the package directions for cooking the peas. Cut the turkey breast into small pieces.

2 Place the turkey pieces and the cooked peas into a food processor and puree, adding a bit of water as needed for consistency. Serve warm.

Chicken and Peaches

We fully expect that you'd probably never think of mixing chicken and peaches together, but children often love the contrasting tastes. This recipe makes 1 cup of puree, but the puree freezes well, so you can make extra and freeze the puree in single-serving containers. (See Chapter 3 for the lowdown on the ice cube freezing method.) The advance preparation makes fixing meals a snap — just thaw, reheat, and serve.

Preparation time: *15 minutes*

Yield: *Two ½-cup servings*

⅓ *cup cooked and chopped chicken breast*   ½ *cup fresh peeled and sliced peaches*

Puree the chicken and peaches until you reach the desired consistency. Serve warm.

Blueberry Steak Puree

This simple recipe combines the sweet taste of blueberry and small bits of steak — sounds weird, but kids love it. It also freezes well, so make extra and portion the leftovers into single servings for later use.

This recipe makes a dark mixture that stains clothes — no white T-shirts for you or your baby with this meal!

Preparation time: *15 minutes*

Yield: *Two ½-cup servings*

½ *cup fresh blueberries, washed*   ⅓ *cup cooked and chopped steak*

Place the blueberries and steak pieces in a food processor and puree. To prevent choking, make sure that you puree until the steak pieces are really small. Serve warm.

Cod and Veggie Puree

Fish is an important meat to bring into your baby's diet even at an early age because fish oil aids in brain development. In fact, fish should be a consistent part of all diets, for both young folks and old folks. If you want a little Einstein, this puree just might help.

Preparation time: *15 minutes*

Yield: *Two ½-cup servings*

¼ cup cooked and finely chopped cod fillet

½ cup finely chopped fresh mixed veggies, cooked according to package directions

⅓ fresh peeled ripe tomato, diced

3 tablespoons formula or breast milk

1 teaspoon butter

1 Mix all the ingredients in a large saucepan and heat until the butter melts. Stir well.

2 Transfer the mixture to a food processor and puree for desired consistency. Serve warm.

Meat and Potato Puree

This recipe is a good combination if your baby seems a bit unsure about eating meat. Keep in mind that a resistance to meat may be due to texture more than taste.

Preparation time: *15 minutes*

Yield: *Two ½-cup servings*

⅓ cup ground beef, cooked and drained

¾ cup peeled, boiled, and mashed sweet potato

2 tablespoons breast milk or formula

½ teaspoon butter

1 Mix all the ingredients in a large saucepan and heat until the butter melts. Stir well.

2 Transfer the mixture to a food processor and puree for desired consistency. Serve warm.

☞ Lentils and Carrot Puree

This hearty recipe is a good meal for your baby, full of carbohydrates and vitamins. Because this recipe makes more than you need, you can simply freeze the extra portions and reheat them later.

Preparation time: *15 minutes*

Cooking time: *1 hour, 15 minutes*

Yield: *Eight ½-cup servings*

¼ pound dry lentils	*4 cups water*
¼ pound raw baby carrots	*Salt to taste*

1 Sort the lentils for stones; throw out the stones and rinse the lentils well. Even lentils sold in a bag (not purchased in bulk) may have stones mixed in with them, so make sure that you sort thoroughly.

2 In a large saucepan, combine all the ingredients. Bring the mixture to a boil, reduce the heat, and simmer for 1 to 1¼ hours, until the lentils and carrots soften.

3 Remove the saucepan from the heat, drain, and pour the mixture into a food processor; puree to desired consistency. Serve warm.

☞ Cinnamon Pear Puree

Cinnamon and pears naturally go together — you can find this combination even in adult desserts — so this puree is a treat for your infant.

Preparation time: *15 minutes*

Yield: *Two ½-cup servings*

⅔ cup skinned and chopped pear	*Pinch of cinnamon*
1 tablespoon apple juice	

1 Boil the pear pieces in water in a small saucepan for 5 minutes or until soft.

2 Pour the pears into a food processor and add the rest of the ingredients. Puree to desired consistency. Serve warm.

Tip: *If you want, add more cinnamon, but strive for a balanced flavor.*

Kicking It Up a Notch: More Complex Meals

As your baby grows to the 10-month stage, the meal options get even more complex as your baby's ability to handle different textures and foods increases. Feeding at this stage requires more options; the recipes in this section help you get started.

⌒ Cheesy Alphabet Pasta

Small pasta shapes, such as alphabet pasta, work well for children this age because the pasta doesn't present a choking hazard. With the combination of cheese, this dish is sure to be a hit.

Preparation time: *20 minutes*

Yield: *Four ½-cup servings*

¼ cup fresh mixed veggies, finely chopped	2 tablespoons butter
1 cup water	⅓ cup cheddar cheese, grated
3 tablespoons alphabet pasta	Salt to taste

1 Steam the veggies in a small saucepan over medium-high heat until tender.

2 While the veggies are cooking, boil the water in a medium saucepan and add the alphabet pasta and butter. Cook the pasta until tender (about 5 minutes) and drain.

3 Add the veggies to the pasta and stir in the cheese until the cheese melts. Salt to taste and serve warm.

Apple Chicken and Veggies

Apples and chicken work well together and have a taste your baby is sure to like. Make an extra-large portion of this recipe and put the extras in the freezer for a quick meal later. Add a side of any fruit or fruit puree in this chapter and you have a complete meal.

Preparation time: *15 minutes*

Yield: *Two ½-cup servings*

1 tablespoon butter	½ ripe apple, cored, peeled, and finely chopped
¼ pound skinless, boneless chicken breast	1¼ cups unsalted chicken broth

1 In a medium frying pan, melt the butter over medium-high heat and sauté the chicken until the center is no longer pink.

2 Add the apple and chicken broth to the cooked chicken and bring the mixture to a boil. Reduce the heat to medium and cook for 10 minutes.

3 Remove the pan from the heat, remove the chicken from the frying pan (reserving the apples and broth), and chop the chicken into small pieces. In a food processor, puree the chicken with the mixture left in the frying pan until well mixed but still chunky.

Ham and Veggie Casserole for Little Ones

This recipe combines meat, rice, and veggies in a kid-friendly casserole. This dish is freezable, so save what you don't serve for a later meal in a pinch.

Preparation time: *15 minutes*

Yield: *Seven ½-cup servings*

1 cup finely chopped fresh mixed vegetables

½ cup shredded cheddar cheese

2 ounces ham, finely chopped

1 cup cooked brown rice

1 cup breast milk, formula, or full-fat cow's milk, depending on child's age

2 heaping tablespoons finely chopped apple

1 Steam the veggies until they're soft (about 5 minutes).

2 Drain the water from the veggies and add the cheese. Stir until the cheese melts.

3 Add the remaining ingredients and puree for a chunky consistency. Serve warm.

Fish and Greens

This healthy meal consists of cod and green veggies and freezes well. Remember, fish oil is a great addition to your baby's diet because it aids in brain development.

Preparation time: *15 minutes*

Yield: *Four ½-cup servings*

1¼ cups water	*¼ cup green peas*
4 ounces cod	*½ cup quick-cooking brown rice*
2 tablespoons finely chopped celery	*2 teaspoons ketchup*
¼ cup green beans	

1 In a large saucepan, combine the water, cod, celery, green beans, peas, and rice.

2 Bring the mixture to a boil, reduce the heat, cover, and simmer for 15 to 20 minutes or until the fish is very tender. Lift the fish out of the mixture with a slotted spoon and slice it into small pieces, checking for bones and discarding any that you find.

3 Drain the rice and veggies and put them in a food processor along with the fish. Puree the ingredients slightly, keeping a chunky consistency.

4 Remove the mixture from the food processor, mix in the ketchup, and serve warm.

Creamy Taters and Chicken

The creamy texture of potatoes and chicken bites will make this quick and healthy meal a favorite! Because the recipe has chunks of chicken, don't fix it until your infant is 10 to 12 months old.

Preparation time: *10 minutes*

Yield: *Two ½-cup servings*

2 teaspoons butter	*¼ potato, baked, peeled, and diced*
1 teaspoon flour	*1 tablespoon grated cheddar cheese*
¼ cup breast milk or formula	
¼ cup cooked and shredded chicken breast	

1 In a small saucepan, melt the butter over low heat, and then stir in the flour and blend well. Add the milk or formula and stir until smooth.

2 Continue cooking over low heat until the mixture thickens. Add the chicken and potatoes.

3 Cook over low heat for 1 minute, and then add the cheese and stir until the mixture is blended and smooth. Serve warm.

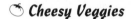 Cheesy Veggies

This creamy veggie recipe is a great addition to your recipe arsenal. Because children often enjoy cheesy foods, they'll love their veggies with cheese. This dish is filling.

Preparation time: *15 minutes*

Yield: *Four ½-cup servings*

½ cup milk

½ cup cottage cheese

¼ cup shredded cheddar cheese

¼ cup peas, cooked according to package directions

¼ cup cooked and diced carrots

¼ cup cooked and diced squash or zucchini

1 In a medium bowl, mix all the ingredients until well blended. The consistency should be somewhat chunky.

2 Before serving, heat the mixture in the microwave or in a large saucepan on the stove over low heat. Serve warm.

Simple Mini-Meatballs

You can chop these meatballs and feed them to your baby when she reaches the 10-month mark. The meatballs are soft enough for your infant to chew them easily, and they're nutritious and easy to make, too. Freeze the extras (no longer than a month) for a quick reheat later.

Preparation time: *10 minutes*

Yield: *4 servings (2 meatballs per serving)*

¼ pound ground beef   *¼ cup rolled oats*

1 Preheat the oven to 350 degrees.

2 Combine the meat and oatmeal in a medium-size mixing bowl.

3 Form the mixture into ½-inch balls and place them on an ungreased baking sheet.

4 Cook the meatballs for 12 minutes or until brown. Serve warm.

Part III

Big Changes Ahead: Feeding Your Toddler

The 5th Wave   By Rich Tennant

"You could call it homemade, but I prefer to call it artisanal toddler food."

In this part . . .

Ah, toddlerhood — the transitional age when your baby is no longer a baby and not quite a full-fledged kid, either. You'll have many joys and many challenges during this time, and you'll find that meals tend to be the same way. However, you can manage your toddler's eating habits and foods with a few tactics and the recipes that you find in this part — for 12- to 18-month-olds, 18-month- to 2-year-olds, and straight-up 2-year-olds.

Chapter 7

First Steps and First Scheduled Meals: 12 to 18 Months

- -

In This Chapter

▶ Exploring the nutritional needs of a 12- to 18-month-old

▶ Satisfying an empty tummy: Main meals throughout the day

▶ Curing the munchies: Quick snacks

- -

*W*elcome to the world of toddlers! The moment you realize that your baby is no longer a "baby" comes as a shock. Babies seem to burst suddenly into toddlers around the age of 12 months without any warning. You'll see your little bundle of joy begin to assert more independence, develop more personality, and yes, voice more opinions on your cooking — meaning your toddler has changing nutritional needs and eating habits.

The good news is toddlerhood brings you plenty of joys as you watch your baby grow, and you'll find that your child's food repertoire grows and develops rapidly. As food choices expand, that means more flexibility in meals and more fun options for your kid and the entire family.

In this chapter, you uncover 15 recipes for children ages 12 to 18 months. You also find advice along the way to help you manage your child who's no longer into "baby food."

Recipes in This Chapter

- ↻ Carrot Muffins
- ↻ Homemade Pancakes
- ↻ Breakfast Pizza
- ↻ Banana Parfait
- ▶ Corn and Chicken Soup
- ↻ Grilled Cheese with Tomato
- ▶ English Muffin Pizza
- ▶ Avocado Turkey Sandwich
- ↻ Cheesy Apple Toast
- ↻ Cheesy Orzo and Veggies
- ↻ Tofu and Pasta Dinner
- ▶ Red Beans and Rice
- ▶ Apple-and-Turkey Meatballs
- ▶ Bow-Tie Pasta with the Works
- ↻ Veggie Fritters
- ↻ Ants on a Log
- ▶ Muffin and Applesauce
- ▶ Orange Banana Smoothie

Understanding a 1-Year-Old's Mealtime Needs

As your baby turns into a toddler, you suddenly become aware that his nutritional needs have also changed. During the previous 12 months, your little one depended on milk (breast or formula) for most of his nutrition, but now, as you're weaning him from formula (he can breastfeed longer if desired), cow's milk (or soymilk, or goat's milk, and so on if you prefer) becomes only a part of his diet.

The transition from a milk-only diet to a diet consisting of a variety of foods can be a bit frightening because you want to make sure that your young toddler takes in all his nutritional needs. The good news is you can make the nutritional transition from baby meals to toddler meals much easier than you may think if you just understand a few basics, which we cover in this section.

Weaning your wee one from breast and bottle

Weaning is a process that takes time, and the time to start is a bit different for each child. Generally, by age 1 a child can make the move from breast milk or formula to full-fat (whole) cow's milk. When you're ready to start weaning, following these steps:

1. **Reduce the number of times each day that your baby is allowed to drink breast milk or formula.**

   Make sure that you don't stop cold turkey, especially if you're breastfeeding.

2. **Dwindle the daytime feedings.**

   This process can take months, more or less, so don't feel like you have to be on a predetermined timeline. The gradual approach is the easiest both emotionally and physically for everyone.

3. **Work toward eliminating the final nighttime nursing.**

   This time can be the most difficult to break because your baby has grown accustomed to nursing and now psychologically needs it. If your baby is having problems giving up the breast or bottle in the evening, follow these steps:

   • Slowly reduce the amount of nursing time over a couple of weeks until there's no more nighttime nursing.

   • Lose the night bottle by simply changing the bedtime routine.

   • Read your child a book to distract her.

If you're breastfeeding, check out *Breastfeeding For Dummies* (Wiley), by Sharon Perkins and Carol Vannais, as an excellent resource. An entire chapter is devoted to weaning your baby.

The fat of the matter

Probably the most important thing you must teach yourself is simply this: Toddlers don't have the same nutritional needs as older children or adults. In fact, your toddler needs more fat and calories and less fiber — basically, the opposite of what *you* need (ah, to be young again)! This advice applies to children 5 years old and younger.

The consensus among health experts is that children under 5 shouldn't be limited in their diets concerning fat and calories, unless your doctor specifically tells you to do so. A lot of parents become worried around the 12th to 15th month because their baby looks chubby. The chubby look is a normal part of a toddler's growth and nothing to be concerned about. Your toddler burns baby fat as he continues to grow and becomes more mobile. But for now, he needs the fat and calories.

In a young child, fat and calories assist the growth of the brain and the nervous system. Without fat and calories to burn, your child's body is forced to burn protein, and protein is necessary for building muscle, so you don't want your child burning protein for energy.

We're not saying that you should feed your baby junk foods that provide only empty calories — you just need to supply a healthy menu of foods, along with a good amount of activity — and Mother Nature will do the rest. The key is to keep your child from a lowfat type of diet, which adults are fond of following. Generally, a 12- to 18-month-old should eat about 1,000 calories a day. Don't be concerned with counting calories, though. Some days your toddler will eat more, and some days she'll eat less. This behavior is normal.

Although a high fiber diet helps prevent cancer and other diseases in adults, it's not good for your toddler. Fiber is a heavy material with few calories, and while it makes you feel full, it doesn't provide the nutritional value your toddler needs. You eat the high fiber diet, but skip it with your toddler.

Managing meals and snacks

One parenting pitfall that you may encounter is the "three meal syndrome." We condition ourselves to eat three main meals a day. However, your child tends to eat smaller meals and snack between meals. This desire is normal and healthy. Don't restrict your child to three meals without snacks — this limitation inhibits your child's nutritional intake. Virtually all children follow the lighter meal method, so don't sweat it. In fact, if your child doesn't eat midmorning and midafternoon snacks, you'll probably notice irritable behavior because your child's blood-sugar levels begin to sag. Snacks are healthy and important!

Wanting to snack between meals is normal, but be sure that your child isn't panhandling between meals. Snacks should be planned and nutritious like meals; allow for plenty of time between snacks and meals so your toddler comes to the table with an appetite.

Making milk a priority

Generally, your 12- to 18-month-old needs 16 to 20 fluid ounces of milk each day. Unless your toddler has an allergy, whole cow's milk (not skim or 2 percent) does the trick. However, some children are a bit resistant to drinking cow's milk. If resistant, try mixing prepared formula or breast milk with whole milk to allow your child to adjust to the taste.

Other options to include calcium in your child's diet that count as "milk" include

- ✔ Cheese
- ✔ Goat's milk
- ✔ Soymilk
- ✔ Yogurt

Include cheese in meals and in snacks, and make delicious smoothies using yogurt. Get creative with milk, cheese, and yogurt so you easily work enough calcium into your toddler's diet if she seems to resist drinking enough from a cup.

Serving fruits and veggies

Throughout this chapter, we mention that the nutritional needs of toddlers differ from older children and adults. However, in the case of fruits and veggies, we're the same. Healthcare professionals recommend consuming five servings of fruits and vegetables each day. This number may seem a bit much and difficult to work into a toddler's diet at first. However, it's not when you consider these opportunities:

- ✔ Have some fruit or fruit juice at breakfast.
- ✔ Serve veggies, such as carrot sticks, and fruit, such as applesauce, with lunch and dinner.
- ✔ Include veggies and fruits as part of snacktime.

Simply put, if *you* make a habit of eating five servings of fruit and vegetables a day, you should have no problem incorporating it into your child's diet as well — and you'll both be healthier.

The case of the testy veggie eater

In a perfect world, we would all munch on our vegetables all day and love every minute of it. However, in the real world, you may have a toddler who's resistant to eating veggies. While this phenomenon isn't unusual, it's a problem worth combating because veggies are an important part of your child's healthy diet.

Here are some suggestions for getting your child to eat those veggies:

✔ **Serve raw veggies.** Many children resist *cooked* veggies but will eat them raw. Consider serving raw veggies with ranch dip at snacktime.

✔ **Stir-fry veggies.** Adding stir-fried vegetables with rice or pasta may help your kids eat up those veggies.

✔ **Serve soup and other dishes with "hidden" veggies inside.**

✔ **Experiment with different veggies.** Find what works, but get those veggies in the diet!

✔ **Allow the addition of sauces, dressings, cheese, butter, and so on.** Sometimes these toppings help mask the veggies for consumption.

✔ **Continue to offer vegetables as your child's tastes change.** Continued exposure is key. Never force-feed any vegetables.

✔ **Introduce veggies before fruit, even when you're pureeing veggies!** It's helpful for your children to get a taste for veggies before fruit, so they don't resist veggies later.

Eating healthy grains

At the 12- to 18-month stage, you need to mix in grains in order to give your child a healthy, balanced diet. Generally, children this age should eat between 5 and 12 servings each day. As you think about grains, think "brown and whole." Stick to brown rice, brown breads, multigrain breads, and other wholesome grains. White breads are the least healthy option for your child.

Common serving sizes are small. For example, ¼ cup rice or pasta is a serving, while ⅓ cup grain cereal or even half a bagel is considered a serving. For more info on serving sizes, see www.mypyramid.gov.

Working meat into the meal

Meat is an important part of any diet, providing necessary protein for strong muscle development. During your child's 12- to 18-month stage, continue to introduce small bites of meat to your child.

You should strive to give your child 2 to 3 ounces of meat per day. Some good serving examples: 1 ounce of beef, poultry, or fish; ¼ cup of beans, lentils, or tofu.

Remembering that toddlers have taste buds, too

Your toddler starts developing a sense of taste and becomes more reactive to food. The sense of taste as well as texture and visual appeal all drive a child to eat (or not eat) in much the same way as adults (think about it, when was the last time you ate something you really didn't like or that looked gross).

The accepting and rejecting behavior is a normal process that your toddler goes through. Your responsibility is to continue to introduce healthy foods (and reintroduce them as your child's likes and dislikes change) and make sure that she has the right daily nutrition. Keep in mind that a new food often has to be introduced several times before your child takes an interest, and also keep in mind that introducing means *offering* the food, not *forcing* it.

Rise and Shine — It's Breakfast Time

Most toddlers love to eat breakfast. Youngsters typically wake up happy and in a good mood (unlike many adults), so the morning is a good time to introduce new breakfast items. In this section, we give you a few breakfast meals to help you get started.

☉ Carrot Muffins

This healthy Carrot Muffin recipe avoids the sugar in most muffins and gives your toddler a tasty breakfast food. In fact, these muffins also work well as a side at lunch or dinner and even for a snack.

Preparation time: *10 minutes*

Cooking time: *20 minutes*

Yield: *12 servings*

1 cup plain, full-fat yogurt	*½ teaspoon baking soda*
½ cup whole milk	*1 teaspoon baking powder*
2 eggs	*½ teaspoon salt*
1 tablespoon maple syrup	*3 medium carrots, grated (about 1 cup)*
1 tablespoon canola oil	*Nonstick cooking spray*
2¼ cups whole-wheat flour	

1 Preheat the oven to 375 degrees and spray a muffin pan with nonstick cooking spray.

2 Whisk together the yogurt, milk, eggs, syrup, and oil until smooth.

3 In a separate bowl, whisk together the flour, baking soda, baking powder, and salt.

4 Add the grated carrots and the yogurt mixture to the flour mixture and stir well.

5 Pour the mixture evenly into the muffin pan and bake for 20 minutes. Cool and serve.

Vary It! *Jazz up your muffins by pureeing fruit and using the puree as a topping. Pineapple works especially well with these muffins.*

🍑 Homemade Pancakes

This recipe puts a healthy twist on simple pancakes. Because the recipe uses both eggs and yogurt, your child gets good nutritional value and will love the taste, too.

Preparation time: *5 minutes*

Cooking time: *20 minutes*

Yield: *7 servings (3 pancakes per serving)*

1 egg	*1¼ cups self-rising flour*
⅔ cup plain full-fat yogurt	*2 tablespoons maple syrup*
⅔ cup milk	*Nonstick cooking spray*

1 Beat the egg and mix it with the yogurt.

2 Stir in the milk, flour, and syrup until the batter is smooth.

3 Spray a frying pan or griddle with nonstick cooking spray and heat on medium-high heat. To check the heat level, put a drop of water in the greased pan or griddle. If the water sizzles, you're ready to cook!

4 Drop a heaping tablespoon of batter in the pan and repeat, leaving space between the pancakes. This method makes pancakes that are 2 to 3 inches in diameter.

5 Cook for 1 minute or until pancake starts to bubble on top. Flip the pancake for another minute of cooking. The pancake should be lightly brown when it's done.

6 Continue to grease the skillet between batches. Serve the pancakes warm with butter and syrup or fruit puree.

Tip: *Have a little fun with these pancakes by making them in different shapes. Pancake cooking molds are available at your favorite kitchen store (or visit* www.cooking.com*).*

Vary It! *Children typically love syrup, but if you're concerned about sugar, many varieties of syrups — including sugar-free syrups — are available at your local grocery store. Give one a try — our children loved the variety! If you start out serving sugar-free syrup, your kids aren't likely to know what they're missing.*

⏱ Breakfast Pizza

This recipe makes a unique breakfast pizza using an English muffin. With this basic recipe, you can easily change it and alter it in a number of ways.

Preparation time: *10 minutes*

Cooking time: *5 minutes*

Yield: *2 servings*

1 English muffin	*Butter (for spreading)*
4 to 5 whole, ripe strawberries or 1 heaping tablespoon pure strawberry jam	*1 egg*

1 Slice the English muffin into two halves and then puree the strawberries in a food processor or blender.

2 Toast the English muffin halves and then butter.

3 Spread the strawberry puree or jam on each of the two English muffin halves.

4 Scramble the egg and cook it until firm (not runny).

5 Place the scrambled egg on each of the muffin halves and serve open-faced style.

Vary It! *Try creating your pizza with fruit instead of eggs. Try small chunks of fruit with cream cheese. You can also serve with small bits of sausage and egg. Make it colorful and it will be a hit!*

⏱ Banana Parfait

Kids think this treat is something special, because the finish product looks cool! But you don't have to tell them that you didn't labor in the kitchen for hours on end (prep is actually quick and easy — a big plus for busy parents). Check out the layered effect in the color section of this book.

Preparation time: *5 minutes*

Chill time: *15 minutes*

Yield: *One 1-cup serving*

½ medium banana	*¾ cup plain, full-fat yogurt*

1 Peel and slice the banana into small pieces.

2 Layer the yogurt and banana slices in a cup: ½ cup of yogurt, then banana slices, and then ¼ cup of yogurt. You can also reserve some banana slices for the top of the parfait if you'd like. Serve chilled.

A Midday Boost: Lunches for Your Little One

As the variety in your toddler's food choices expands, include more options for lunch. The following tried-and-true favorite recipes all provide proper nutrition and are tasty for your growing 12- to 18-month-old.

Avocado Turkey Sandwich

Avocados are great for children this age because they're easy to digest and full of vitamins and healthy fats. Try this yummy avocado and turkey sandwich with your toddler (you may find yourself sneaking a bite). Take a look in the color section of this book to see the finished product.

Preparation time: *5 minutes*

Yield: *1 serving*

Butter	*1 thin tomato slice*
2 slices whole-wheat bread	*2 thin slices fresh avocado*
1 small lettuce leaf	*2 pieces fresh turkey, thinly sliced*

1 Butter one side of each bread slice to taste. Place the bread in a toaster oven, and toast until lightly brown. If you're using a slot toaster, butter the bread after toasting it.

2 On one slice of toast, place the lettuce, tomato, and avocado; and on the other slice, place the turkey.

3 Put the two pieces together, and cut the sandwich into four squares. Serve.

Vary It! *Substitute other condiments for the butter. Try mayonnaise or cream cheese, both of which are tasty choices.*

Corn and Chicken Soup

Chicken soup is a yummy meal for children because they often like the taste, but this recipe takes you much further than the canned variety. The sweet corn greatly adds to the taste of typical canned chicken soup, which tends to be overly salty. This recipe also helps put some additional vegetables in your child's diet.

This recipe is a meal in and of itself, so you don't need another dish to go with it. However, Carrot Muffins (see the recipe earlier in this chapter) are a good pairing with this soup, both in terms of taste and nutrition.

Preparation time: *10 minutes*

Cooking time: *25 minutes*

Yield: *Six ½-cup servings*

3 tablespoons butter	*1 cup chicken broth*
1 celery stalk, finely chopped	*2 skinless, boneless chicken breasts (about 10 ounces total)*
½ medium white onion, finely chopped	
⅓ cup flour	*1¾ cups canned sweet corn, undrained*
1¼ cups milk	*Salt and pepper to taste*

1 Melt the butter in a large saucepan over medium heat. Add the celery and onion and cook for about 6 minutes. Stir in flour and cook for another 2 minutes.

2 In a saucepan, heat the milk over low heat, whisking constantly until the milk is hot.

3 Pour the hot milk into the butter mixture and stir until thickened. Add the chicken broth, heat, and reduce to a simmer.

4 Cut the chicken breasts into small pieces and add to the soup.

5 Simmer for 15 minutes, adding the corn during the last three minutes of cooking. Season with salt and pepper, if desired, and serve.

⟳ Grilled Cheese with Tomato

Did you eat grilled cheese as a child? Odds are good you did. (Or maybe you still do.) Grilled cheese seems to be a favorite among children! Here's a simple recipe you can use time and time again, and it adds extra zing with the tomato and mozzarella cheese.

Preparation time: *3 minutes*

Cooking time: *3 minutes*

Yield: *1 serving*

1 tablespoon butter

2 slices whole-wheat bread

1 slice American cheese

1 tomato slice

2 heaping tablespoons shredded mozzarella cheese

1 Butter one side of one piece of bread and place the bread, buttered side down, in a frying pan over medium to medium-low heat. Place the cheese slice, tomato, and mozzarella cheese on the bread. Butter the second piece of bread and place it on top of the sandwich, buttered side up.

2 Fry the sandwich for 3 minutes on each side or until golden brown. Remove the sandwich from the frying pan, cool slightly, and cut into four quarters and serve.

Tip: *Use a cookie cutter to cut the sandwich into fun shapes. Consider serving with carrot and celery sticks or other nutritious foods that your child can decorate her sandwich with.*

English Muffin Pizza

Here's a simple and healthy English muffin lunch pizza that your toddler will enjoy repeatedly. You have the flexibility to change this recipe in several ways for quick meals with variety. Don't forget to peek at the color section in this book to see the end result.

Preparation time: *3 minutes*

Cooking time: *5 minutes*

Yield: *2 servings*

1 English muffin

4 tablespoons tomato sauce or pizza sauce

4 pepperoni slices

½ cup shredded mozzarella cheese

1 Cut the English muffin into two pieces and place the halves on a baking tray.

2 Evenly place the pizza sauce, pepperoni slices, and mozzarella cheese on the two pieces of English muffin.

3 Toast muffins in a toaster oven until slightly brown and serve warm. If you're using a conventional oven, heat the oven to 300 degrees and cook for 5 minutes or until cheese melts.

Vary It! *If pepperoni isn't your child's thing, try using Canadian bacon, available in small slices like pepperoni. You can also use various vegetables such as mushrooms, onions, and green bell peppers and even fruits such as pineapple for a twist on the traditional pizza toppings. Consider making a dessert pizza with strawberry jam and small bits of pineapple.*

☕ Cheesy Apple Toast

This is a quick meal that even works well for breakfast or a snack. Toddlers tend to love both cheese and apples, and the combination of the two is one that your little tyke is sure to love. Got a finicky eater? This quick recipe often gets the reluctant eater to eat!

Preparation time: *5 minutes*

Yield: *1 serving*

Butter	1 slice American cheese
1 slice whole-wheat bread	½ pureed apple or 2 tablespoons applesauce

1 Butter one side of the bread and place the cheese on top of the buttered side of the bread.

2 Put the bread on a baking tray and place the tray in the toaster oven. Toast the bread until slightly brown and the cheese melts. If you don't have a toaster oven, you can use your regular oven set at about 300 degrees. Cook until the cheese melts.

3 Remove the tray from the toaster and let the sandwich cool slightly. Hot cheese can burn your toddler's mouth.

4 Spread the apple puree or applesauce on top of the cheese. Serve warm.

☕ Cheesy Orzo and Veggies

If you're not familiar with orzo, it's small pasta that looks like barley kernels. If you search the Internet for recipes for kids, you'll find lots of orzo-based recipes, and for good reason — orzo produces a creamy, easy-to-chew pasta that kids seem to like. With this recipe, the orzo will be a hit and you'll get a serving of veggies in as well!

Preparation time: *10 minutes*

Cooking time: *15 minutes*

Yield: *Ten ½-cup servings*

¼ pound dry orzo pasta	2 tablespoons butter
½ cup carrots, peeled and diced	¼ cup grated cheddar cheese
½ cup broccoli, diced	
¼ cup black-eyed peas (or you can substitute another variety)	

1 Place the orzo, carrots, broccoli, and peas in a medium saucepan. Cover with water and boil for 12 minutes or until tender. Drain the water from the saucepan.

2 In a large pan, melt the butter, and add the drained pasta and vegetables, stirring well.

3 Remove the pan from the heat and add the cheese, stirring until cheese melts. Serve warm.

All's Well that Ends Well: Delicious Dinners

Dinnertime can be a great time for family and bonding. With busy schedules, family mealtime is something that's fallen by the wayside, and our culture has forgotten that sitting down to eat together as a family unit is a time for interaction and good communication. We encourage you to make family dinnertime a priority in your home — it leads to healthy eating, good mealtime behaviors, and consistent communication.

With that said, many parents find dinnertime frustrating with a toddler. It's not unusual for toddlers to eat a good breakfast, a decent lunch, but not eat much at dinner. So don't be overly concerned if your toddler tends to pick at her dinner. She'll eat if she's hungry.

Limit juice and milk intake between meals and have snacks far enough before planned meals to allow your child to come to the table hungry enough to eat. Give water for drinks throughout the day because water is less likely to fill your child up.

This dinner section presents some healthy recipes for your toddler (and your family) to enjoy.

☽ Tofu and Pasta Dinner

Pasta is a great food for toddlers because it's a great source of energy (although at times you may want your child to have less energy), and tofu is a healthy alternative to other protein sources. You'll find this recipe quick and healthy for the whole family. The leftovers (if you have any) also freeze well.

Preparation time: *5 minutes*

Cooking time: *10 minutes*

Yield: *Seven 1-cup servings*

4 cups dry pasta (any variety, but orzo is easy for children to eat)

8 ounces tofu, diced (not silken tofu — it won't brown)

3 teaspoons olive oil

1 medium zucchini, grated

Salt to taste

1 Cook pasta according to package directions. Drain water.

2 In a medium saucepan, sauté the tofu in the olive oil until the tofu is slightly brown. The tofu will be wet and doesn't brown easily. Sautéing for 4 to 5 minutes is enough, even if the tofu doesn't seem to brown up.

3 Add the zucchini, cover, and steam for 10 minutes or until the zucchini is soft.

4 Add the pasta, stir, and remove from the heat. Serve warm.

Tip: *If the dish seems a bit dry, add a little more olive oil. You can also add a bit of shredded cheese for extra flavor.*

Red Beans and Rice

Red Beans and Rice can be a staple meal for toddlers because it's high in protein and complex carbs for energy. This dish also avoids the spice of many common versions. As an added bonus, this dish freezes beautifully for a quick thaw and reheat for later use.

Preparation time: *25 minutes*

Cooking time: *1 hour*

Yield: *Ten 1-cup servings*

2 tablespoons vegetable oil for sautéing

½ cup onion, chopped

2 cups hot water

15½ ounces canned kidney beans, drained

2 chicken bouillon cubes

2 cups minute rice, uncooked (or any quick-cook rice)

1 Pour the oil in a large saucepan and add the onion. Sauté the onion until it's slightly brown. Stir in the water, beans, and bouillon. Bring the mixture to a boil.

2 Stir in the rice and cover for 5 minutes. Remove from the heat and let stand for 5 minutes. Serve warm.

Vary It! *If you want to bump up the protein, add precooked crumbled soy sausage (less spicy than regular sausage) to this recipe after you remove from the heat.*

Veggie Fritters

This recipe provides another creative way to help your child eat veggies. Serve this dish not only as dinner but also as a side dish, or freeze the extra portions as a snack — to be served hot or cold later.

Preparation time: *10 minutes*

Cooking time: *10 minutes*

Yield: *About 7 servings (2 fritters per serving)*

1 cup carrots, peeled and grated
½ cup zucchini, grated
½ cup yellow squash, grated
⅔ cup potatoes, grated

2 tablespoons flour
Vegetable oil for frying
Salt to taste

1 Mix the veggies in a bowl with the flour.

2 Form the mixture into 15 round fritters with your hands and place on a clean plate.

3 Heat 2 tablespoons of oil in a frying pan and fry the fritters for about 5 minutes (2½ minutes on each side) on medium-high heat until fritters are golden brown on each side. You can cook about three fritters at a time. After 3 batches, add more oil.

4 Remove each fritter from the pan and place it on a plate covered with paper towel in order to absorb the excess grease. Lightly sprinkle with the salt. Serve warm or cold.

Apple-and-Turkey Meatballs

Apple-and-Turkey Meatballs use ground turkey meat — a healthy alternative and a great source of protein! Toddlers generally eat these meatballs because the turkey is tasty and meatballs are fun finger foods. Your child may also find meatballs fun to play with. Beware a flying meatball at dinnertime!

Preparation time: *15 minutes*

Cooking time: *10 to 15 minutes*

Yield: *8 servings (3 meatballs per serving)*

1 pound ground turkey	*1 egg, beaten*
1 onion, finely chopped	*2 tablespoons thyme*
3 tablespoons fresh breadcrumbs	*Flour for coating*
1 small apple, peeled and finely chopped	*2 teaspoons vegetable oil*

1 Preheat the oven to 350 degrees.

2 In a large bowl, mix the turkey, onion, breadcrumbs, apple, egg, and thyme.

3 Coat your hands with flour and use your hands to form 24 small meatballs. Spread more flour on a plate and roll the meatballs in it until they're lightly coated.

4 Heat the oil in a frying pan and sauté the meatballs until they're golden brown, about 10 minutes. If you use a 10-inch frying pan, you'll be able to cook about five at a time. Feel free to add a bit more oil between batches.

5 Place the meatballs in a casserole dish and cook for 15 minutes.

Tip: *For parents who don't want to cook with oil, thus making the meatballs healthier, skip the sautéing and cook these meatballs in the oven without sautéing. Just extend the cooking time another 10 minutes or so, and then check to make sure they're done.*

Tip: *Double or triple your recipe and freeze the extra meatballs to keep on hand! Freeze the meatballs without the flour coating.*

Vary It! *Serve Apple-and-Turkey Meatballs with spaghetti or almost any other dish, such as rice. You can even eat them by themselves. Try serving these meatballs in a hot dog bun with a little spaghetti sauce for an instant sub sandwich!*

Bow-Tie Pasta with the Works

Farfalle (fahr-FAH-lay) *pasta* is the technical name for bow-tie pasta. But technicalities aside, your toddler will love this dish because it's tasty and colorful. See just how colorful this dish is in the color section of this book.

Preparation time: *25 minutes*

Yield: *Four 1-cup servings*

¼ pound bow-tie pasta	*¼ cup green peas (frozen is fine)*
1 tablespoon butter	*¼ cup carrots, diced (frozen is fine)*
1 tablespoon flour	*½ cup grated cheddar cheese*
1¼ cups milk	*2 slices (about 1 ounce) cooked ham, beef, or chicken, diced*
¼ teaspoon dry ground mustard	

1 Cook the pasta according to the package directions.

2 While the pasta is cooking, melt the butter in a small saucepan and stir in the flour.

3 Whisk in the milk and mustard. Add the peas and carrots, bring back to a boil, reduce the heat, and cook for 3 minutes.

4 Stir in the cheese and remove from the heat, continuing to stir until the cheese melts. Add the meat to the mixture.

5 Drain the water from the pasta, and in a large bowl, toss together the meat and cheese mixture with the cooked pasta. Serve warm.

Vary It! *Substitute other vegetables, such as broccoli, zucchini, squash, and so on for the peas and carrots.*

Quick Cures for the Munchies

Healthy snacks are an important part of your child's diet because they provide consistent nutrition throughout the day. That's no problem when you're making them yourself! Give your toddler fun, quick, and healthy snack options that'll keep her happy. You'll find snack and smoothie options throughout this book, so be sure to look at other chapters as well, but the snacks in this chapter are just right for your 12- to 18-month-old.

○ Ants on a Log

This snack is a classic munchie that is fun to make with your little one. We've put a little twist on this one that you may not be expecting. Celery and cream cheese are both nutritious, and this recipe provides a dose of fun as well.

Preparation time: *5 minutes*

Yield: *2 servings*

1 celery stalk	*16 raisins*
2 tablespoons cream cheese	

1 Wash and dry the celery stalk. Cut the stalk in half in the middle.

2 Fill the celery with the cream cheese, place the raisins in a line on the top of the cream cheese, and serve.

Vary It! *After your child is about 2 years old and you're sure that peanuts don't cause allergies, try this recipe with peanut butter instead of cream cheese.*

○ Muffin and Applesauce

This quick and easy snack is healthy and almost always a hit! In fact, applesauce works great as a topping for all kinds of meals, from muffins to waffles. Because most children like applesauce, it's a great topping to use.

Preparation time: *5 minutes*

Yield: *2 servings*

1 English muffin	*Dash of cinnamon*
1 tablespoon applesauce	*8 raisins*

1 Split the English muffin in half and lightly toast the two halves.

2 In a small bowl, mix the applesauce, cinnamon, and raisins.

3 Spread the mixture over the English muffin and serve warm.

Vary It! *You can vary this recipe by using different bread options, such as pita bread or even a graham cracker. If you use pita bread, toast it in a toaster oven just as you would regular bread.*

Orange Banana Smoothie

This quick and yummy smoothie works well for young toddlers and it's full of complex carbohydrates for energy. Your child will think this smoothie is a treat, but with plenty of vitamins, you'll know it's a good snack option. Check out the color insert for a picture of the final product.

Preparation time: *5 minutes*

Yield: *One ½-cup serving*

½ banana

2 tablespoons plain, full-fat yogurt

2 tablespoons orange juice

1 Place the ingredients in a blender and puree until smooth.

2 Pour the mixture into a plastic cup and serve with a spoon.

Chapter 8

Good Eats for Your Active 18-Month to 2-Year-Old

In This Chapter

▶ Preparing yourself to meet your 18-month- to 2-year-old's mealtime needs

▶ Jumpstarting your toddler's day with breakfast

▶ Striking a balance between lunch and dinner

▶ Meeting the (occasional) needs of the sugar high

As your toddler continues to grow toward the terrible twos, you'll be amazed at the changes. Your growing baby becomes more vocal, mobile, and able to reason and understand what is going on in the world around him. In fact, it's often at this time that new parents become a bit sad because their once tiny baby is asserting his independence (and sometimes defiance).

Rapid growth and change are healthy indications that your child is developing normally and following the transition from babyhood to childhood. During this time, nutritional needs are changing as well. Your toddler not only becomes much more diverse in what she'll eat but also more opinionated about the food she's eating.

In this chapter, you'll add some items to your child's diet that weren't allowed before and discover new nutrition at this stage of the game. Put this collection of tasty recipes to work in your kitchen.

A Whole Lot of Change and Even More Patience

Life involves change. Sure, you know that, but when you're thinking about your toddler, get prepared for a lot of change! Just when you think you have it all figured out, your toddler grows and changes again.

The same can be said for your toddlers eating habits and nutritional needs. You're embarking on a virtual rollercoaster ride of change that requires even more patience on your part. Don't worry, though, we're here to help you survive the ride.

Managing meals and mealtimes

A newborn baby is completely dependent on breast milk or formula for nutrition, but things change quickly. You start introducing solids, still giving milk or formula, but by 18 months of age, your baby is a true eating machine. The digestive system matures and your baby's nutritional needs take a turn. Milk is still part of the diet, just not the *whole* diet. Here's a quick rundown on your child's nutritional necessities at this age:

- ✓ **Milk and other dairy:** Your toddler needs only full-fat cow's milk (whole milk). Don't use 2 percent, lowfat, or skim milk — the fat content is crucial as well as the calcium. Serve 16 ounces of milk or dairy per day, but try not to give more than this amount so your child will be encouraged to eat other foods.

  Some children love milk and will basically try to live on it if you let them. So, monitor the amount of milk consumption to make sure that your toddler is getting enough but not too much. Reserve milk and juice for meals and snacktime, so your child doesn't get full by randomly drinking glasses of milk or juice.

- ✓ **Grains:** 3 ounces per day. Whole grain breads, pasta, brown rice, and oatmeal are all good choices.
- ✓ **Vegetables:** 1 cup per day. Strive for a variety of vegetables, with plenty of green, leafy veggies.
- ✓ **Fruits:** 1 cup per day. Strive for different fruits with any combination.
- ✓ **Meat and Beans:** 2 ounces per day. Lean meats, fish, and any kind of beans are good choices.

Avoid sugary snacks for kids for the same reasons dentists warn you to avoid these kinds of foods — tooth decay and empty calories. Get in the habit of taking care of your child's teeth now, including limiting sugary snacks and using a consistent teeth brushing schedule. Also, avoid juice at bedtime; the sugar attacks your child's teeth while he sleeps.

What to do if your child is choking

At some point in your child's life, he may choke from overeating or eating too quickly and so on. This moment can be every parent's worst nightmare. However, knowing what to do when your little one is choking gives you more confidence (and more time to help) in handling these worrisome situations. **Note:** Our advice doesn't substitute for a certified class, so we highly recommend taking one if you haven't already (see www.americancpr.com to find out more about CPR training). That caveat aside, here are our tips, which are consistent with CPR guidelines:

✔ If your child is coughing and crying, let him continue to cough it out. Don't hit your child on the back because the jolt may move the food and cause a worse obstruction. Your child should get his throat clear in a few minutes; if he continues to have trouble, call your doctor.

✔ If your infant can't breathe (no coughing or crying), lay him face down on your lap with his head hanging down, keeping the head lower than the chest (see the following figure, A). With the heel of your hand, give the infant up to five sharp blows on the back between the shoulder blades (B). Then turn the infant onto his back while supporting the head and give up to five chest thrusts, using two to three fingers over the lower half of the breastbone (C and D). Alternate back blows and chest thrusts until the object is dislodged or the infant becomes unresponsive. If your infant becomes unresponsive, perform CPR and call 911.

✔ If your child (at least 1 year old) can't breathe, use the abdominal thrust method, otherwise called the Heimlich maneuver, if the child is responsive. If the child is unresponsive, call 911. The operator will likely instruct you to perform chest compressions and to check the throat for lodged food.

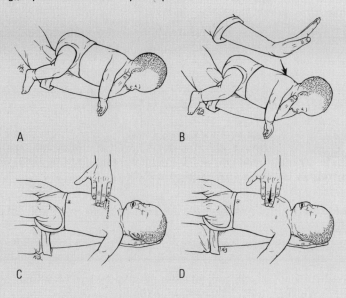

A   B

C   D

In addition to the changes you'll encounter with your wee one's diet, the feeding schedule may seem a little wacky too. One issue you'll likely face is that children often prefer smaller meals with snacks in between, instead of eating three square meals a day. Your child may eat one good meal and seem pickier at others. Don't let this behavior overly concern you or frustrate you at this point. Continue to have mealtime and offer your child meals, but if your tyke seems to eat some meals better than others, don't worry. Just make sure that you're offering healthy, wholesome snacks instead of chips or cookies.

Dealing with the "shoveling syndrome"

As your child grows, she may want to eat too fast and swallow without chewing her food.

Naturally, the shoveling behavior is a choking hazard, so here are some tips to help you out:

- ✔ **Cut food into small pieces.** Your child will have to do more work to shovel the food in. Small pieces helps control the amount your child takes in at one time.
- ✔ **Offer small portions first.** If your child has a serious problem with inhaling his food, limit the amount of food on his plate, and then add more as he eats.
- ✔ **Eat with your child and model good chewing habits.** Your child has a tendency to mimic what you're doing.
- ✔ **Be careful with foods that tend to be choking hazards.** Foods in this category include bread, popcorn, nuts, and hard candy.

Handling tantrums at the table

You'll notice that a furious monster may creep out of your child just before she turns two. At this stage, children don't have the emotional capability to deal with frustrations that you or life in general impose, and as those feelings build up, you're likely to see a variety of reactions:

- ✔ An eruption of screaming and crying for what may seem like no apparent reason
- ✔ A display of emotion (including flying objects) played out like a bad soap opera
- ✔ A body thrown on the floor of the supermarket in a fit of rage

Any of these possibilities and more may occur every day for a period of weeks at a time.

Keep in mind that as frustrating as tantrums are for you, your child is communicating in the only way she knows how. Just remember that tantrums are normal and *not* a reflection on you or your offspring.

Feeding the fire

When it comes to food, you may find yourself at your wit's end because at this stage of the game, your child can eat most foods that you enjoy eating as well, but oftentimes, he refuses. You're dreaming of the time when you fix a meal and everyone sits down at the table and lovingly enjoys the food together. Keep dreaming; just kidding. No really, it can happen. You just need to be firm and set some ground rules.

- ✔ **Make meals that appeal to the entire family.** Strive for a diet that provides a good balance of protein, vegetables, dairy, and grains.

- ✔ **Enforce mealtimes.** Eating together displays good eating habits for your little one.

- ✔ **Place the food on your toddler's tray whether he'll eat it or not.** He may pretend like he's a busboy and sweep the food right off on the floor, but continued efforts on your part show your kid that you mean business.

As much as you strive, you may inevitably encounter the stuck-in-a-rut syndrome, which happens when your child decides that he's going to eat one or two items, but that's all. This decision is a common part of development and not something you should be overly concerned about. It's frustrating when you work hard on a meal and it's not eaten or is thrown across the kitchen, but *c'est la vie.*

If your child is throwing a fit and will only eat a particular item at mealtime, try the following tips:

- ✔ **Make sure to include the beloved food item often with meals.** Try to mix the familiar with the unfamiliar.

- ✔ **Include other options.** Always include a variety of items to coincide with the favored food.

- ✔ **Eat the new food as a model for your child.** This helps your child gain an interest in the new food.

Toddlers eventually become bored with the same food over and over and start trying other items. Although this period can last for a few months, eventually your toddler will move on to other foods.

Never try to bribe your child with *any* food to end his tirade. Using food for rewards or even punishments can lead to a cycle of bad behavior. Your youngster will use you in his moments of madness to get what he wants. He'll know that if he cries, you'll give him a cookie, for example. Always keep the concept of food separate from behavior — this rule sets up a healthy perspective concerning food now and in later years.

In addition, bribing and force feeding may cause your youngster to like foods less. Place foods on a plate in child-size portions and allow your child to decide what and how much to eat. Remember, she may only eat one or two of the items offered. Let her explore by touching, smelling, mashing, and tasting food without it becoming a game. Exposure is more likely to intrigue your child.

Putting out the flames

No, we don't suggest that you throw a bucket of water on your child during a tantrum, although you may want to. Put that bucket down and walk away slowly!

Your tiny tot will eat eventually. No matter how long the tantrum continues, remember a few important guidelines:

- ✔ **Don't give in to unreasonable demands or negotiate with your screaming toddler.** She may scream her head off in her highchair for 15 or 20 minutes or wail in line at the grocery store for that candy bar, and you may want to cave. Don't do it!

- ✔ **Don't walk away.** Walking away only makes your child feel more upset and abandoned. Stay with her and even hold her until the fit passes. Then try to explain to her what happened.

- ✔ **Remember to keep your cool and be consistent.** If your child is simply having a meltdown because she's not getting what she wants, you may find that ignoring the tantrum helps more than applying negative attention. As your toddler discovers that a tantrum doesn't really accomplish anything, she'll soon stop putting forth the energy.

Starting Your Day the Healthy Way

As your child continues to grow, breakfast is a continuing part of a healthy lifestyle. The following recipes give you additional breakfast dishes that you should consider serving to your child for good nutrition and variety. By this age, children can handle more tastes and textures. Also, because they have more teeth, children can chew more effectively. These recipes provide more taste, texture, and require more chewing — all things that your child will enjoy. Also, keep in mind that 18-month- to 2-year-olds can still partake of the breakfast dishes in Chapter 7.

☺ *Zucchini Pear Pancakes*

Most children like pancakes, but you can work in a serving of vegetables and fruit first thing in the morning with these pancakes made with zucchini and pears. Watch out — you may find yourself loving these flapjacks just as much as your child may! This recipe makes several servings, so freeze whatever your child doesn't eat and reheat for later use.

Preparation time: *30 minutes*

Yield: *10 servings*

½ fresh pear, peeled, pitted, and coarsely chopped

Dash of cinnamon

1¾ cups whole-wheat flour

¼ teaspoon salt

1¾ teaspoons baking powder

2 egg yolks, beaten

4 tablespoons melted butter

1¼ cups whole milk

6 tablespoons pear juice

1 cup grated zucchini

Nonstick cooking spray

1 In a blender, puree the fresh pear and cinnamon and set aside.

2 In a separate bowl, stir together the flour, salt, and baking powder. Set aside.

3 In another bowl, mix the egg yolks, butter, milk, and pear juice. Pour the liquid mixture into the flour mixture and blend until smooth. Stir in the grated zucchini until it's coated with the mixture.

4 Spray a griddle or frying pan with nonstick cooking spray and heat the pan on medium heat. Spoon the batter into the pan to form 3-inch diameter pancakes. Cook until the tops of the pancakes form bubbles. Carefully flip each pancake and cook until each side is golden brown. These pancakes are best if cooked thin to help the zucchini cook thoroughly.

5 Remove the pancakes from the griddle (or pan) with a spatula and place on a plate and cover with a clean towel or aluminum foil to retain heat. Continue the process of cooking the batter until all pancakes are made. Remember to grease the pan with nonstick spray in between batches.

6 After all the pancakes are made, place a serving of pancakes on a plate and spread the pear puree on top of them. Serve warm.

Smiling French Toast

Create smiles when your French toast smiles back at your kids. Your children get a kick out of the look of this toast, and you can smile as well because they're getting a complete meal. Enlist the assistance of your toddler to make the faces. This meal is one that you can enjoy making and eating together.

Preparation time: *20 minutes*

Yield: *2 servings*

1 egg	*2 slices whole-wheat bread*
Salt and pepper to taste	*Pat of butter or butter spray*
1 strip of bacon	*4 tablespoons applesauce*
Cooking oil for greasing pan	*40 raisins*

1 Whisk the egg in a bowl until well blended. Lightly salt and pepper and mix again.

2 Cook the bacon per package directions. Set aside.

3 Oil a frying pan and heat on medium-high temperature.

4 Spread the beaten egg with a spoon over both sides of the pieces of bread. Place the bread in the frying pan and flip every minute or so, until the egg coating is light brown on both sides of the bread.

5 Place the bread pieces on a serving dish and lightly spread butter over the top surfaces. Spread the applesauce over the tops of the bread.

6 Create a circle on each piece of French toast with the raisins, which serve as a face. Make the face outline cover most of the toast. Use raisins to create eyes and a nose, and then use half of the bacon strip to create the mouth on each piece of toast. Cut the bacon in the middle so that it will bend to make the mouth "smile." Serve.

Vary It! *Make this recipe without the "French toast" element. Just skip the egg and simply toast the bread, and then start with Step 6.*

☺ Yogurt Delight

If your child struggles with enjoying breakfast, but loves yogurt, this recipe saves the day (or at least the meal). The ingredients in this dish provide calcium and vitamin C and boost your child's energy. This breakfast also works great as a snack.

Preparation time: *10 minutes*

Yield: *Two ½-cup servings*

½ medium banana, peeled

¾ cup plain, full-fat yogurt

2 heaping tablespoons granola or granola mix, any variety

3 small apple or pear slices, peeled and finely sliced

1 In a medium bowl, mash the banana. Add the yogurt and granola and stir well.

2 Place the mixture in a cup, and then place the apple or pear slices on top of the yogurt and serve.

Vary It! *Use other fruits such as oranges and kiwi in this recipe. Make sure the fruit is finely sliced.*

☺ Banana Custard

Banana Custard for breakfast is delicious for both kids and adults, and it's a healthy alternative to other potential sugary choices.

Preparation time: *10 minutes*

Yield: *Four ½-cup servings*

1 cup plain, full-fat yogurt

¾ cup cooked oatmeal

¾ cup prepared vanilla pudding

1 small banana, sliced

1 In a small bowl, stir together the yogurt, oatmeal, and vanilla pudding.

2 Spoon mixture evenly into two plastic cups. Place banana slices on top of the mixture in each cup. Serve warm.

Munching in the Afternoon

Because your 18-month- to 2-year-old is often a snack eater, lunch can sometimes be a challenge, especially if your child has eaten breakfast and perhaps a late morning snack. Yet, lunch is an important meal because you can use it to provide balanced nutrition that your child needs throughout the afternoon. These tempting dishes help your little one want to eat lunch, so put them to work in your kitchen. Little Susie will love the taste, and you'll feel great about providing a healthy meal!

Chicken Quesadilla Triangles

This fun-to-eat food works well as lunch or a snack. It's quick and easy, and you'll be nibbling at it as well! You can freeze the prepared quesadillas for use later. Just store them in a freezer bag and simply reheat in the microwave when needed.

As you make this lunch, consider letting your toddler help you with the preparation. Because quesadillas are made from assembling different parts, it's the perfect meal for your child to help with. This recipe is featured in the color section of this book.

Preparation time: *15 minutes*

Yield: *4 servings*

2 flour or whole-wheat tortillas (burrito size — 14 inches in diameter)

½ cup shredded cooked chicken

1 cup shredded cheddar cheese (or a mixture of cheddar and mozzarella)

1 teaspoon melted butter

1 Preheat the oven to 400 degrees.

2 Lightly brush one tortilla with ½ teaspoon of butter and place the tortilla buttered side down on a baking stone or cookie sheet.

3 Place chicken and cheese on the tortilla. Pile the mixture toward the center of the tortilla to avoid leaks during cooking. Brush the second tortilla with the remaining butter and place on top of the first tortilla, buttered side up.

4 Bake for 10 minutes or until the cheese melts.

5 Remove the tray from the oven and cut the tortilla in four even pieces, making triangles. Serve warm.

Vary It! *Substitute beef or ham for the chicken in this recipe. Make a vegan version using grated carrots, zucchini, yellow squash, onions, and tomatoes.*

⌒ Vegetable Rounds

This recipe is like quiche, but in child-size form. The recipe works well with children because kids tend to like eggs. Vegetable Rounds are full of protein and add a healthy serving of vegetables. Also consider cooking this meal for dinner when you can't get your child to eat anything else and you know that she loves eggs. You can freeze the leftovers and toast them later for a quick meal.

Preparation time: *10 minutes*

Cooking time: *10 minutes*

Yield: *18 servings*

3 eggs	*2 cups frozen cooked mixed vegetables*
1 cup milk	*Vegetable oil*
1 cup self-rising flour, sifted	*Salt and pepper to taste*

1 Preheat the oven to 300 degrees.

2 Mix the eggs and milk in a bowl until smooth and well blended, and then add the flour and mix until smooth. Add the vegetables and stir well.

3 Pour the mixture evenly into well-oiled muffin tins, filling each hole ⅔ of the way full.

4 Bake for 10 to 12 minutes until the tops are golden brown. Salt and pepper to taste. Serve warm with fresh carrot or celery sticks.

Cornflake Chicken Bites

This lunch option served with some veggies may please your child, and it makes a great snack, too. The cornflake coating provides a nice crunch, which is interesting to children, and because it contains whole chicken breast pieces, you can feel good about what's on the inside.

Preparation time: *20 minutes*

Cooking time: *25 minutes*

Yield: *About 10 pieces, 2 pieces per serving*

2 cups cornflakes

½ cup shredded cheddar or mozzarella cheese

1 split boneless chicken breast, cooked and skinned

½ stick of butter

Nonstick cooking spray

1 Preheat the oven to 375 degrees.

2 In a medium bowl, coarsely crush the cornflakes. Don't grind them into a powder. Add the cheese to the cornflakes and mix.

3 Cut the chicken breast into bite-size pieces — about 10 pieces, depending on how large you want them to be.

4 Melt the butter in a small saucepan or in the microwave in a microwave-safe bowl. Dip the chicken pieces in the butter, and then press the chicken in the cornflakes and cheese to make sure that the mixture sticks to the chicken.

5 Place the chicken chunks in a baking pan (sprayed with nonstick cooking spray) and bake for 25 minutes or until the chicken is cooked through and no longer pink in the center. You may need to turn the chicken after 10 minutes to keep the browning even. Serve warm.

⏱ Fruit Salad

This fruit salad works great as a side dish for lunch or dinner. Many parents never think about cottage cheese for little tykes, but this healthy salad is a good alternative to other basic salads, and the pineapple gives the whole salad a different taste. This recipe is one that your toddler may need to try a few times in order to get used to the taste and the texture. Freeze the leftovers and allow to thaw for a quick lunch option.

Preparation time: *10 minutes*

Chill time: *15 minutes*

Yield: *Eight 1-cup servings*

24 ounces cottage cheese

8-ounce container frozen whipped topping, thawed

6-ounce package orange flavored gelatin mix

2 11-ounce cans mandarin oranges, drained

20-ounce can pineapple chunks, drained, or you can finely chop two apples instead

Mix all the ingredients in a large bowl and chill for 15 minutes before serving.

Vary It! *You can substitute other fruit options as desired (try adding some bananas).*

Tip: *If your little tyke is a little squeamish about the texture of cottage cheese, you can use a mixer to blend the cottage cheese until the texture is more like sour cream.*

Drumming Up Dinner

Dinner can often be a bit of a challenge for this age group. Kids that tend to eat an afternoon snack are often uninterested in dinner, but these delicious recipes help alleviate that problem.

Naturally, dinner is the last meal of the day, providing balanced nutrition for your child before he goes off to sleep, so it's important to work with your child to establish a pattern of healthy meals and healthy snacks. Just remember that some children are often uninterested in dinner. If you're having this problem, watch out for oversnacking or milk or juice intake before dinner. Work to establish a pattern that keeps your child from eating or drinking milk or juice for at least an hour and a half before dinner.

Mushroom Chicken

This standard chicken "bake" recipe works well for dinner, and you can freeze the leftovers for use later.

Preparation time: *5 minutes*

Cooking time: *25 minutes*

Yield: *Four 1-cup servings*

4 skinless, boneless chicken breast halves	*¼ cup whole milk*
1 can condensed cream of mushroom soup	

1 Preheat the oven to 400 degrees.

2 Place the chicken in a 9-x-12-inch baking dish.

3 Mix the soup and milk together in a bowl, then pour the soup evenly over the chicken. Cover and bake for 25 minutes. Cut the chicken into bite-size pieces. Serve warm.

Tip: *Consider heating a bit of cream of mushroom soup and spooning it over the chicken at serving time to make the chicken even juicier.*

☺ Cheesy Rice and Broccoli

If your child is a bit unhappy about broccoli, and let's face it — sometimes kids scrunch their noses at veggies — this cheesy rice mix should change those attitudes from grim to glad. If you don't serve this dish by itself, it also makes a great side.

Preparation time: *15 minutes*

Yield: *Six ½-cup servings*

10-ounce package frozen broccoli florets	*1 cup water*
1 cup instant rice	*1 cup shredded cheddar cheese*

1 In a medium saucepan, combine broccoli, rice, and water.

2 Bring to a boil, and then remove from the heat and cover for 5 minutes. The water should absorb into the rice and broccoli.

3 Stir in the cheese until it's melted. Serve warm.

Stuffed Potatoes

This variation of twice baked potatoes is more kid friendly with all the extra stuffed items, and it works in a good serving of vegetables. You may find yourself loving this recipe too!

Preparation time: *20 minutes*

Cooking time: *1½ hours in the oven or 15 minutes in the microwave*

Yield: *2 stuffed potatoes, 4 servings*

2 regular baking potatoes, cleaned and scrubbed

1 tablespoon olive oil

6 sliced canned mushrooms

1 tablespoon frozen corn

2 tablespoons frozen green peas

1 tablespoon milk

1 teaspoon butter

2 slices American cheese

1 slice turkey, ham, or chicken, shredded

Salt and pepper to taste

1 Preheat the oven to 400 degrees.

2 Bake the potatoes for 1 hour or until soft. You can also prick the potatoes with a fork and microwave on high for about 8 minutes, saving the oven time.

3 Heat the oil in a frying pan on medium heat and sauté the mushrooms, corn, and peas, stirring frequently for 3 to 4 minutes. Remove from heat and place in a bowl.

4 Cut the baked potatoes in half lengthwise and scoop out the centers, making sure to keep the skins intact. Place the inside of the potatoes in the bowl with the sautéed vegetables. Set the potato skins aside.

5 In a separate bowl, add the milk, butter, cheese, and meat together and salt and pepper to taste and stir well.

6 Refill the potato skins with the mixture. Rebake the potatoes in the oven or microwave; about 25 minutes in the oven and 10 minutes in the microwave on high heat. Serve warm.

Quick Fish Fillets

Fish is an important part of any diet because it contains essential fatty acids that your body uses in a number of ways, including brain development and normal brain function. This isn't only true for children but also for adults. Get in the habit of eating fish meals with your children, and this quick fish fillet is a great place to start.

Preparation time: *15 minutes*

Yield: *4 to 5 fillets, 1 fillet per serving*

4 ounces cod or halibut	*½ cup breadcrumbs or crushed cornflakes*
1 egg, beaten	*2 tablespoons olive oil*

1 Wash the fish and cut away any skin or fat. Cut in 4 or 5 even pieces.

2 Crack the egg in a small bowl and whisk the egg to combine the yolk and the egg white. Place the breadcrumbs in another bowl.

3 Dip the fish in the egg and coat both sides. Then roll the fish in the breadcrumbs. Make sure that the fish is completely coated.

4 Heat the oil in a frying pan on medium-high heat and fry the fish for 5 minutes or until golden brown. Serve with cooked or raw vegetables or another side of your choice.

Tip: *Serve the fish with ketchup or mayonnaise. Don't feel that your child has to eat fish without any condiments. The important thing is that he eats it!*

Quick and Easy Turkey Chili

Here's a quick chili dish with a twist: It uses turkey meat, which is less fatty than hamburger or other chili meat. Chili can be a bit spicy, which kids aren't acclimated to, but our toddlers loved this version because it's blander than typical chili.

Preparation time: *15 minutes*

Yield: *Three 1-cup servings*

½ pound ground turkey

14-ounce can pinto beans, undrained

14-ounce can diced tomatoes, undrained

10½-ounce can condensed tomato soup

1 soup can water (10½ ounces)

1 teaspoon chili powder

Salt to taste

1 Over medium heat, fry the turkey in a large frying pan until brown, about 8 to 10 minutes. Drain extra grease if necessary.

2 Stir in all remaining ingredients and bring to a boil, then reduce heat, stirring occasionally. Serve warm with crackers, carrot sticks, and ranch dressing.

Succumbing to Your Toddler's Sweet Tooth

We pretty much all love desserts, and there are millions of goodies to choose from. Your child may have a similar sweet tooth, and if that is the case, the recipes in this section may help curb that craving while still providing nutrition and not just empty calories.

We love these recipes because they're yummy and fun to make. Get your child to help you make them! Enjoy!

Sweet Potato Cookies

Sweet potatoes are really a perfect food. They taste great and are a good source of potassium, iron, vitamin A, and vitamin E, not to mention fiber. Try to work sweet potatoes into both your child's diet as well as your own diet, and these cookies are a great way to do it! Head to the color section to see these cookies.

Preparation time: *10 minutes*

Cooking time: *10 minutes*

Tools: *Parchment paper*

Yield: *15 servings, depending on size*

¾ cup butter, softened	1½ cup flour
½ cup sugar	1 teaspoon baking powder
¾ cup packed brown sugar	¼ teaspoon cinnamon
1 egg	¾ cup rolled oats
1 cup peeled, cooked, and mashed sweet potato	1 cup raisins

1 Preheat the oven to 350 degrees.

2 Using a hand-held mixer, mix the butter, sugar, and brown sugar until well blended. Add the egg and sweet potato and stir well by hand. Add all the other ingredients and stir.

3 Place parchment paper on a cookie sheet. Drop teaspoon-size drops of cookie dough onto the parchment paper. You can make the drops a little larger if desired.

4 Bake for 10 to 12 minutes. Remove from the oven and allow to cool on the cookie sheet.

Vary It! *Add ¼ cup crushed pecans (for older children only) to this recipe; however, don't give nuts to children under 2 years old.*

Gummy Worm Mud

Around the age of 2, children start to enjoy things that seem gross. This fascination is a normal part of a child's development and in many ways will last into the teen years. This snack is made from chocolate pudding and a couple of gummy worms, which you can buy in the snack aisle of your grocery store. This recipe is best for children 2 years old and older because gummy worms can be a choking hazard for smaller children. Check out the color section of this book for a picture of the finished product.

Preparation time: *20 minutes*

Chill time: *15 minutes*

Yield: *Four ½-cup servings*

1 box of chocolate pudding mix	*1 package of gummy worms, any kind*

1 Make the pudding according to the package directions. Remember, always use whole milk.

2 After the pudding has chilled, spoon a serving (serving size on package directions, about ½ cup) into a plastic cup or dish.

3 Place two gummy worms on the top of the pudding. Press one end of the worms down into the pudding slightly to make it look like the worms are crawling around in the pudding. Serve with a spoon.

Vary It! *Crumble a chocolate sandwich cookie and sprinkle it on the top of the pudding. This variation makes the pudding look like dirt! Your child may think it's funny and be intrigued enough to eat it.*

Tip: *This recipe contains a lot of sugar. Cut down on the sugar by purchasing sugar-free pudding or sugar-free gummy worms.*

Setting a good mealtime example

From ages 18 months to 2 years old, children begin to mimic their parents. That's quite a change because in the early months of life, your baby seems mostly oblivious to what you're doing, aside from the occasional smile. However, children soak up information like a sponge throughout their entire life, so learning primarily comes from you, the parent.

As your child grows, remind yourself constantly that your every move is being watched, and behaviors, both good and bad, pass from you to your kid. Check your behavior and make sure that you're modeling what you want to see. Keep the following points in mind:

✔ **Your child is rapidly studying and learning your language at this time.** Even if your child doesn't speak well, he knows what you're saying, and he's in the process of discovering words and speech behavior

(screaming, quiet voices, and so on) from his primarily caregivers. Use mealtime as an opportunity to teach your child words about eating and food (also, remember to watch your language — toddlers can pick up bad words at this age.)

✔ **Your child is naturally curious about food.** As you eat, try to model good eating habits. Let your child see you eating a wide variety of healthy foods, and he may want to try those foods as well. Get out of the habit of giving your child one food while you eat something else.

✔ **Model table manners and behavior.** Your child often looks like he's slept in the food that he's eaten, but modeling table behaviors (eating with silverware *at* the table) and manners (saying please and thank you) will soon rub off on your youngster.

Vanilla Apricot Squares

These treats are delicious, and everyone in your family is likely to enjoy the vanilla and apricot taste. You can also freeze any leftover squares for a quick dessert at a later date.

Preparation time: *20 minutes*

Cooking time: *20 minutes*

Yield: *36 servings*

2 tablespoons butter	*½ cup flour*
¾ cup sugar	*1 teaspoon baking powder*
2 eggs	*1½ cups vanilla wafers, crushed*
2 egg whites	*Nonstick cooking spray*
1 teaspoon vanilla extract	*Confectioners' sugar for dusting*
1¼ cups chopped dried apricots	

1 Preheat the oven to 350 degrees.

2 In a medium bowl, beat the butter and sugar until well blended. Beat in the eggs, egg whites, and vanilla until well blended.

3 In a food processor, combine chopped apricots and flour until blended. Add baking powder and vanilla wafers to the food processor and blend. Stir the dry mixture into the egg mixture until combined.

4 Coat an 8-x-8-inch square baking pan with cooking spray. Pour the batter into the pan and bake in the oven for 40 minutes. Dust with confectioners' sugar and cut into squares when cool.

Chapter 9

Tasty Meals for 2-Year-Olds

. . . .

In This Chapter

▶ Saving your sanity at mealtime

▶ Smiling your way through breakfast

▶ Focusing your efforts on lunchtime

▶ Winding down the day with dinner

▶ Icing the cake: Desserts

. . . .

Recipes in This Chapter

▶ Piggy in a Blanket

↻ Cheesy Eggs and Toast

↻ Fruity Toast Sticks

▶ Tex-Mex Roll-Ups

▶ Cheesy Ham and Peas

▶ Crazy Open-Faced Ham Sandwich

▶ Chicken and Veggie Quesadillas

↻ Stuffed Apple

▶ Pizza Meatloaf

↻ Pasta Veggie Casserole

▶ Crab Patties

▶ Cheeseburger Tator Tot Bake

↻ Stuffed Celery

▶ Corn Chowder with Beef

▶ Frozen Peanut Butter Bananas on a Stick

▶ Banana Split

▶ Fruity Shake

▶ Frozen Fruit Slush

▶ Simple Rice Pudding

You very well may find yourself running head to head with your 2-year-old at the table, but you have plenty of options and steps to take to make mealtime a blast for your youngster and nutritionally balanced to boot.

Throughout this year of your child's life, you'll find that she'll become more and more opinionated about what she'll eat. She may want only mac and cheese every meal of the day, every day of the week, and she may become hopelessly devoted to peanut butter and crackers. Don't jump on the phone to call Dr. Phil, though — the pickiness and preference for the same foods over and over are normal. To guide you in your efforts to feed your child the best foods (without losing your sanity!), in this chapter, we give you the rundown on what's most important to keep in mind when preparing nutritious meals for a balanced diet, how to cook for your 2-year-old to keep him happy yet healthy, and how to get your little one involved so mealtimes are bonding times as well. To get you started, we give you plenty of tempting recipes that help you and yours get over this nutritional hump.

The Great Balancing Act: Mealtimes versus Your Sanity

Because you're likely to have your hands full with your 2-year-old child, you may find it difficult to focus on the types of foods you serve your tot as well as the amounts you feed him — you may end up in situations where you're tempted to slide a box of cookies his way, just to keep him happy and fed. But fret you shouldn't — this section tells you all you need to know about feeding your 2-year-old so you know what to expect and how to entice your growing child with the right amounts of healthy foods, all the while maintaining your sanity.

Welcome to the land of small meals and snacks

Small meals and snacks are likely becoming the norm for your 2-year-old — your toddler prefers several small meals a day at this point, as she's not quite ready for the three-meal-a-day plan. In fact, eating three smaller meals a day and nutritious snacks in-between is healthiest for adults as well, but we tend to eat three larger meals in order to manage our time and lives better. Your toddler, however, eats when he's hungry, which tends to be every few hours. During this stage of life, you should continue offering three balanced meals per day with balanced, healthy snacks in-between. Keep in mind that young children play hard, so they burn a lot of energy and may suddenly seem to be starving to death. This is why balanced meals with healthy snacks are so important.

Figuring out mealtime foods and portion sizes

One of the questions that parents often face with children who are 2 years old is "How much do I give my child in a typical meal?" Your child doesn't need as much as you may think, but it's important to give the right amount. Giving too little food may cause your child to finish mealtime with a tummy that's not quite full, which means she'll be ready for another mini-meal in an hour or two. Too much, and your child may become overwhelmed with the amount of food on her plate and then won't want to eat at all. We had this issue with our youngest daughter. If her plate was too full, even with foods that she liked, she tended not to eat well. A full plate is overwhelming to some kids, so keep this point in mind as you make your child's plate.

Food portions

Remembering how much food to provide your toddler at mealtime is as easy as following the "⅓ cup rule," which is also recommended by the USDA's MyPyramid for Kids (for more information on MyPyramid for Kids see Chapter 2). Generally, ⅓ cup of any dish is enough to satisfy your child's hunger and his nutritional requirements. If he child wants more, you can always give him an additional portion after he's eaten his initial serving — keep in mind, though, that seconds should usually be half of ⅓ cup, because most of the time your youngster's tummy will be almost full after the initial serving.

Don't get in the habit of giving your child too much food or he'll get in the habit of eating everything. Naturally, this behavior can lead to obesity. At this stage in the game, portion control becomes important.

Beverage portions

In addition to keeping track of the quantity and types of food you're giving your child, you also need to monitor drinking habits. Because your child is so active, she's likely to act like a camel at this age, meaning she'll tank up on liquid before or during the meal, especially if you serve juice or some other drink your child likes. The end result: Your child fills up on liquid instead of eating food, which means her nutritional needs won't be met, and she'll also be hungry again sooner.

To avoid filling up on liquid before mealtime, limit your child's drinks to water the hour before a meal — she's less likely to overfill on water than on sugary (and tasty!) juice. Don't worry about how much water you give — your child can't drink too much water!

Ensuring nutritional balance

Like growing children of any age, 2-year-olds have some specific nutritional needs, but you'll also find that a well-balanced diet for a 2-year-old is much the same as a well-balanced diet for adults. Strike a balance between protein, grains, vegetables, and dairy. If you're wondering what your child needs per day in terms of servings, keep these handy points in mind:

- **Grains:** 4 to 6 servings of bread, cereals, or starches, such as ½ cup brown rice, cereal, or a slice of whole-wheat bread. Remember, stick more to whole-wheat products for the best nutritional value.

- **Vegetables and fruits:** Four to six ½-cup servings per day. Include a variety of different fruits and veggies.

- **Milk or other dairy products:** Four 4-to-6-ounce servings; for example, one serving may be a glass of milk or perhaps a ½ cup of yogurt. At age 2, it's a good idea to go ahead and move your child to lower fat milk, such as 2 percent.

- ✔ **Meat and beans:** Two ½-to-1-ounce servings; for example, one serving may be a 1-ounce serving of fish or chicken breast. Your child can have red meat, and you don't have to over worry about what types of meat you give. However, fish and chicken breast are good choices.

- ✔ **Fats or oils:** 1 to 3 teaspoons per day. This extra category is recommended by the USDA, yet you're not going to feed your child a teaspoon of oil. You don't have to worry about meeting the needs of this category if you feed your child a balanced diet because the oil needs will be met within the diet. Just remember that oils, such as olive oils, are a healthy part of the diet and your child will get the oil content from condiments such as mayonnaise and salad dressings.

Overcoming pickiness and making mealtime fun

It's not rocket science, but sometimes getting your youngster at this age to eat what you cook may prove challenging, to say the least. You may have a bit of a tough time getting your 2-year-old to eat healthy foods — or even to eat at all. If you approach your little one with some patience and keep her interests in mind, your ride may be a much smoother one. Always keep in mind that it's your responsibility to offer a good variety at scheduled times, but it's your child's decision whether to eat what is offered and how much. Also remember that it may take 10 to 20 exposures to a food before a child will even want to try it.

Managing under- or overweight children

When your child reaches the age of 2, you may get concerned that your chunky baby is becoming a lean machine. This thinning out is normal, and children this age often shed the baby fat and become a bit skinny looking as they grow taller and play harder. Keep offering balanced meals and healthy snacks. If your child is eating and has plenty of energy, you're in good shape. If your precious one frequently seems a little dreary and refuses to eat, make an appointment with your pediatrician.

On the other end of the spectrum are overweight children. Most children who are overweight at 2 years of age are heavy because of higher fat diets and a lack of activity. Lose the sugary snacks and fatty foods, such as chips, and start preparing the meals, snacks, and desserts found in this book. Also, limit television and other sedentary activities. Your child needs to be up and moving instead of being passively entertained. Your pediatrician may also give you additional dietary suggestions that help you make healthy lifestyle changes for your child, depending on your child's specific health needs. If you are concerned that your child is too skinny or overweight, always check with your pediatrician.

Rely on visual appeal

Especially at age 2, children become very sensitive to how their food looks. If a dish doesn't visually appeal to your child, for whatever reason, your child may have problems taking a bite. In fact, even some of the dishes he liked when he was younger may suddenly be under scrutiny.

To overcome picky eater syndrome, it's a good idea to think visually as you prepare your child's food. Toddlers respond well to fun shapes and sizes, especially anything that seems unusual, and they like vivid, bright colors. Of course, not every dish or food lends itself to such creativity — you can't win every battle with presentation alone! Here are some ideas that we've found helpful with our little ones, and you can find more information and some specific recipes for picky eaters in Chapter 14:

- ✔ Use fruit to create a smiling face on a plate (and string cheese for hair).
- ✔ Use a cookie cutter to cut out fun shapes in your pancakes.
- ✔ Garnish healthy smoothies and shakes with a little fruit, such as grapes or thin strawberry slices.
- ✔ Use carrot sticks and other raw veggies to build a fence or a wall around the meal.
- ✔ Include color in the meal to attract your child's eye.

Get your child involved

Another way to entice your toddler at the table is to let her help out with the prep work. Even at age 2, your child isn't too young to help in the kitchen. Children gain knowledge by watching you, so consider allowing your toddler to

- ✔ Help arrange napkins on the table
- ✔ Stir a mixture with a wooden spoon
- ✔ Pour the dry contents into the bowl
- ✔ Scrape the bowl with a spatula
- ✔ Help wash the dishes or place them in the dishwasher

In Chapter 11, you find some great recipes that lend themselves to youngster participation.

If your toddler isn't ready to help with any prep work or isn't interested yet, you can even have him play with spoons and other safe kitchen items — your kid may love to make noise with a pot and a wooden spoon. While you get a meal ready, tell him what you're doing and use the time to build his vocabulary, introducing each item and its name as you cook, and he discovers more about eating and food.

Curing Morning Tummy Grumbles

At this stage of the game, your child can go two ways with breakfast: he'll either love it or hate it. These recipes are geared toward getting your child to love it! The following recipes are often favorites for 2-year-olds. You have a lot of flexibility with food. Food allergies and intolerances aren't so much of a concern at this point, and your child has gotten used to more textures, flavors, and colors of food.

Piggy in a Blanket

Toddlers enjoy these tasty little roll-ups, mostly because they're fun to eat. This quick recipe is easy to make and a healthy choice for a breakfast food to help start your little one's day on the right foot. Add a side of fruit and you have an even more nutritious meal.

Preparation time: *5 minutes*

Cooking time: *15 minutes*

Yield: *16 roll-ups, 2 per serving*

1 can refrigerated croissant dough	*16 sausage links*
8 slices American cheese	*2 tablespoons butter*

1 Preheat oven to 375 degrees.

2 Unroll croissant dough, separate pieces, and cut each triangle piece in half lengthwise (so each piece is still a triangle).

3 Cut each slice of American cheese into 2 strips.

4 Wrap each sausage in a strip of the cheese and then wrap in the croissant. To wrap the croissant, place the sausage at the bigger end of the triangle and roll the dough toward the tip of the dough. Place the wraps with the tip facing down on a cookie sheet. This placement keeps the dough from unrolling during cooking.

5 Melt the butter in a microwave-safe container. Lightly brush all sides of the dough with the butter. Bake for 15 minutes, turning about halfway through cooking time to ensure even browning. Remove from heat and allow to cool. Serve warm.

☺ Cheesy Eggs and Toast

This kid-friendly version of a traditional breakfast meal — eggs and toast — is easy to make, and the kids enjoy the visual appeal made with different shaped cookie cutters. You may already know that getting kids to eat can sometimes be a challenge. So it's helpful to make the food interesting on their level (See "Overcoming pickiness and making mealtime fun," earlier in this chapter, for suggestions on making meals interesting.) Check out the color section of this book for a picture of the final product.

Preparation time: *10 minutes*

Tools: *Small cookie cutters, any shape*

Yield: *1 serving*

2 slices whole-wheat bread, toasted	*1 large egg*
Butter	*1 slice American cheese*

1 Shape the toast into bite-size pieces with the cookie cutters. Lightly butter the toast pieces.

2 In a small bowl, beat the egg until well blended. Pour the egg in a frying pan, stirring as it cooks. When eggs are about halfway cooked, add the American cheese. Finish cooking the eggs; remove from the heat.

3 Place eggs in a pile in the middle of a child-size plate. Arrange toasted shapes around the eggs. Serve warm.

☁ Fruity Toast Sticks

Need a quick and healthy breakfast for your hungry toddler? These toast sticks are great for the whole family because they contain whole-wheat bread, peanut butter, and fruit. They taste yummy and provide good nutrition to start the day.

Preparation time: *5 minutes*

Yield: *8 servings (2 sticks per serving)*

4 slices whole-wheat bread	*1 large banana, sliced*
2 tablespoons peanut butter	*Honey*
Raisins	

1 Spread each piece of bread thinly with the peanut butter. Slice the bread into 4 sticks.

2 Add desired amount of raisins on top of the peanut butter. It's a good idea to push the raisins down into the peanut butter.

3 Place the toast sticks on a baking tray and toast them to your desired darkness in a toaster oven. Remove from the toaster and add the sliced bananas. Drizzle with honey. Allow toast to cool and serve.

Scaling the Midday Hump: Lunchtime!

Lunchtime meals are important for your toddler because he's active during the morning hours. Keep in mind that many toddlers are a bit resistant to lunch if they've eaten a good breakfast and a snack, so make sure that your child isn't grazing during the morning hours and tanking up on milk.

A good lunch helps your child have a better afternoon by keeping solid nutrition flowing through her body. She'll also more likely take a good nap with a full tummy. Take a stab at the recipes in this section to beef up your lunchtime menus.

Tex-Mex Roll-Ups

With chicken breast and veggies, this dish is a true, balanced meal wrapped in a tidy package. Head to the color section to see the finished product.

Preparation time: *15 minutes*

Yield: *2 roll-ups, 2 servings*

2 flour or whole-wheat tortillas	*¼ cup shredded lettuce, divided*
¼ cup refried beans, divided	*¼ cup chopped tomato, divided*
¼ cup diced cooked chicken breast, divided	*¼ avocado, peeled, pitted, and diced, divided*
¼ cup grated cheddar cheese, divided	

1 Place each tortilla on a microwavable plate and spread half of the refried beans evenly on each. Sprinkle equal amounts of the chicken and cheese on the tortillas. Microwave for 15 to 30 seconds until cheese melts.

2 Allow to cool slightly. Add the remaining ingredients and roll up each tortilla.

Vary It! *You can use regular pinto beans instead of refried beans, but the refried beans act as a "glue" to help hold the ingredients in the roll-up.*

Cheesy Ham and Peas

Cheese always gives a dish a creamy texture, which is appreciated by children. With this recipe, the cheese gives the ham extra flavor and helps your child eat his peas, which children often resist. It's a quick and easy lunch!

Preparation time: *20 minutes*

Yield: *Eight ½-cup servings*

2 cups frozen sweet peas	*1 tablespoon butter*
1 cup diced, cooked ham	*3 slices American cheese*
2 tablespoons whole milk	*Salt and pepper to taste*

1 Cook the peas according to package directions, and then put the peas in a microwavable casserole dish. Gently stir in the ham chunks.

2 Add the remaining ingredients and salt and pepper to taste.

3 Cover the dish with a moist paper towel and place in the microwave. Cook on medium-high heat for 2 to 3 minutes, stirring every minute.

4 Remove the dish from the microwave and gently stir. Let set for 2 to 3 minutes before serving. Serve warm.

Crazy Open-Faced Ham Sandwich

With this simple recipe, you'll give your child something healthy to eat and some fun to boot — kids love the smiley face on top. Have your child help you with this recipe.

Preparation time: *20 minutes*

Yield: *1 serving*

1 teaspoon mayonnaise	*1 string-cheese stick*
1 slice whole-wheat bread	*1 baby dill or sweet pickle, sliced in thin, round circles*
1 slice deli ham	*1 thin slice tomato*

1 Spread the mayonnaise on one side of the bread and place the ham slice on top of the mayonnaise.

2 Separate the cheese stick into thin strings. Place the strings of cheese around the top of the bread to look like hair for your smiley face.

3 Place two slices of pickle on the ham for the eyes of the sandwich. With another slice of pickle, cut out a triangle for the nose. Place the nose on the sandwich.

4 Cut the slice of tomato in half to create the smile for the face, and complete the smiley face by placing the tomato on the sandwich. Serve.

Chicken and Veggie Quesadillas

Quesadillas are a great way to mix nutritious meat and veggies in a package that children are favorable to. We like quesadillas as a lunch item because of the good nutrition and quick cook time. Add this recipe to your arsenal!

Preparation time: *10 minutes*

Yield: *4 wedges, 2 pieces per serving*

6-inch tortilla, flour or whole-wheat	*1 tablespoon cooked mixed vegetables*
3 tablespoons shredded cheddar cheese	*1–2 tablespoons of finely chopped, cooked chicken breast*

1 Place the tortilla on a microwave-safe plate. Sprinkle all the ingredients evenly on the tortilla. Fold the tortilla in half and microwave for 40 seconds or until cheese melts.

2 Cut the quesadilla into four wedges and serve warm.

 **Stuffed Apple**

This recipe is a bit different than standard lunch fare, and kids are often intrigued by it because they get to dig the inside of the apple out with a spoon. At first glance, the stuffed apple seems like a snack, but because it contains peanut butter and fruit, it provides a nutritional lunch with plenty of vitamins and protein. You can also use the Stuffed Apple as a snack, or you can combine it with other recipes, such as the Vegetable Rounds recipe.

Preparation time: *20 minutes*

Yield: *1 serving*

1 medium apple	1 teaspoon cream cheese
2 tablespoons smooth peanut butter	Raisins, optional
½ ripe banana, peeled	

1 Wash the apple and core it, creating a hole in the top and coring out the meat. Make sure there is no hole in the bottom. The idea is to scoop out ½ to ¾ of the inside to create a mostly empty center, essentially turning the apple into a "bowl."

2 In a small bowl, finely mash the banana. Add the peanut butter and cream cheese and mix well.

3 Spoon the mixture into the apple. You can top the hole with raisins if you like. Serve with a spoon.

Tip: *If you don't want to waste the inside of the apple you have carved out, just mash the good parts into small pieces and mix them into the peanut butter and cream cheese. This option adds a little more crunch to the mixture!*

Tempting Your Toddler at Dinnertime

As adults, we look forward to dinner. Dinner signals the end of the day (for most of us) and food tends to be relaxing. From your child's point of view, dinner is simply another meal, and depending on how well your child has eaten the other meals of the day, she may be more or less hungry. This behavior is normal, so keep providing healthy meals and snacks.

Snow Flake Lake

Banana Parfait (Chapter 7);
Yogurt Pineapple Pops (Chapter 11)
© T. J. Hine Photography

Peaches and Cheese Sandwich;
Peanut Butter and Jelly Waffles (Chapter 10)
© T. J. Hine Photography

Clockwise from left: Fruit Kebabs (Chapter 11);
Peanut Butter and Apple Toast (Chapter 14);
Cheesy Eggs and Toast (Chapter 9)
© T. J. Hine Photography

Gummy Worm Mud (Chapter 8);
Bow-Tie Pasta with the Works (Chapter 7)
© T. J. Hine Photography

English Muffin Pizza;
Avocado Turkey Sandwich (Chapter 7)
© T. J. Hine Photography

Sweet Potato Cookies (Chapter 8);
Vegetable Chow Mein (Chapter 10)
© T. J. Hine Photography

Clockwise from left:
Meat and Veggie Kebabs (Chapter 10);
Orange Banana Smoothie (Chapter 7);
Stuffed Burgers (Chapter 11)
© T. J. Hine Photography

**Before and After: Tex-Mex Roll-Ups (Chapter 9);
Chicken Quesadilla Triangles (Chapter 8)**
© T. J. Hine Photography

In this section, we include dinnertime meals that are tempting to children, combining common ingredients with a few new twists. In fact, you may find that other members of your family enjoy these dishes as well.

Pizza Meatloaf

This meatloaf isn't Grammy's dry meatloaf. This meatloaf packs a juicy punch! Your toddler, along with the rest of the family, is sure to enjoy this unique and delicious dish. As an added bonus, the leftovers, which are freezable, make delicious meatloaf sandwiches.

Preparation time: *15 minutes*

Cooking time: *30 to 40 minutes*

Yield: *8 servings*

Nonstick cooking spray

1 pound extra-lean ground beef or ground turkey

¼ cup breadcrumbs

1 egg

1 cup pizza sauce, any variety

1 teaspoon dried Italian seasoning

1 cup grated mozzarella cheese

1 Preheat the oven to 425 degrees.

2 Spray a medium-size casserole dish with nonstick spray.

3 In a medium mixing bowl, combine the meat, breadcrumbs, and the egg. Add ¼ cup of the pizza sauce and the Italian seasoning and mix well. Add ½ cup of the cheese and mix well. Pat the mixture together to create a loaf and place it in the casserole dish.

4 Bake for 30 to 40 minutes. You may need to adjust the bake time slightly depending on the size of your casserole dish. Deeper casserole dishes typically require a bit more bake time.

5 Remove the dish from the oven and test the meatloaf to make sure that it's cooked all the way through (no pink showing). You can test it with a meat thermometer, or simply cut a portion of the meatloaf and check for a brown center.

6 Top the loaf with the remaining pizza sauce and mozzarella cheese. Continue cooking the meatloaf for 5 to 10 minutes.

7 Remove the dish from the oven and allow the meatloaf to sit for 10 minutes before slicing. Serve warm with a side salad or fresh veggies.

ᗧ *Pasta Veggie Casserole*

This pasta veggie casserole is delicious, and your children, along with the not so small members of your family, will love this one. The leftovers also keep well in the freezer.

Preparation time: *15 minutes*

Cooking time: *45 minutes*

Yield: *8 servings*

16-ounce package penne pasta	*4 cups milk*
2 cups chopped frozen broccoli	*½ cup grated Parmesan cheese*
1 cup sliced canned mushrooms	*5 tablespoons chopped fresh basil, divided*
1 cup chopped green bell pepper	*⅓ cup breadcrumbs*
1 tablespoon butter	*2 tablespoons grated Parmesan cheese*
1 onion, chopped	*Nonstick cooking spray*
1 clove garlic, minced	*Salt and pepper to taste*
¼ cup flour	

1 Preheat the oven to 350 degrees.

2 Cook the pasta according to package directions. Stir in the broccoli, mushrooms, and green bell pepper, and cook for 6 to 8 minutes, or until pasta is al dente — slightly firm in the center. Drain off the water and set aside.

3 Melt the butter in a medium saucepan over medium-high heat. Sauté the onions and garlic for 1 to 2 minutes. Stir in the flour and milk and cook for 5 minutes or until the mixture coats the back of a metal spoon. Remove the pan from the heat and stir in ½ cup Parmesan cheese and salt and pepper to taste. Add the pasta and stir well.

4 Coat a 9-x-13-inch baking dish with cooking spray, combine mixtures and 4 tablespoons of basil. Sprinkle the top with the breadcrumbs, 2 tablespoons of Parmesan cheese, and the remaining 1 tablespoon of basil.

5 Bake for 45 minutes or until the top of the casserole is golden brown. Serve warm.

Crab Patties

No, this recipe isn't from the famous land under the sea that serves Crabby Patties, but you can sing the Spongebob Squarepants theme song while making your own at-home version of the crab patty. The crunchy texture is often a hit with kids; the patties are easy to make and fit well with most other side dishes or veggies that you choose to serve. Freeze the leftovers and use them with other meal options as well.

Preparation time: *25 minutes*

Yield: *16 servings*

¼ cup softened butter

5 ounces (about 1½ cups) shredded cheddar cheese

8 ounces cooked crab meat or imitation crab meat

¼ cup mayonnaise

½ teaspoon minced garlic

8 English muffins, split

1 Preheat the oven to the broiler setting.

2 In a medium bowl, mix together the butter and cheese. Add in the crab meat, mayonnaise, and garlic.

3 Arrange the split English muffins with the cut side facing up on an ungreased cookie sheet. Spread the crab mixture over the English muffins.

4 Broil the muffins until the cheese melts. Serve warm.

Cheeseburger Tator Tot Bake

Toddlers often love tator tots, and this meal works well as a main course. Extra servings can be frozen for leftovers to reheat easily for lunch.

Preparation time: *15 minutes*

Cooking time: *40 minutes*

Yield: *8 servings*

2 pounds lean ground beef

½ medium onion, chopped

Salt and pepper to taste

Garlic powder to taste

10¾-ounce can condensed golden mushroom soup

10¾-ounce can condensed cheddar cheese soup

16-ounce package frozen tator tots

2 cups shredded cheddar cheese

1 Preheat the oven to 375 degrees.

2 Cook the ground beef and onion in a skillet over medium-high heat. Stir occasionally. When the beef is no longer pink and the onion is translucent, remove the skillet from the stove and drain off the excess grease. Season to taste with salt, pepper, and garlic powder.

3 Return to the heat, and stir in the mushroom and cheese soups until well blended. Heat thoroughly, and remove from the stove. Transfer the mixture to a 9-x-13-inch baking dish. Cover the ground beef mixture with a layer of frozen tator tots.

4 Bake for about 40 minutes. When the tots are golden brown, remove the casserole from the oven, and sprinkle the cheese over the top. Return the dish to the oven, and bake until cheese melts. Serve warm.

☺ Stuffed Celery

This recipe works as a side dish for just about any meal. Kids love the look of the stuffed celery and the addition of nuts adds a unique taste.

Preparation time: *15 minutes*

Chill time: *15 minutes*

Yield: *15 celery bites, 3 pieces per serving*

8-ounce package cream cheese, softened

2 tablespoons sour cream

¼ cup chopped walnuts

20 green olives with pimentos, chopped

4 celery stalks, cut into 1-inch pieces

1 In a small bowl, mix the cream cheese and sour cream. Stir in the walnuts and chopped green olives.

2 Spread the mixture into the bite-size celery pieces, place on a plate and chill for 15 minutes. Serve.

Vary It! *Leave out the nuts if you have a child that is allergic or doesn't like nuts.*

Corn Chowder with Beef

This recipe is quick and easy and a great meal, especially on those cold winter days. This meal is very hearty, and with a simple side dish of salad and bread, you have a complete meal. The rest of your family will enjoy this recipe as well!

Preparation time: *15 minutes*

Cooking time: *50 minutes*

Yield: *Ten 1-cup servings*

1 pound ground beef	15-ounce can creamed corn
1 onion, chopped	15¼-ounce can whole kernel corn, undrained
5 potatoes, washed, peeled, and cubed	2 cups milk
5 cups water	

1 In a skillet over medium-high heat, cook the beef with the onions until the meat is completely brown and no pink remains.

2 In a large stock pot, cook the potatoes in 5 cups of water (add a bit more if necessary), until they're tender — approximately 20 minutes.

3 Add both kinds of corn, milk, and the beef mixture to the pot of potatoes. Simmer for 30 minutes and serve warm.

Capping Off a Good Meal with Dessert

Dessert is a course that typically comes at the end of the meal (although you may have been caught a time or two trying to dip into the pudding or swipe a cookie hot out of the oven). The word dessert comes from the Old French word *desservir,* meaning "to clear the table." While your little one may only want to clear the table in one fell swoop (and not by eating) for the sweets to come, remind him that dessert is a treat. You can feel good about serving the desserts found in this section because while the sweetness tempts your youngster, the healthiness of each recipe ensures that your child is getting the proper daily nutrition. Put the following year-round desserts to work for you in your kitchen.

Frozen Peanut Butter Bananas on a Stick

These treats are a perfect dessert because most kids love peanut butter and bananas, and they love popsicles, too, which these are, in a way. Let your little one help you make this treat!

Preparation time: *5 minutes*

Chill time: *4 hours in the freezer*

Yield: *1 serving*

1 small banana   *2 tablespoons creamy peanut butter*

1 Peel and cut the banana in half lengthwise.

2 Place two tablespoons of peanut butter on one of the halves using a butter knife or a plastic spatula if your kid is helping. Smooth peanut butter from one end to the other.

3 Place the other half of the banana on the half covered with the peanut butter to make a "sandwich."

4 Insert the popsicle stick into the end of the banana.

5 Wrap the banana in a piece of wax paper and place it in a freezer bag or wrap it in aluminum foil.

6 Place the banana in the freezer for 4 hours.

7 Remove the banana from the freezer and peel away the layers of foil and wax paper.

Tip: *Make sure you use wax paper or the peanut butter will stick to the foil.*

Vary It! *Dip the banana in melted chocolate before placing it in the freezer.*

Banana Split

If you love banana splits, you'll love this version as well. You can use ice cream as usual, but you can also make this recipe healthier with frozen vanilla yogurt. Combined with the fruit, it's a delicious cold treat that your toddler will love.

Preparation time: *10 minutes*

Yield: *1 serving*

1 small banana

1 scoop frozen vanilla yogurt or ice cream

3 strawberries, washed, dried, and sliced

1 teaspoon of flaked coconut

Whipped cream for topping

1 Peel the banana and cut it in half lengthwise.

2 Place one scoop of yogurt or ice cream in a plastic serving dish and place the bananas on each side of the ice cream.

3 Top the yogurt or ice cream with the sliced strawberries; sprinkle with coconut, and top with a dollop of whipped cream. Serve with a spoon.

Fruity Shake

This fruity shake is made with yogurt and fresh fruit, so it's a healthy alternative to other snacks.

Preparation time: *5 minutes*

Yield: *Two 8-ounce shakes*

6-ounce can pineapple juice, chilled

6-ounce can peach nectar, chilled

½ cup cold milk

1 small banana, peeled and sliced into small pieces

6 strawberries, washed, dried, and sliced

1 Place all the ingredients, except three slices of strawberries, in a blender and blend until smooth.

2 Pour blended shake into a plastic cup and place the remaining pieces of strawberry on top for a garnish. Serve with a straw.

Tip: *Throw a couple of ice cubes in the blender to thicken the shake if you want.*

Frozen Fruit Slush

Slushy desserts are often a favorite for children. Notice how many fast-food restaurants serve some kind of slushy drink. This frozen fruit slush is a great snack that's more nutritious than the fast-food version.

Preparation time: *5 minutes*

Chill time: *2 hours in the freezer*

Yield: *About 8 servings, depending on the size of cups you use*

15-ounce can crushed pineapple	*12-ounce can frozen orange juice concentrate*
4 medium bananas cut into small slices	*1½ cups water*

1 Mix all the ingredients until the orange juice is melted and pour the mixture into small plastic cups.

2 Place the cups in the freezer and freeze for 2 hours (until slushy). Serve with a spoon.

Simple Rice Pudding

This rice pudding is simple and healthy for your 2-year-old. This quick dessert also works well for children as young as 9 months.

Preparation time: *5 minutes*

Cooking time: *10 minutes*

Yield: *Four ½-cup servings*

1 cup white rice, cooked	*2 drops vanilla extract*
1 cup warm milk	*1½ tablespoons sugar*

Combine all the ingredients in a saucepan and cook over low to medium heat for 10 minutes or until the mixture is smooth and warm, and then serve.

Part IV

Welcoming Your Child to the Big People's Table

The 5th Wave   By Rich Tennant

"I find it easier to say 'No' if I imagine them saying, 'Mommy, can I have the latest over-hyped, over-priced, commercial exploitation of an obnoxiously adorable cartoon character?'"

In this part . . .

About the time that your child reaches the age of 3, he begins to eat more foods that the whole family loves. Although you'll continue to deal with some age-appropriate issues, your recipe repertoire can easily grow and change. In this part, we provide plenty of recipes to help you keep up with your growing weed (tot, rather), from ages 3 to 5. You discover how fun it is to cook with your child (and get some appropriate recipes to involve your kid in the kitchen — see Chapter 11). Take a look at Chapter 12 for ideas devoted to meals for the entire family.

Chapter 10

Enticing Your 3- to 5-Year-Old

- -

In This Chapter

▶ Meeting the ever-growing needs of your child

▶ Counting the calories all the way out the door:
  Daycare nutrition

▶ Waking up the nutritious way

▶ Growing up on good lunches and dinners

▶ Adding a little sweetness to your life

- -

As your child reaches the ages of 3 to 5, you'll
likely find that mealtimes get easier — your
child can more clearly communicate to you what
he wants, and he's more likely to be open to a
greater variety of foods because he has more
options in terms of tastes and texture. These years
can also be challenging, though, because your
child may be more opinionated about what he will
or won't eat. From a nutritional point of view,
these years continue to be important as your child
grows and matures, so you need to keep an edu-
cated eye on what you're serving him and how
much. With delicious and nutritious recipes, such
as those we provide in this chapter, you can make
sure that your child is getting what he needs for
healthy growth with little to no fuss on his end.

Recipes in This Chapter

- ↻ Peanut Butter and Jelly Waffles
- ↻ Peaches and Cheese Sandwich
- ↻ Blueberry Whole-Wheat Waffles
- ▶ Cheeseburger Soup
- ▶ Homemade Stuffed Corn Dogs
- ↻ Vegetable Chow Mein
- ▶ Southwestern Tortilla Roll-Ups
- ▶ Meat and Veggie Kebabs
- ▶ Homemade Chicken Nuggets
- ▶ Super Quick Chicken Enchiladas
- ↻ Veggie Burritos
- ▶ Chicken Lo Mein
- ▶ Cupcake Family
- ▶ Lemon Ice
- ▶ Double Chocolate Éclair Pie
- ▶ Carrot Banana Smoothie
- ▶ Watermelon Slushy

Leaving the Toddler Years Behind

By the time your child turns 3 years old, the often-difficult toddler behavior
starts to pass. You find that your child's temper tantrums seem to be subsid-
ing and even completely passing, which makes mealtime all the more pleas-
ant for everyone involved. As your child continues to grow, she needs a
healthy and varied diet, much like yours. You have more flexibility with the
foods you offer because your child already has a full set of teeth. However, a

3- to 5-year-old isn't mature enough to create her own diet, so eating nutritiously continues to be an important part of the parental focus. In the following sections, consider your child's needs — in regard to both structure and nutrition — at this stage of life.

Settling into a routine

At this stage, three meals a day with a few healthy snacks in-between continue to be the normal eating schedule for your tyke. Your child may be in daycare and starting pre-kindergarten during this time of his life, and you won't be there to feed him every time his tummy grumbles, so chances are that your child will even be better behaved and happier in general with the schedule you establish early on. Children this age tend to prefer the same basic routine every day — ever wonder why he wants to read the same books and watch the same cartoon movie over and over?

Naturally, you need to serve breakfast, lunch, and dinner. Ideally, at this age your child should have about three healthy snacks per day, 2 hours before each meal. Try to avoid the habit of giving your child a snack an hour or less before a meal because your child is less likely to eat the actual meal. Also, be wary of providing too much milk or juice — children at this age will panhandle for them in lieu of eating food!

Here are a few tips to help you keep your child's eating schedule on track:

- **Keep a consistent schedule.** As much as possible, breakfast, lunch, and dinner need to be at the same time every day. This routine helps your child develop a desire to eat. This process does take time.

- **Eat together.** Try to make mealtime a family event, so it's something everyone does together at the same time. Mealtime is as much about socialization as it's about food, and your toddler learns from older children and adults.

- **Avoid the exotic.** Children tend to like the same things over and over. This is a normal part of a child's development and isn't something you should be overly concerned about. Keep mixing in new foods, but now isn't the best time for foods that are exotic.

- **Don't fight it.** Some days your child eats well at mealtime and others he doesn't. This behavior is normal, so don't let the table turn into a battleground for your kiddies. If your child won't eat, don't worry. Finish your meal, and then at the next snacktime, offer something healthy.

- **Watch out for milk and juice.** If your child tanks up on milk and juice an hour before mealtime, he won't eat the meal. Try to keep the hour before mealtime free of milk and juice or any kind of snack. Offer water between meals, as little Billy may be thirsty.

> ✔ **Be patient.** As with all things, patience with your child's eating habits and routine is something that takes time and should be handled with gentleness on your part. Food shouldn't be a negative issue with your child or a source of discipline or reward.

Upping the variety in your child's diet

Your child's diet at this age and beyond becomes much like yours. You need a good variety of nutrition instead of the same thing every day, which is really true from the time your baby starts eating a variety of solids. The good news about this age is that you have more flexibility because your child can simply eat a larger variety of foods. Keep mixing it up! Offer new foods and be sure to serve a familiar food with an unfamiliar food. This tactic makes the addition of new foods easier for you and your little one.

At the same time, don't make life more complicated than necessary. If your child can't stand lima beans, choose another kind of beans or vegetable altogether. In other words, choose your food battles wisely. Even if your child doesn't like a particular food, it's still a good idea to offer it from time to time, because your child's likes and dislikes change a lot. Who knows — lima beans may suddenly be the new trendy food!

So what does your 3- to 5-year-old need in terms of nutrition and servings? As a general rule, you can follow the USDA's MyPyramid for Kids (head back to Chapter 2); specifically, a 3-year-old of average weight and activity level should have the following amounts per day:

✔ **Grains:** 4 to 5 ounces per day, at least half coming from whole grains. Typical servings equal one slice of bread, a cup of cereal, or ½ cup of rice or pasta.

✔ **Vegetables:** 1½ cups of any vegetables.

✔ **Fruits:** 1 cup (or a bit more) of any fruit.

✔ **Milk:** 2 cups. If your child doesn't like milk, serve 1 cup of yogurt or 2 ounces of cheese, but continue to offer milk at meals for exposure.

✔ **Meat and Beans:** 3 to 4 ounces per day.

One common situation that parents face is when a child loves milk — not just likes it, but *really* loves it. This desire is great for your child's bone growth, but remember that your toddler shouldn't have milk as a substitute for food. In fact, cow's milk, although rich in calcium, is low in iron and other nutrients, so your child needs the varied nutrition that well-rounded meals and snacks bring. (Generally, by age 3, you can use 2-percent or skim cow's milk.) If your child frequently wants milk but not food, limit the amount of milk you offer throughout the day and don't offer milk at mealtime.

Odds are that between the ages of 3 and 5, your child becomes more interested in sugary cereals and other not-so-nutritious foods due to television commercials and other such advertising. You can acknowledge those desires, but continue to provide healthy meals instead of giving in to the marketing hype. It's okay to allow your child to have these products from time to time, but don't let them become the norm.

The Most Important Meal: Breakfast

Breakfast is the most important meal of the day for your growing child, so always be sure to offer it and keep the meal enticing. Remember to offer your child healthy meals, but don't force your child to eat. With the breakfast dishes in this section, however, you'll probably find that your child will gobble them down with no encouragement from you!

☉ Peanut Butter and Jelly Waffles

This heavier breakfast provides a kid favorite of peanut butter and jelly with a waffle. Remember to include options for a meal that is healthier: high protein, whole-wheat waffles, natural peanut butter, and pure-fruit preserves.

Preparation time: *10 minutes*

Yield: *1 serving*

2 waffles, homemade or any prepackaged variety	1 tablespoon peanut butter
	1 tablespoon jelly or preserves

1 Toast the waffles according to the package directions, or cook homemade waffles as desired.

2 Spread the peanut butter on one side of one waffle and the jelly on one side of the other.

3 Place the waffles together to form a sandwich, cut into four squares, and serve warm.

Tip: *Make extra waffles (if you're whipping them up from scratch) and freeze them for a quick reheat when your child is requesting this recipe.*

☺ Peaches and Cheese Sandwich

Have you heard of pineapple and cottage cheese for breakfast and even tomatoes and cottage cheese for lunch? Well, this delicious breakfast combines a different kind of cheese with fruit: fresh peaches and ricotta cheese. The two flavors offset each other well, as the cottage cheese versions do, and the dish also provides a boost of protein to get your child going in the morning. Whip up this concoction for a healthy snack, too.

Preparation time: *10 minutes*

Yield: *1 serving*

2 slices whole-wheat bread

¼ cup ricotta cheese

½ cup fresh peaches, peeled and sliced

⅛ teaspoon cinnamon

1 On one slice of the bread, spread the ricotta cheese and top with fruit. Sprinkle the cinnamon on top of the fruit.

2 Place the bread on a baking tray and toast both slices in a toaster oven until the plain slice is brown and the slice with cheese has melted cheese.

3 Remove from the heat, and place the plain slice of bread on top of the fruit to form a sandwich. Cut into squares or other shapes as desired. Serve warm.

◌ Blueberry Whole-Wheat Waffles

Our children love waffles, and that seems to be a common theme among kids everywhere. These waffles are whole wheat, giving your child more nutrition than a typical waffle, and the sweet blueberry taste is sure to be a hit.

Preparation time: *25 minutes*

Yield: *5 servings*

¾ cup flour	2 eggs
¾ cup whole-wheat flour	1 cup milk
4 teaspoons baking powder	2 tablespoons vegetable oil
2 tablespoons sugar	½ cup fresh blueberries, washed

1 Preheat the waffle iron.

2 Sift together both types of flour, the baking powder, and the sugar.

3 With a mixer, blend in the eggs, milk, oil, and blueberries to create a smooth batter with a few small lumps of blueberries.

4 Spray the waffle iron with nonstick cooking spray and pour ¼ cup of batter on the iron; cook for about 2 minutes, repeating this step until you run out of batter. Serve warm with regular maple syrup or flavored syrup, if desired.

Nifty Lunches for a Growing Kid

Children at this age love creative lunches, because food is more interesting to eat when it looks cool. You'll find that the recipes in this section help you incorporate a variety of lunch options that your 3- to 5-year-old will love.

Cheeseburger Soup

If your child is a bit resistant to eating soup, this delicious and filling soup may do the trick. Because the soup is so cheesy, it's not like eating plain old soup. In fact, our kids aren't big soup fans, but they love this hearty lunch.

Preparation time: *1 hour*

Yield: *Four to six ½-cup servings*

½ pound lean hamburger meat	1 teaspoon salt
½ cup diced onion	2 cups reduced-sodium beef broth
1½ cups canned, stewed tomatoes	3 tablespoons butter
1½ cups frozen sweet corn	¼ cup flour
2 cups peeled and diced potatoes	1¾ cups milk
2 teaspoons Italian seasoning	2 cups shredded cheddar cheese

1 In a medium-size skillet over medium-high heat, brown the hamburger meat and onion. Remove the skillet from heat and drain the excess grease from the meat. Place meat and onion mixture in a medium-size pot. Add the tomatoes, corn, potatoes, Italian seasoning, salt, and beef broth.

2 Bring the mixture in the pot to a boil, and boil for 2 minutes. Reduce the heat to a simmer. Simmer for 15 minutes or until potatoes are cooked all the way through.

3 Melt the butter in a microwave-safe bowl, and stir in the flour. After the flour and butter have been thoroughly combined, stir in the milk until the mixture is smooth.

4 After the soup has simmered for 15 minutes, gradually whisk in the butter mixture. Bring to a boil, stirring constantly. Boil for 2 minutes and reduce the heat to a simmer.

5 Stir in the cheese, and stir constantly until cheese melts. Remove from the heat and allow the soup to sit for 5 minutes before serving.

Homemade Stuffed Corn Dogs

Corn dogs seem to be a favorite for kids of all ages (even you big kids: a.k.a. adults). One great aspect of this recipe is control: You control what goes in the coating for the dogs because you make it yourself. You'll also enjoy this recipe because it freezes well, which saves you time later when you need a quick meal for a fussy child.

Preparation time: *15 minutes*

Cooking time: *35 minutes*

Tools: *Rolling pin*

Yield: *10 servings*

Nonstick cooking spray

1⅔ cup flour

⅓ cup yellow cornmeal

3 tablespoons sugar

1 teaspoon baking powder

¼ teaspoon salt

¼ teaspoon dry mustard

⅔ cup warm water

2 tablespoons vegetable oil

10 turkey or all-beef hot dogs

10 slices American cheese

10 wooden Popsicle sticks

2 tablespoons milk

1 Heat the oven to 350 degrees. Spray a cookie sheet with nonstick cooking spray.

2 In a medium bowl, combine the flour, cornmeal, sugar, baking powder, salt, and dry mustard. Stir in the water and oil. Continue to stir until the dough pulls away from the sides of the bowl.

3 Sprinkle some flour on a clean, dry surface, and remove the dough from the bowl and place it on the floured surface. Lightly flour your hands, and knead the dough for 4 to 6 minutes. Dough will become smooth. Place the dough back in the bowl and cover with a clean towel. Let the dough rise for 10 minutes.

4 Remove the hot dogs from the package, and with the tip of a sharp knife, cut 4 slits lengthwise along the hot dog. Make sure that the slits don't cut all the way through the hot dog because you still have to insert the Popsicle stick.

5 Cut each slice of cheese into 4 thin slices. Stuff the slices into the slits of each hot dog.

6 Remove dough from bowl and place on lightly floured surface. Roll dough out with a floured rolling pin. Cut strips of dough into 5-x-4-inch rectangles. You don't have to be exact. Keep in mind you will need to have 10 strips of dough (one for each hot dog).

7 Gently insert a Popsicle stick into each stuffed hot dog, about half way. Wrap each stuffed hot dog in a strip of dough. Tightly press edges together to make sure that you have a tight seam.

8 Brush corn dogs on all sides with milk. Place the corn dog seam side down on prepared cookie sheet.

9 Bake for 35 minutes or until golden brown. Remove from heat and allow to sit for 5 minutes before serving. Remember, the corn dogs contain melted cheese inside; you don't want your child's mouth to get burned by the melted cheese that will come out when they bite into it. Serve with your child's favorite condiment.

🍑 *Vegetable Chow Mein*

Chow mein is a great lunchtime meal, and if you introduce foods such as chow mein early, you may greatly expand your child's food repertoire. Another great point: Chow mein can easily find its way into your menu more often than you may think. Stir-fried veggies can work as an entire meal, as they do in this recipe, but they also work great as a side dish for all kinds of other recipes. This recipe is quick and easy and is featured in the color section of this book.

Preparation time: *30 minutes*

Yield: *Five 1-cup servings*

¼ pound fine Chinese egg noodles

1½ tablespoons sesame oil

½ peeled and crushed garlic clove

1⅓ cups shiitake mushrooms

1¼ cups sugar snap peas

½ cup baby corn on the cob, cut into small bites

4 green onions, finely chopped

1 cup chopped zucchini

4 tablespoons soy sauce

1 tablespoon brown sugar

1 Cook the noodles according to the package directions. Drain and set aside.

2 In a large frying pan or wok, over medium-high heat, heat the sesame oil. Add the garlic and stir fry it for about 20 seconds, and then add the mushrooms, peas, and corn. Stir fry for 4 minutes.

3 Add the onions and zucchini and cook for 5 minutes, stirring regularly. Add the soy sauce and brown sugar and stir well for 1 to 2 minutes. Stir in the noodles and serve.

Southwestern Tortilla Roll-Ups

Get a taste of the Southwest with this quick meal! This recipe gives you plenty of cooking flexibility, because you can vary the ingredients however you like. Get your toddler involved: She'll have a good time helping you make this quick and easy lunch.

Preparation time: 10 minutes

Yield: 1 serving

1 flour tortilla, burrito size

2 tablespoons grilled hamburger meat

2 tablespoons ranch-style beans

2 tablespoons cheddar cheese

On the tortilla, place the meat, beans, and cheese. Roll into a burrito and toast in a toaster oven until the cheese melts. Cut the burrito into four pieces and serve warm.

Vary It! Serve the roll-ups with a dipping sauce, such as cheese or ranch dressing.

Grown-Up Dinners Fit for a Child

Dinner is always a great way to end the day, and as a parent, you may find yourself spending more time on preparing dinner for your family than on any other meal. The toddler dinners in this section are all tasty and full of nutrition — the perfect way to end the day.

Meat and Veggie Kebabs

We love kebabs because they have a beautiful visual appeal for both children and adults (for more suggestions on the appearance of meals, see Chapter 18). This recipe makes two small kebabs on toothpicks. Serve these to your toddler with a side of pasta and you'll have a healthy, tasty meal!

Let your child help out with the preparation for this recipe. He'll enjoy poking and spearing the meat and veggies with the little toothpicks. Because the order of ingredients isn't important, your child can make many different combinations of kebabs.

Preparation time: 15 minutes

Yield: 2 kebabs, 1 per serving

4 small chunks cooked, skinless chicken, ham, or turkey

2 large black olives

2 cherry tomatoes

2 bite-size chunks yellow squash or zucchini

2 tablespoons melted butter

Spaghetti sauce for dipping

1 Set the oven to broil.

2 Thread the meat, olives, tomatoes, and squash or zucchini onto two toothpicks in any order.

3 Place the kebabs on a foil-lined baking dish and brush all sides with the melted butter.

4 Broil for about 3 minutes or until the vegetables are slightly browned. Serve your kebabs warm with a side of spaghetti sauce for dipping.

Tip: *Use small cocktail sausages instead of chunk meat. The sausages are precooked, which will speed up the preparation of the meal.*

Vary It! *Adjust the ingredients as desired. Use different veggies or meats. Or go all vegetarian. Mix it up and have some fun!*

Homemade Chicken Nuggets

Chicken nuggets are a favorite with kids, and you'll find this recipe to be quick and easy (and cheesy). Notice that this recipe makes a larger portion. Your prep time may be a little longer for this recipe, but you end up with a larger batch of nuggets for your work. Simply freeze the extras for a quick lunch option when you're short on time.

Preparation time: *30 minutes*

Marinating time: *30 minutes*

Yield: *20 to 30 pieces*

2 pounds boneless, skinless chicken breasts	*½ cup crushed cornflakes*
3 tablespoons margarine or butter, melted	*⅓ cup grated Parmesan cheese*
1 teaspoon Worcestershire sauce	*Shortening*

1 Cut the chicken in 1-inch square pieces. Combine the chicken, melted margarine, and Worcestershire sauce. Marinate the mixture in the refrigerator for 30 minutes.

2 Preheat the oven to 450 degrees.

3 Combine the crushed cornflakes and Parmesan cheese in a large bowl.

4 Remove the chicken pieces from the marinade and press the chicken into the cornflake and cheese mixture until well coated. Arrange the chicken on a greased cookie sheet.

5 Bake for 7 to 9 minutes. Remove the chicken from the oven and serve warm.

Super Quick Chicken Enchiladas

Chicken enchiladas are a popular dish among all ages, but you'll find that 3- to 5-year-olds are a bit sensitive to spices and flavors. Therefore, this recipe is blander for your toddler's taste buds. This freezer-friendly recipe has the added bonus of a quick fix, so make extra for those times you're in a hurry and when your kid needs something to eat, now!

Preparation time: *15 minutes*

Yield: *8 enchiladas, 2 per serving*

1 tablespoon of cooking oil	*¼ cup mild salsa (avoid chunky varieties)*
3 chicken breast halves, cut into small pieces or chunks	*14½-ounce can condensed cheddar cheese soup*
14½-ounce can condensed cream of chicken soup	*8 6-inch tortillas*

1 In an oiled skillet, cook chicken pieces over medium heat for about 5 minutes until the chicken is browned and cooked all the way through (when you cut a piece of the chicken, the center shouldn't have pink meat).

2 Add the chicken soup and salsa and stir together until the mixture is hot. Spoon ¼ cup of the mixture into each tortilla and roll up the tortilla.

3 Place tortillas in a 2-quart microwavable dish. Pour cheese soup over tortillas.

4 Heat in the microwave for 3 minutes or until hot. Serve warm.

☙ Veggie Burritos

Kids often like eating burritos because they like to eat with their hands. Although we aren't advocating a total abandonment of table manners, sometimes it's just more fun to leave the silverware in the drawer. These burritos are easy to make, and you can adjust the ingredients depending on what you have on hand. Isn't flexibility a wonderful thing?! Try out this recipe and see the reaction you get from your children.

Preparation time: *15 minutes*

Cooking time: *5 minutes*

Yield: *3 servings*

1 cup refried beans	*1 ripe avocado, mashed*
1 cup cooked brown rice	*⅓ cup tomatoes, finely chopped*
3 tablespoons mild salsa	*3 large flour or whole-wheat tortillas*
2 cups grated cheddar cheese	

1 Preheat the oven to 300 degrees.

2 Heat the refried beans in a small microwave-safe bowl in the microwave until hot.

3 Mix the beans, rice, salsa, and cheese in a bowl until well blended. Add in the avocado and tomatoes and mix well.

4 Evenly divide the mixture between the three tortillas and roll up. Put the tortillas in a baking dish and bake for 5 to 10 minutes, until hot. Serve warm.

Chicken Lo Mein

This mild lo mein makes a great dinner meal (or even lunch) because it's full of nutrition and quick to make. This recipe may stretch your child's palatal interest, but it's bland enough to entice a 3- to 5-year-old. The peanut butter taste makes this one a hit with kids.

Preparation time: 15 minutes

Yield: Six 1-cup servings

½ pound whole-wheat pasta	4 tablespoons water
2 tablespoons peanut oil	½ garlic clove, crushed
¼ teaspoon sesame oil	1 chicken breast, cooked and diced
2 tablespoons smooth peanut butter	⅓ cup grated carrot
1 tablespoon soy sauce	¼ cucumber, grated

1 Prepare the pasta according to package directions.

2 While the pasta is cooking, in a medium bowl, combine both oils, the peanut butter, soy sauce, water, garlic, and chicken. Mix well.

3 Drain the pasta and add to the mixture. Add the carrot and cucumber and stir. Serve warm.

Tantalizing Toddler Treats

We love desserts (who doesn't?), and your child will enjoy a sweet treat from time to time. We recommend that you don't let dessert become a daily habit in your home, because doing so sets up the expectation that all meals should end on a sweet note. Instead, use these recipes periodically, no more than twice per week.

In this section, we've included some of our favorites, and they're all rather easy to make. Enjoy!

Cupcake Family

This basic cupcake recipe takes on a new meaning when you and your child decorate the cupcakes to represent the members of your family. The time spent in the kitchen gives you quality time with your little one. You'll love talking with your child about what each person in the family looks like and how you should decorate the cupcake to represent your Uncle Steve. As you cook with your child, expect a lot of fun and laughter.

Preparation time: *40 minutes*

Yield: *12 servings*

18.5-ounce box yellow cake mix, any brand	*3.14-ounce package plain M&M candies*
16-ounces container vanilla frosting	*2 red licorice bootlaces, cut in 2-inch pieces*
Food coloring, any color	*3 ounces plain chocolate*

1 Make the cupcakes according to the package directions. Allow them to cool.

2 Mix the frosting and add the food coloring, whichever color you choose, if desired. Ice the cupcakes.

3 Add M&M candies for the eyes and noses and cut pieces of the licorice to form the mouths.

4 In a small bowl, melt the chocolate and then drizzle it on the cupcakes to form hair. You can add beards and mustaches in the same way. Serve.

Vary It! *Vary the decorations in any way you like. Use the chocolate drizzle to add glasses, dimples, and any other family characteristics. You can also use strawberry topping to create red hair or butterscotch to create blonde hair. The fun is trying to create a resemblance of each family member.*

Tip: *A piping bag makes the icing decorations much easier to form. Consider picking one up at your favorite discount store.*

Lemon Ice

When the hot summer days leave your 3- to 5-year-old sweaty and tired, this quick lemon ice treat will be a welcomed, refreshing surprise.

Preparation time: *30 minutes*

Chill time: *2 hours in the freezer*

Tools: *Popsicle trays*

Yield: *About 5 servings, depending on the Popsicle trays used*

1½ cups hot water	*1¼ cups freshly squeezed lemon juice*
1½ cups sugar	*1 cup cold water*

1 Combine the hot water and sugar in a saucepan and cook over medium heat for 5 to 8 minutes, until syrupy.

2 Allow the syrup to cool slightly, and then add the lemon juice and cold water and mix well. Pour the mixture into Popsicle trays and freeze until firm, about 2 hours.

Double-Chocolate Éclair Pie

Any chocolate lover in your family is sure to love this éclair pie, and the good news for you is you can prepare it in only minutes! This is one of our kids' favorites.

Preparation time: *25 minutes*

Chill time: *1 hour*

Yield: *15 servings*

2 sleeves graham crackers	*8 ounces thawed whipped topping*
5.1-ounce package instant vanilla pudding	*16 ounces milk chocolate cake frosting (2 containers)*
2½ cups cold milk	

1 Cover the bottom of a 9-x-13-inch baking dish with a layer of the whole graham crackers. You'll need to break some of them into pieces in order to cover the bottom.

2 Remove the lid and foil seal from one container of frosting and microwave on high for 30 to 45 seconds.

3 Carefully remove the frosting from the microwave and stir. Pour the frosting over the layer of graham crackers in your baking dish.

4 In a large mixing bowl, whip the pudding mix and milk for 3 minutes on high speed with an electric mixer. Gently fold in the whipped topping.

5 Spoon the pudding mixture on top of the frosting and graham cracker layer in the baking dish. Add a layer of whole graham crackers on top of the pudding layer. Again, you'll need to break a few crackers into pieces to completely cover the pudding layer.

6 Remove the lid and foil seal from the second container of frosting and microwave on high for 30 to 45 seconds. Carefully remove the frosting from the microwave and stir. Pour the frosting over the top of the graham cracker layer.

7 Place the dessert in the freezer for 1 hour. Loosely cover the dish with foil so the foil doesn't stick to the chocolate. Cut and serve.

Tip: You can serve this dish after freezing for one hour, but it's better if it chills in the refrigerator overnight because the graham crackers become soft.

Carrot Banana Smoothie

This smoothie can actually be given to children all the way down to 1 year of age, but we like this one because you work in the carrot juice, so it's not just a fruit smoothie. Try it out!

Preparation Time: *5 minutes*

Yield: *Four 1-cup servings*

1 cup carrot juice	*1 small ripe banana*
1 cup apple juice	*6 ounces full-fat plain yogurt*

Put all the ingredients in a blender and blend until the juice reaches the desired consistency. Pour the mixture into a plastic cup and serve with a straw or spoon.

Tip: If you own a juicer, for an all natural, healthy drink use fresh carrots and apples and juice the fruit in your machine until you have enough juice to fill the 1-cup measurements.

Watermelon Slushy

On a hot summer day, this slushy is sure to be hit with kids of all ages.

Preparation Time: *20 minutes*

Chill time: *30 minutes*

Yield: *Five 1-cup servings*

2 cups seeded watermelon chunks	*¼ cup water*
6-ounce can frozen lemonade concentrate	*1 cup ice*

1 Put the watermelon chunks in a bowl and chill them in the freezer until they're very cold or almost frozen, about 30 minutes.

2 Put the watermelon and the rest of the ingredients in a blender and blend until you get the slushy consistency you desire. Add more ice if necessary.

3 Pour the mixture into a cup and serve with a straw or spoon.

Chapter 11

Cooking with Your Little One

Cooking with your little one is a great activity that has many parents discovering the benefit of quality time spent together. Our kids love to cook with us in the kitchen, and we highly recommend that you make it a regular activity in your home as well.

Keep in mind that your child generally won't be able to get involved in the cooking process until the age of 3. However, the kitchen can be a fun place even for younger children. Let your youngster play with spoons and other safe kitchen items while you're cooking, and explain the processes as you go along so you're still routinely spending time with your tots while you're in the kitchen.

We know what you may be thinking: Is cooking with a child a complicated, potentially disastrous combination? It certainly could be, but with the simple, fun-to-prepare recipes in this chapter, you can pretty much bank on the fact that it won't be.

The Benefits of Cooking with Your child

As you think about spending time in the kitchen with your youngsters, you can probably think of several immediate benefits — primarily the extra time you'll get to spend together. As your child helps you cook, she's more likely to be willing to try new foods as she helps prepare them, and she'll understand why cooking is important. Yet, there's more to these immediate benefits than meets the eye.

You get quality time together

Spending quality time with your children is one of the most important aspects of being a parent. Sure, you need to take care of countless other details to raise your youngster, those being absolutely essential as well — feeding your baby, changing his diapers, that sort of thing. But a growing child has emotional and psychological needs, too, and when you can kill two birds with one stone, so to speak, showing your child that she's important to you by spending quality time with her and getting a meal ready at the same time, you're doing an excellent job of multitasking (a concept well familiar to most parents).

Another great aspect of cooking is the artistic nature of it, the process of creating something and enjoying the end product. So when you get your child involved, you're not only taking care of routine business as well as spending time together, but also you're creating together. If you use the recipes in this chapter, the process, as well as the final result, will be rewarding to you both.

You can give your child a solid nutritional foundation

If you prepare healthy meals with your child alongside you, you can teach a lot about what foods are healthy and what foods should serve as an occasional treat. As you cook healthy meals with little Joey, he'll become more familiar with individual items in the kitchen. Teach him about veggies, grains, milk products, meats, and other foods.

Use this time to educate him on the food pyramid (we discuss the MyPyramid for Kids in Chapter 2) and why these groups of foods are important for good health.

You help to instill a love of cooking

If you love to cook, chances are that someone initiated that interest and you caught on — and you may want to do the same for your child. Your youngster can become active in the kitchen even as a toddler simply by playing with spoons. As your little one grows, he can start helping you with simple tasks, such as pouring ingredients into a bowl. Young children love to organize things and help out when they feel like they can. These simple "hands-on" tasks and spending time with you in the kitchen may lead to a lifelong love of cooking.

You help develop language and motor skills

The kitchen is a learning laboratory for your child. Think about it: Basically everything you do in school you put to work in the kitchen. From language to math to art, the kitchen is arguably the most interdisciplinary room in your house. As you get involved in meal preparation, be sure to think in terms of education. Instead of simply preparing food, try to reinforce various skills. Keep these ideas in mind:

✔ **Language:** Focus on new words. Teach the names of ingredients and the names of different kitchen tools (such as "blender" and "spatula," or whatever you call them in your native tongue). Practice teaching new words and reiterating old ones each time you're in the kitchen. Don't try to teach everything at once, though; focus on a few key items, and when your child can easily recognize them, call them by name, and tell you what they're used for, move on to a few new words.

✔ **Math:** The kitchen is the perfect place to work on basic math skills, such as addition and subtraction. Even if your son is only 3 years old, you can help him practice counting by asking questions such as "How many eggs do we have?" Older children can work with recipe items and amounts, which is often great addition and subtraction practice.

✔ **Sequence:** Because most recipes require that you complete a series of steps in order to create them, the kitchen is the perfect place to focus on following directions and helping your child discover that order is a common (and important) part of any task.

As you work through a recipe, it's important that you read the ingredients and steps out loud with your kid, in much the same way that you'd read a book. This action reinforces reading and learning and helps your toddler understand how the entire recipe works as a whole. In other words, don't just give your kid the pieces of the whole while you assemble the recipe — instead, let her enjoy the entire experience.

✔ **The five senses:** The kitchen is the perfect place to explain and explore the five senses. Children are hands-on learners by nature, and the kitchen is a good place to work on texture, smell, and sight. Ask your child what she thinks of the various ingredients and then of the finished product. By having her describe them to you and helping her along the way, you're increasing the number of descriptive words in her vocabulary.

✔ **Cause and effect:** Especially at ages 4 and 5, toddlers begins to grasp relationships and how one thing affects something else — a prime time to talk about cause and effect. You can discuss what happens to dough when it goes into the oven, for example, or what may happen if you leave the butter out of a recipe and put an apple in instead.

As you cook with your child, you help him develop fine motor skills as well. Let him mix, flip, or knead, for example, and show him how to manage different utensils — he'll love it.

Taking Precautions before You Begin

The kitchen can be a fun place for your children, but it can also be dangerous. Before you get your youngster involved in cooking, take some precautionary measures to make sure that the kitchen is safe, including the following:

✔ **Lock the cabinets and drawers.** Make sure that all cabinets and drawers are outfitted with locking mechanisms that allow *you* to open the cabinet but not your curious kid.

✔ **Keep out all poisonous substances.** You shouldn't keep poisons of any kind in the kitchen. The list includes household cleaners, ant or pest poisons, and detergent, bleach, and so on. Put all household cleaners and other hazardous items in a utility room or other safe area away from your children and away from all food.

✔ **Carefully monitor the tasks you let your kids do.** Almost all recipes (including some of the recipes in this chapter) require the use of a knife, so you need to take a look at each recipe and determine what tasks you need to accomplish and what tasks you can delegate. At ages 3 and 4, toddlers shouldn't use any electric appliances. By age 5, he can start with the electric mixer because it's a safe appliance (and by age 5, he's strong enough physically to manage it).

✔ **Tell your child what she can and can't eat.** Use your time in the kitchen to explain which ingredients are good to eat by themselves and which ingredients aren't good unless they're in a recipe. For example, raw eggs aren't healthy and don't taste good, and that bottle of vanilla extract smells wonderful, but it doesn't taste good on its own.

✔ **Beware the bacteria!** *Never* allow children to handle any potential bacteria-carrying food, such as raw eggs or meat. This task should be left to the adult.

Getting Started: The Game Plan

As you're getting ready to cook, take note of a few tips that will help the process go smoothly. After all, when you cook with your child, you want the event to be positive for both of you, and you can help make that happen by first getting your ducks in a row. Consider the following steps:

1. **Choose the recipe.**

   Before you do anything, choose a recipe that you want to cook with your little tyke, and take a look at the ingredients to make sure that you have everything on hand. You may want to allow your child to be a part of the selection process as well. If you do, give her a choice of three options, instead of overwhelming her with a book of choices.

2. **Prepare the work area.**

   Your kitchen is set up for you — not your kids. With that thought in mind, you may have to do more of the preparation at the kitchen or dining room table. Another option is to get your hands on a bar stool so your child can work next to you at the counter.

3. **Open this book.**

   We recommend that you keep this book (or — gasp! — another cookbook of your choice) on the counter as you cook. It's a positive moment for your child to see you learning and following instructions from a book.

4. **Get all ingredients and tools ready.**

   You should get everything ready before you call the kids into the kitchen. When they arrive in the kitchen, review all the ingredients and cooking tools.

5. **Dole out the tasks.**

   If you have more than one child and want to involve them all in the meal preparation, split up the tasks based on age and what each child is able to do. We highly suggest that you don't have more than four kids helping you out at one time, though — if you have a big family, consider alternating who gets to help out at different meals. Too many people in the kitchen tend to create confusion, and too many tasks to oversee at one time may lead to botched recipes and accidents.

6. **Wash your hands.**

   Before you get started, teach good kitchen hygiene. Everyone should wash their hands thoroughly.

Preparing Main Meals and Sides

Although you may tend to gravitate toward desserts when you cook with your child, you may like cooking some main meals as well. In fact, we recommend that you take this approach instead of letting every cooking time be about desserts and fun foods, because you want to convey a balanced approach to cooking. The recipes in this section are particularly good choices because they aren't overly complicated, and they provide different levels of activity that kids can help with.

Barbecued Franks and Beans

Here's a basic franks and beans recipe that your toddler is likely to love to make and eat! The use of brown sugar and vinegar gives you the barbecued taste without the barbecue! Children age 2 and up can help with this recipe.

Preparation time: *20 minutes*

Cooking time: *40 minutes*

Yield: *Twelve ½-cup servings*

2 15-ounce cans of pork and beans

½ cup loosely packed brown sugar

1 teaspoon white vinegar

1 teaspoon Worcestershire sauce

10 hot dogs

1 Preheat the oven to 350 degrees. Thoroughly mix all the ingredients except the hot dogs in a shallow baking dish.

2 Cut the hot dogs into pieces or simply slice them in half. Place the hot dogs on top of the ingredients in the baking dish.

3 Bake for 30 to 40 minutes. Remove the pan from the oven and serve warm.

✆ *Green Bean Casserole*

Green bean casserole is a common side dish found around American tables, and this easy version of the recipe is a great way to involve your child in a more formal dish. Children 2 and up can help with this recipe.

Preparation time: *15 minutes*

Cooking time: *15 minutes*

Yield: *Twelve ½-cup servings*

14.5-ounce can green beans, drained	*Salt and pepper to taste*
10.75-ounce can cream of mushroom soup	*2.8-ounce can French fried onions*
2 tablespoons sour cream	

1 Preheat the oven to 350 degrees. Mix together the green beans, soup, and sour cream in a bowl. Salt and pepper to taste.

2 Pour the mixture into a 9-x-13-inch casserole dish. Bake for 25 minutes or until the casserole is bubbly.

3 Remove the dish from the oven, and sprinkle the French fried onions on top. Return the dish to the oven and bake for 5 to 10 more minutes until the onions brown slightly. Serve warm.

☺ Vegetable Primavera

This vegetarian version of a basic Italian dish is a great source of energy for your child (thanks to all the carbohydrates in the pasta). Because it freezes well, you can also use the leftovers as a side dish with other meals. Children 3 years and older can help cook this recipe.

Preparation time: *20 minutes*

Yield: *Seven 1-cup servings*

4 cups diced vegetables, any variety	*2½ cups cooked spaghetti noodles*
28-ounce jar spaghetti sauce, plain or vegetable	*1 cup shredded Parmesan cheese*

Mix the vegetables and spaghetti sauce in a medium-size pot. Cover the pot and let the sauce simmer until the vegetables are cooked to the desired tenderness. Serve warm over the spaghetti noodles and sprinkle the cheese over the sauce.

☺ Counting Fruit Salad

This colorful fruit salad is simple to make, but kids like it because you work on your counting skills to make it. And, you can change these ingredients in terms of amount or use other ingredients as desired.

Preparation time: *15 minutes*

Chill time: *15 minutes*

Yield: *Ten 1-cup servings*

1 handful (about ⅓ cup) finely shredded colby or American cheese	*6 apple slices*
2 handfuls finely sliced banana slices	*7 orange slices*
3 tablespoons orange juice	*8 watermelon cubes*
4 tablespoons of nondairy whipped topping	*9 seedless grapes, quartered*
5 kiwi slices and 5 pineapple chunks	*10 marshmallows*

Count out all the ingredients with your child as you place them in a large mixing bowl. Gently stir all the items together and then chill the salad for 15 minutes before serving.

Vary It! *If you have children over the age of 2, add about 10 pecan halves to this recipe. The nuts add an extra crunch to this fruit salad.*

Everyday Treats

Most children enjoy a good dessert and snack from time to time, and in conjunction with a healthy diet, that desire is okay. Don't get carried away, though. This section gives you some desserts, treats, and snacks that are fun to make with your kids, and when eaten in moderation, the treats won't destroy healthy eating habits.

Caramel Rice

This quick and easy dessert is a simple one you can make with your kids. Children older than 2 years can help with this recipe.

Preparation time: *20 minutes*

Yield: *10 servings (2 treats per serving)*

8 tablespoons butter	*5 cups crispy rice cereal*
14-ounce can sweetened condensed milk	*Confectioners' sugar for dusting*
14-ounce package caramels, unwrapped	

1 Over medium heat, melt the butter in a large saucepan and then add the milk. Allow the mixture to become hot again (not boiling). Add the caramels and stir the mixture until the candy is completely melted. Add the crispy rice cereal and stir until completely coated.

2 Remove the pan from the heat and drop the mixture by the spoonful onto wax paper.

3 After the treats have cooled, dust them with confectioners' sugar and serve.

☺ *Homemade Pretzel Shapes*

Here's some good news if your child loves soft pretzels: They're easy to make at home and can be molded into a variety of different shapes. Let your toddler's imagination go wild. Follow this simple recipe and have fun with your youngster.

Preparation time: *15 minutes, plus 30 minutes for rising*

Cooking time: *15 minutes*

Yield: *5 servings*

1½ cups warm water	*2 cups whole-wheat flour*
1 package yeast	*4 cups flour*
1 tablespoon sugar	*Nonstick cooking spray*
1 tablespoon salt	*1 beaten egg*

1 In a large bowl, mix water, yeast, sugar, and salt. Stir in wheat and white flours with a wooden spoon to form dough. Knead the dough until smooth. (See Figure 11-1 for the illustrated process. Remember to place the dough on a floured cutting board before kneading and use small amounts of flour to dust the dough as needed if it gets sticky.)

2 On a flour-dusted table or cutting board, roll out the dough until it's about ½ inch thick. Cut and form into any desired shapes. Allow the dough to sit for 30 minutes so it can rise a bit.

3 Preheat the oven to 425 degrees. Spray a cookie or baking sheet with nonstick cooking spray. Place shapes on cookie or baking sheet, and then brush dough with a beaten egg and add a sprinkle of salt.

4 Bake the dough for 15 minutes or until golden brown. Allow the pretzels to cool before removing them from the pan — they're fragile when hot! Serve slightly warm.

Kneading Dough

Figure 11-1: How to knead dough.

To knead dough, press down with your palm...

Fold the dough over and rotate ¼ turn

Repeat steps 1 + 2 until dough is soft and elastic. *voilà!*

Pecan Turtles

Your family will enjoy this delicious, chocolaty recipe, but it contains nuts, which makes it a potential choking and allergy hazard. Children should be over the age of 2 before eating or helping with this recipe. You can freeze the leftovers for later enjoyment.

Preparation time: *45 minutes*

Yield: *15 servings (2 treats per serving)*

2¼ cups packed brown sugar

1 cup butter

1 cup light corn syrup

⅛ teaspoon salt

14-ounce can sweetened condensed milk

1 teaspoon vanilla extract

1½ pounds whole pecans

1 cup (6 ounces) semisweet chocolate chips

2 tablespoons shortening

1 In a medium saucepan, mix the brown sugar, butter, corn syrup, and salt. Heat the mixture over medium heat until the sugar is dissolved. Add the milk and continue to cook until the mixture stiffens a bit.

2 Remove the pan from the heat and stir in the vanilla. Fold in the pecans.

3 Line a cookie sheet with wax paper and drop spoonfuls of the mixture to create the candy. Refrigerate the candy until it's completely cool.

4 In a microwave-safe bowl, melt the chocolate and shortening in the microwave and mix well. Remove the candy from the refrigerator and drizzle chocolate over the candy. Return the cookie sheet to the refrigerator again until the candy is completely cool and the chocolate has hardened. Serve.

Crispy Rice and Peanut Butter Logs

This peanut butter–based snack is one your kids will love because it's yummy and fun to make. It (obviously) contains peanut butter and nuts, which contain potential allergens, so please make sure that your child doesn't have a nut allergy and is older than 2 years old before letting him pop this treat in his mouth.

Preparation time: *15 minutes*

Chill time: *15 minutes*

Yield: *3 servings*

1 cup crunchy peanut butter

2 tablespoons butter, softened

1¼ cups sifted confectioners' sugar

3 cups crispy rice cereal

¾ cup finely chopped pecans

½ cup melted milk chocolate

1 In a large mixing bowl, stir together the peanut butter, butter, and confectioners' sugar. Add the cereal and mix well. The cereal may get a bit crushed in the mixing, but that's okay.

2 Shape the dough into three 7-x-2-inch logs and place them on wax paper. If you want to make the logs a bit shorter, but thicker, that's fine.

3 Cover the logs with the melted chocolate and sprinkle with the chopped pecans.

4 Chill the logs until firm (15 minutes or so). Cut the logs into bite-size pieces and serve.

Ice Cream Igloos

When you think of hot summer days, do you crave something cold on your tongue? Do you think of swerving into the neighborhood ice cream shop and indulging in a cool treat? If so, try making this fun recipe with your child (if she's over age 2).

Preparation time: *7 minutes*

Yield: *1 serving*

4 graham crackers (still connected)

½ cup chocolate frosting

1 scoop vanilla ice cream

1 Stack the graham crackers on a plate.

2 Put the icing in a piping bag. If the icing seems too thick, mix in a tablespoon of warm water and stir.

3 Place one scoop of vanilla ice cream on the graham crackers. Decorate the ice cream scoop with the icing to create a door, a window, or bricks.

Strawberry Yogurt Pie

This quick and easy no-bake pie will be a real hit and it's fun to cook with your child because its quick and colorful. This recipe calls for strawberries, but you can use any flavor and fruit that you prefer. Children 2 years old and older can help with this recipe. Also note that some children, especially those under 2 years, have allergic reactions to strawberries. Serve this pie only after you've eliminated the possibilities of strawberry allergies.

Preparation time: *10 minutes*

Chill time: *30 minutes*

Yield: *6 servings*

2 8-ounce containers of strawberry flavored yogurt

2 cups whipped nondairy topping

9-inch graham cracker pie shell

1 cup fresh sliced strawberries

1 In a large bowl, combine the yogurt and whipped topping until well mixed. Spoon the mixture into the pie shell.

2 Place sliced strawberries on top of pie in a decorative fashion. This stage is where your creativity can come alive. Chill for 30 minutes and serve.

Fruit Kebabs

These quick and easy kebabs are a healthy snack, and the fact that the fruit is on a kebab makes the snack even more interesting to your child. Children like to remove one bite at a time. Because you're using toothpicks, we recommend that helping hands 3 years old and above help with this recipe because of the potential danger. Keep in mind that you can also freeze this recipe for a frozen fruit treat. Check out the kebabs in the color section of this book (and try to keep yourself from drooling).

Preparation time: *5 minutes*

Yield: *7 servings*

6 banana slices	*6 pineapple slices*
6 peach slices	*3 cherries*
6 apple slices	

Thread the fruit on toothpicks as desired. Serve with supervision.

Vary It! *Brush the fruit with a bit of honey for an extra tinge of sweetness.*

Yogurt Pineapple Pops

With a simple Popsicle tray, you can make all kinds of pops with your children. Because you're making these treats from scratch, you control the ingredients, so you know what is going into your little one's tummy. Experiment with all kinds of varieties.

Preparation time: *10 minutes*

Chill time: *2 to 3 hours in the freezer*

Tools: *Popsicle tray*

Yield: *6 servings*

2 cups full-fat plain yogurt	*1 can frozen pineapple juice (or other combos, such as orange-pineapple), thawed*
½ cup canned crushed pineapple, packed in its own juice and drained	

Mix all the ingredients together and stir well. Fill the Popsicle tray and freeze, generally 2 to 3 hours.

Tip: *Multiply this recipe easily and store extras in the freezer for a quick snack for the little ones.*

Holiday Eats

Holidays are always a time of year that people begin thinking about baking gifts for others or baking treats for around the house. Holiday treats are fun to cook with kids to get your family excited about the upcoming festivities. The recipes in this section are a few of our favorite holiday recipes that we enjoy preparing with the entire family.

Festive recipes from winter to spring

The spring and Easter holiday also provide a great opportunity for cooking with kids because the colors typical for that time of year presents a wide array of variations. Try these recipes to get you started!

Yummy Valentines

Think about when you were a kid. You raced out to the store with one or both of your parents to pick out the perfect paper valentines to pass out to your classmates. Many of those cute little cards had pictures of candy hearts and heart cookies. Did the pictures look so good that you wanted to eat them? Well, while eating the paper may add a little fiber to your diet, why not make real edible valentines for your family and friends to enjoy? This recipe works great for children 2 and older.

Preparation time: *15 minutes*

Yield: *1 serving*

1 whole graham cracker	*Candy hearts*
Red icing	*Decorating gel*

Place the graham cracker on a plastic or paper plate and cover the cracker neatly with red icing. Outline the graham cracker with candy hearts or other candy decorations. Use the decorating gel to write a valentine message in the center. Serve.

Tip: *These crackers get soggy after a few hours, so they're best enjoyed shortly after they're made. If you're sharing with others, whip them up shortly before a Valentine's Day party or use this recipe as an activity for all the kids to enjoy.*

Vary It! *If you're using this recipe for a kid's party, use different colors of icing or get white icing and food coloring so the children can whip up their own colors. Have different kinds of Valentine's Day candy on hand as well.*

Chocolate and Peanut Butter Bird Nests

This old recipe representing renewal and rebirth still provides great holiday fun and doesn't require any baking. Easter is a lively springtime holiday, and your kids will enjoy the fun they have making these bird nests. Make sure to reserve this recipe for children 2 and older. If you don't eat them all at once (we highly discourage overindulging!), you can freeze the extra treats for later use.

Preparation time: *30 minutes*

Chill time: *15 minutes*

Yield: *15 servings*

1 cup butterscotch chips

½ cup peanut butter chips

1 tablespoon shortening

1½ cups chow mein noodles, coarsely broken

Marshmallow birds for garnish

1 Line a cookie sheet with wax paper.

2 In a medium microwave-safe bowl, microwave the butterscotch, peanut butter chips, and shortening on high for 1 minute. Stir well and add additional time, if necessary, until all ingredients are melted and well blended. Add chow mein noodles and stir to coat the noodles.

3 Drop heaping spoonfuls on the cookie sheet and form slightly to create a bird nest shape. Adjust the size of the bird nests as desired, which naturally impacts the yield.

4 Let the nests stand until firm. Garnish with marshmallow birds, which are typically available at any grocery store during the Easter season.

5 Cover with plastic wrap and refrigerate (at least 15 minutes) until ready to serve.

Hidden Treasure Cupcakes

Your child will love making these Easter cupcakes because they hide a chocolate egg inside. The jelly beans present a choking hazard, so this recipe is intended for children older than 3 years. If you like the idea of these cupcakes but have toddlers under age 3, leave out the jelly beans. You can store the extra cupcakes in an airtight container for 5 days or freeze them for later use.

Preparation time: *30 minutes*

Tools: *Muffin pans and paper liners*

Yield: *24 servings*

Shortening for greasing	*2 eggs*
2¼ cups all-purpose flour	*1 teaspoon vanilla extract*
2½ teaspoons baking powder	*1¼ cups milk*
1 teaspoon salt	*24 small chocolate eggs or kisses*
⅔ cup margarine, softened	*16-ounce container strawberry frosting*
1 cup packed brown sugar	*Jelly beans*
¾ cup white sugar	

1 Preheat oven to 350 degrees. Grease 24 muffin tins or use paper liners for easier cleanup.

2 Sift together the flour, baking powder, and salt. Set aside.

3 In a large bowl, cream together the margarine, brown sugar, and white sugar until light and fluffy. Beat in the eggs one at a time, and then stir in the vanilla. Beat in the flour mixture alternately with the milk, mixing until incorporated.

4 Fill each muffin cup ⅓ full, and place the chocolate candy in the center of each. Top with the remaining batter until the cups are ⅔ full.

5 Bake the cupcakes for 18 to 20 minutes or until golden brown. Remove from the oven and allow to cool. Ice with strawberry frosting and garnish top with a few jelly beans. Serve.

Gelatin Eggs

This easy recipe is perfect for spending some quality time with your children during the Easter season. Have your 2-year-old (or older) help out with the prep on these eggs.

Preparation time: *30 minutes*

Chill time: *2 hours in the refrigerator*

Tools: *Egg-shaped cookie cutter*

Yield: *7 servings (2 treats per serving)*

2 cups boiling water

1 packet unflavored gelatin

8 ounces whipped topping

6-ounce package flavored gelatin (any flavor desired)

Shortening

Decorating gel

1 In 1 cup of boiling water, add unflavored gelatin and stir until the gelatin is completely dissolved.

2 After the mixture cools, mix in the whipped topping. Add another cup of boiling water, and then stir in the flavored gelatin and mix well.

3 Pour into a lightly greased 9-x-13-inch baking pan and refrigerate for two hours. In order to make the eggs easier to remove, consider lining the dish with plastic wrap.

4 Cut gelatin mixture into egg shapes and decorate with decorating gel. Serve.

July 4th recipes

July 4th is a time to celebrate and have fun, and it's the perfect opportunity to cook something festive with your child. Here are a couple of fun recipes to get you started.

Star and Stripes Cookies

Simple cookies become festive with the right icing. Kids love the colorful look of these treats. This recipe works well with children over 2 years of age.

Preparation time: *30 minutes*

Tools: *Star-shaped cookie cutter*

Yield: *12 servings*

12 sugar cookies (premade, homemade, or from premade dough), cut into star shapes

16-ounce container vanilla frosting

Red and blue food coloring

1 Prepare cookies according the package directions and cut them in star shapes by using a cookie cutter. You can use any size cookie cutter you want, but the larger shaped stars are easier to decorate.

2 Divide the icing into three different bowls. Place 2 drops of red food coloring into one bowl and 2 drops of blue food coloring into another bowl. Mix the coloring in and add more food coloring to get the right red and blue colors.

3 Using three different piping bags, decorate the cookies alternating red, white, and blue stripes. Serve.

Tip: *Purchase store-bought sugar cookies to save the time of baking your own, and then use the cookies cutter to make the star shapes.*

Quick Flag Cake

Make a cake that looks like a flag without a lot of fuss. Your child will love the colorful design and it's a great teaching opportunity as well because you can talk about the American flag: what it represents, its shape, and the meaning of its design.

Preparation time: *45 minutes*

Chill time: *15 minutes*

Yield: *15 servings*

1 box yellow cake mix (and ingredients listed on the box)

8-ounce container whipped topping

2 pints fresh strawberries

½ cup fresh blueberries

1 Bake the cake according to the package directions. You want to follow the baking instructions for the 9-x-13-inch baking pan and not the instructions for a layer cake.

2 After the cake cools, smoothly spread whipped topping over the cake.

3 Wash the strawberries, remove the stems, slice them in half, and arrange the fruit on the cake as the stripes. Use the blueberries for the stars. Chill for 15 minutes; cut and serve.

Vary It! *If you can't find fresh blueberries, use frozen ones or even blackberries instead.*

Halloween recipes

Halloween is a natural time to have some scary fun in the kitchen. Here are a couple of recipes that will get you started, and you can find a plethora of Halloween recipes on the Internet by searching on any Internet search engine.

Frightful Brownies

Turn a simple brownie mix into Halloween fun with this recipe. Brownies work well with younger children because your child can spend more time decorating instead of cooking.

Preparation time: *40 minutes*

Yield: *8 servings*

8-x-8-inch tray of prepared brownies (no icing)

5 chocolate sandwich cookies, crushed

16-ounce container milk chocolate frosting

5 tablespoons nondairy whipped topping

5 cookies of your choice, cut in half (oblong cookies, such as Nutter Butters, work best)

Decorating gel

Candy corns and small candy pumpkins for additional decoration

1 After the brownies have cooled, mix the sandwich cookies and frosting in a bowl (reserve 2 teaspoons of the frosting for Step 3). Leave the mixture a bit chunky to resemble dirt.

2 Spread the frosting mixture on the brownies, and cut the brownies into squares. Arrange squares on a serving tray as desired.

3 On the bottoms of the cookie halves, smear a bit of the reserved frosting and stick the cookie in the brownie, so the cookie sticks out vertically, resembling a tombstone. Decorate with decorating gel so that it resembles a tombstone.

4 Use dollops of whipped cream to create fluffy ghosts and the decorating gel to add facial features. Use candy corn, small candy pumpkins, or other decorating candy for additional toppings.

Eyeballs in a Bowl

For a healthier alternative to Halloween treats, try this quick and easy recipe with your child. Beware: The eyes may be watching you.

Preparation time: *20 minutes*

Yield: *Eight ½-cup servings*

1 package of prepared gelatin, cherry flavor	*16 to 20 dark grapes, quartered*
2 to 3 tablespoons of nondairy whipped topping	

1 Prepare the gelatin according to the package directions.

2 Spoon the gelatin into serving dishes. Create more or fewer servings as desired.

3 Create two eyes with the whipped topping on top of the gelatin in each dish and then place two grapes on each dollop of whipped topping to create the iris of the eyes. Serve.

Green Witch Punch

This green, but yummy, punch will be a hit with kids at any Halloween party. Leftover servings can be frozen for later use. Children 2 years and older can help with this recipe.

Preparation time: *20 minutes*

Yield: *Ten 1-cup servings*

6-ounce package lime gelatin	*Ice cubes*
2 cups boiling water	*2 cups lime sherbet, slightly softened*
2 cups cold pulp-free orange juice	*1 orange, peeled and thinly sliced*
1 liter seltzer, chilled	

1 In a mixing bowl, add the gelatin to the 2 cups of boiling water and stir for a few minutes until completely dissolved. Add the orange juice and allow the mixture to cool for 10 to 15 minutes.

2 Transfer the mixture to a punch bowl, and a few minutes before serving, add all other ingredients and stir well. If the punch needs to be colder, add more ice.

Vary It! *Make this punch more intriguing by making ghoulish ice cubes! In a bowl, mix water and green food coloring until you have a light green color. Pour into ice cube trays, add a gummy worm or a gummy bug (such as flies) to each ice cube, freeze, and serve these ice cubes in the punch.*

Christmas recipes

The Christmas holidays are the quintessential time to cook with your children in the kitchen. Use the break that children and family typically get around the holidays to make delicious treats together. You'll find entire Web sites dedicated to Christmas cooking, so be sure to check them out (search on any search engine). Here are a few favorites to get you started.

Instant Gingerbread House

You can create a gingerbread house from scratch, but let's face it, most of us probably like decorating the house, not cooking it. That process is a long and grueling task. This quick recipe gives you and your little one (of 3 years or older) a miniature gingerbread house with no cooking involved.

Preparation time: *30 minutes*

Yield: *1 serving*

7 graham crackers	*Decorating candy (jelly beans, M&Ms, licorice)*
16-ounce container vanilla frosting	

1 Place one graham cracker on a sturdy plate.

2 Use a piping bag to squeeze a thick bead of icing around the outside of the graham cracker. If you don't have a piping bag, place the icing in a freezer bag and simply cut away a small portion of one corner. Squeeze the bag and the icing comes out clean and neat.

3 Use four graham crackers to create the walls. Place icing at each corner to create a seam to hold the walls together.

4 Use the two remaining graham crackers to create the roof, again using the icing to hold the graham crackers together.

5 Use the icing to create a door and windows on the house and then create roofing tiles. Let your imaginations go wild. Finally, decorate the house with candy as desired.

Melting Snowballs

This simple cookie looks like a snowball and it melts in your mouth like snowflakes. Try out this recipe with your little ones who are 2 years old or older.

Preparation time: 10 minutes

Cooking time: 20 minutes

Yield: 6 servings (2 treats per serving)

2 cups butter (Don't substitute margarine)	½ teaspoon pure vanilla extract
3 cups flour	1 cup confectioners' sugar
½ cup cornstarch	Nonstick cooking spray

1 Preheat the oven to 350 degrees.

2 Cream the butter with a wooden spoon and add the remaining ingredients and mix well.

3 Spray a cookie sheet with nonstick cooking spray, and roll spoonfuls of the dough between your hands to form 1-inch balls. Place the dough balls on the cookie sheet.

4 Bake the cookies for 20 minutes. Cool the cookies and roll in the additional confectioners' sugar. Serve.

Chapter 12

Appealing Meals to Suit the Entire Family

Ah, family mealtime. You picture a perfect table, delicious food, candles, and a soft glow in the room. Then reality strikes! Sometimes, especially if you have young children, a family meal can be a stressful event. You have to juggle the nutritional needs and desires of a diverse group of people, and when you have a small child, you have to take into consideration what meals are appropriate for him or her. After all, you don't want to prepare multiple meals, but you want your family to eat together — you need recipes that will work for both! So to ease your load and make the stressful times more enjoyable, this chapter provides a collection of recipes that are perfect for feeding the entire family.

The Importance of Eating Together

You already know the basic premise of family meals: The family that eats together stays together. As parents ourselves, we, your humble authors, couldn't agree more with this philosophy. Naturally, life gets hectic sometimes, and we don't always eat together as a family — but as a general rule, we try to share as many meals as possible, and eating together is more of a norm in our house than not.

For ages, psychologists have agreed that sharing a meal together reinforces a family's bond. Of course, family meals won't fix all your family's problems, but they do have some important benefits:

- ✔ **They foster open communication.** In a day and age where different schedules and activities, along with TV, seem to steal time away from families, mealtime can be an informal time of bonding between family members of all ages, just by giving you the opportunity to talk to each other (after you've swallowed, of course!). It's important to get your child involved in this communication and bonding time right from the start — this process creates a pattern of open and healthy communication in your tyke's life.

- ✔ **They give you a chance to train your child to use manners.** A super benefit of sharing meals together is the behavior training your children get just by watching you. You can easily and gently reinforce table manners as you eat together — a great time for kids to learn to serve themselves by helping fix their own plate. Rather than determining portion control, give your youngsters some freedom and flexibility to eat more of the dishes she wants. If you're serving healthy meals, you don't need to worry about portion sizes too much.

- ✔ **They help you avoid the "shifting meal" syndrome.** Perhaps you're familiar with this all-too-common scenario, where everyone in the family eats at different times. When you don't eat as a family, you often end up trying to fix a bunch of different dishes at different times, depending on everyone's needs and schedules. Or else you don't have a clue what your children are eating, because they help themselves as they have time. If you can make mealtime a family gathering, you avoid this problem and essentially save yourself a lot of hassle.

- ✔ **They lend themselves to good nutrition.** This last point is an obvious one: If your family eats prepared meals together, you're likely to eat more nutritious, well-balanced meals than when you're grabbing something on the run (but if you have to eat on the go, check out Chapter 15 for some tips and recipes designed for busy times).

The Do's and Don'ts of Family Meals

So you're convinced that family meals are a great idea, but you're not quite sure what you should and shouldn't do — especially if your family isn't yet in the habit of eating together. Fret no more — in this section, we blaze the trail toward family-meal-planning greatness.

Do be flexible

Don't paint yourself into a Norman Rockwell scene — life is hectic for many people, so you need to be flexible when trying to gather the troops. Realize that sometimes, other priorities will interrupt family mealtime so that it seems an impossible feat. Just remember that it's okay to forgo the community meal once in a while, but don't let it become the norm. If some other priority interrupts your family time more often than not, take a hard look at your family's schedule and see if you can make some other items a bit more flexible to accommodate a regular mealtime — after all, family mealtime is just as important as business meetings and sports practices. You need to strike a balance between family meals and the demands of real life, but try to make sure your family eats at least one meal together per day, five days a week.

Don't get hung up on dinner

Family dinnertime tends to be difficult in many cases because of scheduling — Timmy has basketball practice, Meagan has tap-dance classes, you have late meetings, and so forth. If you find that getting everyone around the dinner table on a consistent basis is a challenge, why not do family breakfast? Sure, you'll need to get up a little earlier than normal, but if you plan a couple of days per week to be family breakfast day, your children likely will (eventually!) get on board and will look forward to it.

Speaking of breakfast, it works great as a family meal for two important reasons. First, breakfast is the most important meal of the day, so a family meal around the breakfast table is always a great start to a new day. Also, many of the breakfast recipes that we provide in this chapter are freezable, so you can make them in the evening and quickly warm them up before breakfast. No need to make everything from scratch at 5 a.m.!

Do include everyone

The idea of preparing a meal for a whole family may make you groan as you think about all the work involved. Instead, think of the meal as your family's time to be together and to help each other. Give tasks to everyone and expect everyone to help with the cooking *and* with setting up and cleaning up. When everyone helps, you all work together as a family, which in turn builds expectations and keeps you or your spouse from being the servant, fostering teamwork within the family.

Getting your family on board isn't difficult after you set the precedent for it. Now is the time to be firm — show them that family meals are important and aren't optional, and you need their help. In fact, our children help with most meals — even our 4-year-old helps set and clear the table. Her particular job is to rinse the silverware and put it in the dishwasher. You can find a job for even a 3-year-old, such as putting out napkins for family members and such, so no excuses.

Need help getting family members on board? Give them some control. Plan your weekly menu on Sunday afternoon and make it a family gathering. Discuss the menu and take requests (within reason). This way, your entire family has ownership of the meals because they've all helped choose the foods you'll eat. You don't have to turn your home into a democracy, but an open forum never hurts.

Don't try to be a gourmet cook every day

We live on the practical side of life, and we think that you should too. Some days you have extra time to spend on a special family meal, and on those days, by all means, go for it! In many cases, though, you need something healthy and realistic, and in others, you need something really quick! In this chapter, our recipes are practical and down-to-earth (read that: fast and easy). And as a bonus, because we know the busyness of family life and the struggle of meal preparation all too well, we've made sure that many of the recipes in this chapter (and throughout the book, in fact) work well for freezing and reheating on those busy days.

Do set aside outside disturbances

Inevitably, mealtime won't always be the picture-perfect, completely focused family time that you hope it will be. Several distractions commonly put a damper on family bonding 'round the table. To make time for quality family time, eliminate common disruptions. Here's our advice on how to avoid them:

- ✔ **Ditch the TV.** If you absolutely have to have background noise, pop in an unobtrusive CD that the family will enjoy, preferably one without words.

- ✔ **Leave homework for another time.** Homework should be done before the meal or after, not during.

- ✔ **Put your pets outside or in a separate room.** We love our pets, but they always seem to want attention during mealtime.

- ✔ **Turn on the answering machine.** A good rule of thumb is to not answer the phone while you're eating, with no exceptions. If the call is important, the caller will leave a message, and you can call that person back after you've had your family time.

- ✔ **Keep neighborhood children at bay.** If you have older children who regularly play with kids in your neighborhood, you need to make sure the neighbor kids know when they shouldn't come by.

Rising with the Roosters: Family Breakfasts

We love family breakfast because it's a time that we get to spend together and a way that we like to start off our day. Although we don't eat breakfast as a family every day, we try to from time to time, especially on Saturday mornings. If you've never tried breakfast as a family meal, you should give it a shot — you might like it! We include recipes in this section that work well for family breakfast time and brunch as well.

Smiley Face Omelets

We include our favorite ingredients in this recipe, but we often lose the onions and mushrooms for our children when we make them. Tailor yours depending on what each family member likes.

With a little additional time, your kids can take the cooked omelet, spend a few minutes decorating the outside with jelly to make a happy face, and then dig in. (A piping bag is a great tool for this art project.)

Preparation time: *25 minutes*

Yield: *4 servings*

6 eggs	*Cooking oil or spray*
Salt and pepper as desired	*1 cup cooked, chopped ham, sausage, or bacon (or a combination)*
½ cup chopped onions	
½ cup chopped green bell pepper	*1 cup grated cheddar cheese*
½ cup sliced mushrooms	*½ cup grape jelly (or any other variety)*
¼ cup mild salsa	

1 In a large bowl, beat the eggs until well blended and add salt and pepper as desired.

2 In a separate bowl, combine the onions, green bell pepper, mushrooms, and salsa. Mix well.

3 Oil a griddle or frying pan and heat over medium heat. Pour ¼ of the blended eggs into the pan. As the eggs cook, flip them over so that the other side begins to cook.

4 On half of the egg, add ¼ cup of meat, ¼ cup cheddar cheese, and ¼ of the vegetable mixture.

5 Bend the egg in half to cover the ingredients and then flip it, continuing to cook until the omelet is golden brown and the cheese melts. Repeat Steps 1 through 5 for the other three omelets.

6 Put some jelly in a piping bag (or just put it in a sandwich bag and snip away one corner). Allow your children to use the jelly to create eyes, a nose, and a smiling mouth on the outside of the omelet. Serve.

Sausage and Egg Casserole

You can find plenty of variations of this recipe, but in many cases, you'll find that sausage and egg casseroles contain such ingredients as half-in-half, salsa, Worcestershire sauce, and such. Although yummy for adults, your children tend to avoid this dish if the taste is too overwhelming. This simple recipe works best for everyone.

Preparation time: *20 minutes*

Cooking time: *25 minutes*

Yield: *Seven 1-cup servings*

Shortening	*⅔ cup milk*
8-count can crescent rolls	*Salt and pepper to taste*
1 pound pork sausage	*2½ cups grated cheddar cheese*
5 eggs	

1 Preheat the oven to 350 degrees.

2 Grease a 9-x-13-inch baking dish and place the crescent rolls in the bottom, rolled out flat. They can overlap as needed.

3 In a large skillet, over medium-high heat, brown the sausage. Drain the excess grease and spread the sausage evenly on top of the crescent rolls.

4 In a medium bowl, whisk together the eggs, milk, salt, and pepper, and then pour into the baking dish. Top with cheese and bake for 30 minutes or until the cheese melts and is bubbly.

Vary It! *Substitute turkey sausage for the pork sausage for a healthier casserole. Also, you can add a spoonful of salsa for extra taste, which the older children and adults in your family may enjoy.*

Quick Breakfast Burritos

If you want to have breakfast with the family but you don't have a lot of time to cook, you can make this dish in a flash.

Preparation time: *15 minutes*

Yield: *4 servings*

4 burrito-size flour or whole-wheat tortillas

4 eggs, scrambled

½ cup mild salsa

½ pound sausage, cooked and crumbled

1 cup shredded cheddar cheese

Evenly divide all the ingredients among the tortillas, roll each tortilla to form a burrito, and warm the burritos in the microwave for 20 to 30 seconds. Serve warm.

Snowflake Pancakes

Here's a from-scratch pancake recipe that includes a quick craft your kids can do while the family is getting ready for breakfast. (See the sidebar "How to make a paper snowflake" for the craft instructions.)

Preparation time: *15 minutes*

Yield: *About 5 servings*

1 cup flour

2 teaspoons baking powder

¼ teaspoon salt

1 egg

1 cup milk

1 teaspoon melted butter

Cooking oil

1 cup confectioners' sugar

1 paper snowflake template (see sidebar for instructions)

1. In a bowl, sift together the flour, baking powder, and salt. Beat in the egg. Add the milk and butter and stir well.
2. Heat an oiled griddle to medium-high heat and spoon out the batter to form pancakes. We prefer medium pancakes and use about ¼ cup of batter for each pancake.
3. Flip the pancakes as they brown and make sure that the pancake is golden brown on both sides. If necessary, re-oil the griddle and repeat Steps 2 and 3.

4 Place the pancake on a plate and put the paper snowflake template on top of the pancake. Put the confectioners' sugar into a shaker and shake generously over the template. Remove the template and you'll have a snowflake design on the pancake. Serve with your favorite syrup.

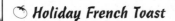 *Holiday French Toast*

This wonderful French toast recipe is the perfect breakfast or brunch for holiday mornings when the family is together, but in truth, it's perfect any time! Don't feed this meal to children under 2 years old due to the chance of nut allergies.

Preparation time: *30 minutes*

Yield: *8 servings*

8-ounce package cream cheese, softened

2 tablespoons sugar

1 teaspoon vanilla	*6 eggs*
½ teaspoon cinnamon	*1 cup half-and-half*
½ cup chopped pecans	*1 cup strawberry preserves*
1 loaf thinly sliced bread, any kind	*½ cup confectioners' sugar*
Oil for cooking	

1 In a bowl, mix the cream cheese, sugar, vanilla, cinnamon, and pecans until well blended and fluffy.

2 Take two pieces of bread. On one, spread a tablespoon (or a bit more) of the filling and place the second piece of bread on top to form a sandwich.

3 Oil a griddle or frying pan and heat to medium high.

4 Beat the eggs and half and half until well blended. Take a sandwich and submerge it in the egg mixture until well coated.

5 Fry the sandwich on both sides until the egg coating is golden brown.

6 Heat the cup of strawberry preserves until runny. Drizzle over the cooked French toast and dust with confectioners' sugar. Serve.

How to make a paper snowflake

To make a paper snowflake, you need an 8½ x 11 sheet of standard typing or copy paper and a pair of scissors with a sharp point for accurate cutting. See the figure following these steps for a visual aid, and get to work.

1. Cut one end off of the paper so you have a perfect square.

2. Fold the piece of paper so you have a big triangle.

3. Fold the triangle in half to make a smaller triangle.

4. Hold your triangle with the longest side at the top and fold the right-hand corner toward the middle until it's directly above the bottom point of the triangle and the right-hand side is in a straight line extending from the bottom corner. Press down firmly on the edge.

5. Fold the left-hand corner toward the middle until it touches the right-hand point and press down firmly.

6. Flip the paper over, and cut off and discard the two points whose sides meet and are sticking up in a straight line. You should be left with a triangle.

7. Begin cutting shapes into the triangle in any pattern you like (spikes, swirls, or a mixture). Be careful not to cut the folds completely or you'll have several little pieces of paper instead of one snowflake.

8. Unfold the paper and you have a unique snowflake!

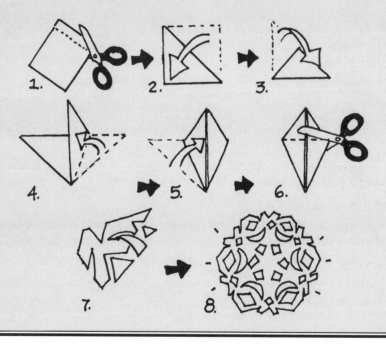

Family Lunches You Can Make in a Flash

These lunch meals are perfect for everyone in the family if you have time for family lunches on weekends or any other days of the week. Also, we're including only dishes that are quick and simple, because we know what it's like to be parents, and we know you're probably short on time.

Turkey Soft Tacos

Soft tacos are a great lunch option because you can stuff your tortillas with healthy food. Also, you can quickly make changes to a younger child's taco without altering the rest of the family's meal.

Preparation time: *20 minutes*

Yield: *4 servings*

2 cups turkey breast, cooked and finely chopped

2 cups shredded cheddar cheese

4 burrito-size flour or whole-wheat tortillas

1 cup drained black beans

1 cup corn, cooked

1 cup fresh, diced tomatoes

Ranch dressing to taste

1 Combine the turkey and cheese in a microwavable bowl and microwave for 20 seconds or so until the cheese melts. Stir.

2 Heat the tortillas in the microwave for 20 seconds or until warm.

3 Spoon even amounts of the turkey and cheese mixture onto each flour tortilla.

4 Evenly divide the remaining ingredients among the four tortillas and add ranch dressing to taste. Roll the tortillas into burritos and serve.

Cheesy Beef and Noodles

Here's a quick, warm, and hearty lunch, and it freezes well to boot.

Preparation time: *30 minutes*

Yield: *Six 1-cup servings*

1 pound ground beef	1 cup sliced green onions
2 cups medium egg noodles, uncooked	1 cup water
½ cup ranch-style beans	½ cup mild salsa
1 cup corn, cooked	2 8-ounce cans no-salt-added tomato sauce

1 In a medium skillet, thoroughly brown the beef over medium-high heat. Drain the grease.

2 Add all the remaining ingredients to the skillet and stir well.

3 Bring the mixture to a boil, reduce the heat, and simmer for 15 minutes or until the noodles are soft. Serve warm.

Vary It! *Add a dollop of sour cream and a bit of shredded cheddar cheese on top for extra flavor.*

Hearty Meatballs

Meatballs are a popular food, and we think they're great for all ages. Try adding marinara and Parmesan cheese and putting them in a sub roll to make a healthy sandwich or try incorporating them into a pasta dish. They're a snap to make (and you can make extra and freeze the leftovers).

Preparation time: *25 minutes*

Yield: *6 servings, 4 meatballs per serving*

2 pounds ground turkey	¼ teaspoon oregano
1 cup soft breadcrumbs	¼ cup chopped onion
¼ teaspoon garlic salt	1 teaspoon Worcestershire sauce
Pepper to taste	

1 Preheat the oven to 350 degrees.

2 In a large bowl, mix all the ingredients until well blended. Form the mixture into meatballs about an inch in diameter.

3 Place the meatballs in a large, greased baking pan and bake for 35 to 45 minutes, until cooked through. Remove the pan from the oven and serve warm.

Watercress and Carrot Burgers

These grilled burgers make a great summer lunch, or you might enjoy them any time of the year! Make extra burgers and freeze them.

Preparation time: *30 minutes*

Tools: *Grill, gas or charcoal*

Yield: *5 to 7 servings, depending on size*

¾ pound ground beef	*1 small onion, finely chopped*
½ pound ground turkey	*3 tablespoons chopped fresh parsley*
½ cup dried breadcrumbs	*Salt and pepper to taste*
½ cup grated carrots	*4 tablespoons olive oil*
1 cup watercress, finely chopped	

1 Combine all ingredients in a large mixing bowl.

2 Form hamburger patties, roughly ¾-inch thick and 4 inches in diameter.

3 Heat the grill to high and grill the patties, flipping to make sure that both sides are done. Depending on your grill's heat, cooking takes about 5 minutes for a medium-rare burger.

4 Serve on hamburger buns with any desired salad dressing, relish, fresh tomatoes, or other desired fixings. Serve fresh pineapple on the side.

Chicken Apple Salad Sandwiches

For a lighter lunch, this chicken apple salad will satisfy, and it's easy to make. The crunchy apples mixed with the tangy mayo or ranch dressing is a delicious combination.

Preparation time: *15 minutes*

Yield: *4 servings*

2 cups diced apple

2 cups cooked and diced boneless, skinless chicken breast

4 tablespoons chopped green bell pepper

4 tablespoons mayonnaise or ranch dressing

¼ cup chopped pecans

½ cup corn, cooked

¼ cup chopped black olives

1 small head lettuce, any variety, chopped

Salt to taste

Combine all the ingredients in a large bowl and mix well. Serve with croissant rolls or the bread of your choosing.

🍅 Pesto Veggie Soup

This hearty soup is perfect for a cold winter day (and it's a good way to bump up the veggie servings for your children). You can make a homemade pesto for this recipe or buy it premade at your grocery store. We give you a recipe for making it yourself following this recipe.

Preparation time: *5 minutes*

Yield: *Five 2-cup servings*

2 large leeks, chopped and well cleaned

2 medium carrots, peeled and diced

1 white potato, peeled and diced

3 tablespoons water

8 cups canned vegetable broth

½ cup orzo

6 ounces green beans, cut into ½-inch pieces

15-ounce can white kidney beans, rinsed and drained

Salt and pepper to taste

2 tablespoons freshly grated Parmesan cheese

1 Prepare the pesto (see the following recipe) and set it aside.

2 Combine the leeks, carrots, potato, and water in a large stockpot. Cover and cook over medium-low heat until the vegetables are almost tender (about 8 minutes). Stir occasionally.

3 Add the vegetable broth and bring to a boil. Stir in the orzo and boil uncovered until the orzo is almost tender (about 12 minutes). Stir often.

4 Add the green beans; reduce the heat to low and simmer until the beans are tender (about 6 minutes).

5 Stir in the kidney beans; simmer until heated through (about 3 minutes). Season with salt and pepper.

6 Divide the pesto among five bowls. Ladle the soup over the pesto and stir. Sprinkle with 2 tablespoons of Parmesan cheese and serve warm.

🍅 *Presto Pesto*

Preparation time: *10 minutes*

Yield: *3 cups*

2 cups packed, fresh basil leaves	*3 tablespoons chopped pine nuts or walnuts*
¼ cup fresh, grated Parmesan cheese	*3 garlic cloves, finely minced*
¼ cup olive oil	

Mix all the ingredients in a food processor and puree until it forms a thick paste.

Gathering around the Table: Family Dinners

In this section, we give you some of our favorite family meal entrees. These entrees are versatile, and most of them freeze well for future use. They may take a little more time to prepare than the lunches in the preceding section, but the extra time requirement is worth it in the end — trust us.

Veggie and Chicken Calzone

Calzones are basically stuffed pizzas that look like a turnover and make a good family meal because they appeal to almost everyone, especially this veggie and chicken variety. You can freeze any leftovers for later use.

Preparation time: *25 minutes*

Cooking time: *20 to 25 minutes*

Yield: *8 servings*

1 cup canned corn, drained	*1 teaspoon salt*
1½ cups fresh, chopped broccoli	*1 teaspoon pepper*
½ cup finely chopped onions	*10¾-ounce can condensed cream of chicken soup*
½ cup finely chopped red bell pepper	
1 cup shredded mozzarella cheese	*2 tablespoons butter*
1 cup shredded cheddar cheese	*1 tablespoon Italian seasoning*
2 cups cooked cubed or shredded chicken	*2 10-ounce packages refrigerated pizza dough*
2 teaspoons minced garlic	

1 Preheat the oven to 350 degrees. In a large bowl, mix together all the ingredients except for the last three until well combined and set to the side.

2 In a small bowl, cream together the butter and Italian seasoning.

3 Roll out each pizza dough according to the package directions. Place one pizza dough on a pizza stone or pan and, using a pastry brush, lightly butter the top of the dough with the butter and Italian seasoning mixture.

4 Spoon the chicken mixture into the center of the dough and gently spread it out, leaving a ¼-inch lip around the edge so you can attach the top layer of dough.

5 Take the second pizza dough and lay it on top of the mixture. With moistened fingers, gently press the edges of the top and bottom layers of dough together forming a tight seal.

6 Brush the top of the dough with the remaining butter and bake for 20 to 25 minutes or until golden brown.

7 Remove the pan from the oven and allow the calzone to sit for 5 minutes before serving. Cut into 8 pieces and serve warm.

Honey-Lime Grilled Chicken

We love this tasty grilled chicken recipe because of the sweet and sour zing of the honey and lime, and your kids will enjoy it as well. Leave space in your freezer, because the leftovers freeze well for future servings.

Preparation Time: *30 minutes*

Marinate Time: *1 hour*

Tools: *Grill, gas or charcoal*

Yield: *6 servings*

1½ cups honey	*¼ cup lime juice*
⅓ cup soy sauce	*6 boneless, skinless chicken breast halves*

1 In a large bowl combine the honey, soy sauce, and lime juice.

2 Place the chicken breasts in an extra large, heavy-duty resealable plastic bag. If preferred, chicken breasts can be marinated in a shallow glass dish.

3 Pour the marinade over the chicken and seal the bag. If using a glass dish, cover with plastic wrap. Refrigerate for 1 hour.

4 Prepare the grill for medium heat.

5 Remove the chicken from the bag and shake off the excess marinade.

6 Grill the chicken breasts for 8 to 10 minutes or until the juice runs clear.

Tip: *If you so desire, you can also prepare the chicken as stated in the recipe and bake for 15 minutes at 350 degrees until cooked through. You can then grill the baked chicken for 3 minutes.*

Fresh Vegetable Soup

This fresh vegetable soup will make everyone in your family happy — it's perfect on cold winter days and freezes well so you can make a batch and use the leftovers when you need a quick meal.

Preparation time: *15 minutes*

Cooking time: *15 minutes*

Tools: *Dutch oven, optional*

Yield: *Eight 1-cup servings*

1 medium zucchini

1 tablespoon olive oil

½ cup mushroom slices

½ cup carrot slices

½ cup celery slices

2 large, ripe tomatoes, coarsely chopped

2 14½-ounce cans chicken broth or vegetable broth

1 teaspoon ground cumin

¾ teaspoon fresh thyme leaves, or ¼ teaspoon dried thyme

2 tablespoons prepared pesto (see the Presto Pesto recipe, earlier in this chapter)

Salt and pepper to taste

1 Cut the zucchini in half lengthwise and slice it into ¼-inch-thick pieces, and then set it aside.

2 In a large heavy saucepan or Dutch oven, heat the oil over medium-high heat. Add the mushrooms, carrots, and celery and cook for 3 to 4 minutes, stirring constantly, until the vegetables start to brown.

3 Add the zucchini slices, chopped tomatoes, broth, cumin, thyme, pesto, and salt and pepper.

4 Cover the pot and bring the mixture to a boil; cook for 15 minutes, or until the vegetables are tender. Serve.

Baked Ham

You may think of baked ham as a holiday chore or something you buy at a specialty shop around the holidays, but you can enjoy ham any time with this delicious recipe. It's quick to prepare and always a winner with the family, and best of all, the leftovers are freezer friendly.

Preparation time: *25 minutes*

Cooking time: *2 hours, 50 minutes*

Yield: *6 servings*

2-pound whole, fully cooked ham

2 teaspoons whole cloves

1½ cup packed brown sugar, divided

1 teaspoon dried parsley

1 cup pineapple juice

⅓ cup honey

8-ounce can sliced pineapple, drained

1 Preheat the oven to 350 degrees. Remove the skin from the ham and trim any fat.

2 Score the surface of the ham with a sharp knife, making diamond shapes about ½-inch deep. Insert a clove into every other diamond.

3 Place the ham on a rack in a shallow roasting pan. (This raises the ham off the baking pan to ensure that the bottom doesn't burn.)

4 In a small bowl, mix ¾ cup of brown sugar with the parsley. Pat the mixture on the top and sides of the ham, and then pour the pineapple juice around the ham in the baking dish. Bake uncovered for 1 hour. Baste often.

5 Remove the ham from the pan and set it aside. Drain the pan of the juices left from baking, reserving ¼ cup of the juice.

6 Create a ham glaze by combining the honey, the remaining brown sugar, and the reserved pan juices in a bowl. Mix until well blended.

7 Return the ham to the pan and spoon half of the glaze over the ham. Place the ham in the oven and bake uncovered for 20 minutes.

8 Remove the pan from the oven and place the pineapple slices on the ham. Drizzle the ham with the remainder of the glaze and bake it for 30 minutes, or until a meat thermometer reads 140 degrees. Let the ham stand for 15 minutes before carving.

Surprise Family Meatloaf

This recipe is a classic, with its sweet taste from the brown sugar and the crunchy surprise of bacon under the sauce.

Preparation time: *30 minutes*

Cooking time: *1 hour, 15 minutes*

Yield: *6 servings*

For the meatloaf:

1½ pounds lean ground beef

1½ cups crushed butter-flavored crackers

1 small onion, chopped

1 egg

1 cup ketchup

¼ cup packed brown sugar

½ teaspoon salt

½ teaspoon garlic powder

6 slices American cheese

3 slices bacon

For the sauce:

1 cup ketchup

1 teaspoon salt

2 tablespoons prepared yellow mustard

½ cup packed brown sugar

1 Preheat the oven to 350 degrees.

2 In an extra-large bowl, combine the ground beef, crackers, onion, egg, ketchup, brown sugar, salt, and garlic powder. Mix well.

3 Press half of the mixture into a 9-x-5-inch loaf pan. Tear three slices of cheese in half and lay them on top of the meat in the pan. Place three slices of bacon lengthwise on top of the cheese. Pat the remaining meat mixture into the pan.

4 Bake the meatloaf for 1 hour or until cooked through.

5 While the meatloaf is baking, prepare the sauce by placing all the sauce ingredients in a medium-size bowl and mix well. Make sure that all the sugar is thoroughly incorporated into the sauce and set the sauce aside.

6 Remove the meatloaf from the oven and place the remaining slices of cheese on top of the cooked meatloaf.

7 Top the meatloaf generously with the sauce and bake for an additional 15 minutes. You'll have extra sauce left over, which you can use if you want to top the meatloaf on your plate.

8 Remove the meatloaf from the oven and allow it to sit for 10 minutes before slicing and serving.

Stuffed Burgers

How about a hamburger with a little kick? We love these stuffed burgers because they taste so different than your run-of-the-mill burger — the onion soup mix is the key ingredient. Check out the final product in the color section of this book.

Preparation time: *30 minutes*

Tools: *Grill*

Yield: *4 servings*

1½ pounds lean hamburger meat	*1 teaspoon salt*
1 envelope dry onion soup mix	*4 slices American cheese*
1 egg	*4 hamburger buns*
½ cup ketchup	

1 Preheat the outdoor grill to high heat. You can also cook these burgers on an indoor grill or in a frying pan.

2 In a medium-size bowl, combine the meat, soup mix, egg, ketchup, and salt.

3 Divide meat into 8 parts, forming a patty with each part. The patties should be thin.

4 Put a slice of cheese on four of the patties, making sure that the cheese doesn't go past the edges of the patty. If it does, tear the cheese into pieces. Place the other four patties on top of the cheesy ones, and form a seal around the cheese with the meat. This part is crucial if you want to keep the cheese from leaking out while cooking.

5 Cook for 4 to 5 minutes on each side or until cooked through.

6 Toast the buns if desired and assemble the burgers with desired condiments.

○ *Veggie Casserole*

This veggie casserole is a perfect choice for a summertime dinner because it's light and boasts a variety of fresh summer veggies. Consider serving this casserole with a side of cold fruit.

Preparation Time: *25 minutes*

Cooking time: *45 minutes to 1 hour*

Yield: *Six 1-cup servings*

¼ cup olive oil	Salt and pepper to taste
3 small zucchini, cut into small slices	8 ounces processed cheese, cubed
3 small yellow squash, cut into small slices	5 eggs
2 green bell peppers, cut into small strips	1 cup heavy cream
2 red bell peppers, cut into small strips	2 tablespoons flour
2 sweet onions, sliced	2 cups seasoned breadcrumbs
1 teaspoon garlic powder	1 cup fresh, grated Parmesan cheese

1 Preheat the oven to 350 degrees.

2 Heat the olive oil in a large skillet over medium-high heat. Add the zucchini, squash, green and red bell peppers, and onions; cook, stirring occasionally until slightly softened. When the vegetables are tender, drain the skillet of the excess liquid and arrange in the bottom of a large glass baking dish.

3 Season the veggies with the garlic powder and salt and pepper. Evenly distribute the cheese cubes on the veggies.

4 In a medium-size bowl, whisk together the eggs, cream, and flour.

5 Pour the egg mixture into the baking dish and sprinkle the breadcrumbs and Parmesan cheese on top.

6 Bake for 45 minutes to 1 hour or until bubbling hot. Serve warm.

Baked Ziti

Ziti is macaroni pasta that is shaped into long, thin tubes. This recipe gives you a great Italian dish with a rich taste and the cheesy texture that everyone in your family will love. This recipe makes more than a typical family needs in one meal, but you can freeze the leftovers for later, saving you cooking time down the road.

Preparation time: *45 minutes*

Cooking time: *1 hour and 30 minutes*

Yield: *12 servings*

8 ounces uncooked ziti	*1 egg*
1 pound ground beef	*15-ounce container ricotta cheese*
26- or 28-ounce jar spaghetti sauce	*¼ cup Parmesan cheese*
1 teaspoon Italian seasoning	*2 cups shredded mozzarella cheese, divided*
1 teaspoon garlic powder	

1 Preheat the oven to 350 degrees. Cook the pasta according to the package directions. Remember to cook *al dente.* After the noodles are cooked, drain and set to the side.

2 In a large stockpot, cook the ground beef thoroughly, drain the excess grease, and return the meat to the pot.

3 Stir in the spaghetti sauce, Italian seasoning, and garlic powder; simmer on low for 10 minutes.

4 While the meat sauce is simmering, combine the egg, the ricotta and Parmesan cheeses, and 1 cup of mozzarella in a large bowl and mix well. Toss in the pasta and mix until it is well coated with the cheese mixture.

5 Grease a 13-x-9-x-2-inch baking dish; spoon a thin layer of the meat sauce on the bottom of the casserole dish. Follow with a layer of pasta, then another layer of meat sauce. Layer until the pan is close to full. Meat sauce needs to be on the top of the casserole.

6 Cover and bake for 45 minutes. Top the casserole with the remaining mozzarella cheese and bake for 10 minutes or until the cheese is melted. Let the casserole stand for 15 minutes before serving.

Ending on a Sweet Note

We have this basic philosophy — strive to eat a healthy, well-balanced diet. But an occasional, no-holds-barred dessert is certainly not a crime. As with all things in life, strive for balance, and teach your kids that delicious desserts are fine on occasion.

We provide our favorite family desserts in this section. Be sure to get your children in on the cooking action — they'll have fun and so will you!

Banana Cake

We love this banana cake recipe because it tastes great, is easy, and is rather versatile because you can also use the batter to make muffins instead. Leave out the nuts if you have children under the age of 2.

Preparation time: *10 minutes*

Cooking time: *40 minutes*

Yield: *8 servings*

Shortening or nonstick cooking spray	1 cup sugar
Flour for coating	¾ cup packed light brown sugar
2½ cups flour	2 eggs
1 tablespoon baking soda	4 ripe bananas, mashed
1 pinch salt	⅔ cup buttermilk
½ cup unsalted butter	½ cup chopped walnuts

1 Preheat the oven to 350 degrees. Grease and flour two 8-inch round pans.

2 In a small bowl, mix the flour, baking soda, and salt. Set aside.

3 In a large bowl, cream together the butter, white sugar, and brown sugar until light and fluffy. Beat in the eggs one at a time. Mix in the bananas.

4 Add the flour mixture to the creamed mixture, alternating with the buttermilk. Stir in the chopped walnuts.

5 Pour the batter into the prepared pans. Bake for 30 minutes. Remove from the oven, and place on a damp towel to cool before serving.

Tip: *You can ice this cake if you want — a plain vanilla frosting works great. For a richer taste, consider a cream cheese frosting.*

Blonde Brownies

This classic blonde brownie recipe uses vanilla instead of chocolate, but the walnuts and semisweet chocolate chips really give the brownies a flavor punch. They aren't as heavy as chocolate brownies, but you can add butterscotch topping for extra flavor. For your kids who are younger than 2, skip the walnuts in this recipe.

Preparation time: *20 minutes*

Cooking time: *20 to 25 minutes*

Yield: *10 servings*

1 cup sifted flour

½ teaspoon baking powder

⅛ teaspoon baking soda

½ teaspoon salt

½ cup chopped walnuts

⅓ cup butter

1 cup packed brown sugar

1 egg, beaten

1 tablespoon vanilla extract

⅔ cup semisweet chocolate chips

Nonstick cooking spray

1 Preheat the oven to 350 degrees.

2 In a medium-size bowl, combine the flour, baking powder, baking soda, and salt. Sift all the ingredients together and then add the walnuts. Mix well and set aside.

3 Melt the butter in a medium-size microwave-safe bowl and add the brown sugar and mix well.

4 Add the egg and vanilla and blend well. Add the flour mixture a little at a time, mixing well.

5 Spread in a 9-x-9-x-2-inch greased pan. Sprinkle the chocolate chips on top of the batter. Bake the brownies for 20 to 25 minutes. Let the brownies cool before serving.

Orange Dreamsicle

This refreshing frozen dessert is great any time of the year, and we recommend that you make it before summer sets in and store it in the freezer. Before serving, let it soften in the refrigerator for about 30 minutes.

Preparation time: *35 minutes*

Chill time: *4 hours and 5 minutes*

Yield: *12 servings*

1 cup butter	*1 cup coconut flakes*
2 cups flour	*1 quart orange sherbet, softened*
½ cup sugar	*1 quart vanilla ice cream, softened*

1 In a large frying pan, melt the butter over medium-high heat. Add the flour, sugar, and coconut to the pan and mix well.

2 Cook for 3 to 4 minutes or until the mixture is golden brown and crumbly, stirring constantly. Remove the mixture from the heat and set ¼ cup of it aside.

3 Place the mixture in an ungreased 13-x-9-x-2-inch baking dish. With the back of a wooden spoon, press the mixture into the bottom of the pan, making a crust.

4 Place the crust in the freezer for 5 minutes.

5 In a large bowl, mix the sherbet and ice cream together. Spread the mixture onto the crust.

6 Sprinkle the ¼ cup of reserved crust on top of the dessert. Place in the freezer for 4 hours and serve.

Part V
Fast Fixes for Mealtime Hurdles

In this part . . .

As a parent, you're likely to deal with some mealtime challenges with your growing child. In this part, you tackle those challenges head on, one by one. You explore food-related issues and allergy problems and find recipes to help you overcome these obstacles. You also uncover a collection of tempting dishes for your picky eater and an assembly of recipes that help you feed your child healthy food when you're on the run.

Chapter 13

Dealing with Food-Related Challenges

*Y*ou have a baby. That baby needs to eat. You provide food. That's it. It sounds simple enough, right? Unfortunately, we don't always get to live in that simplistic, idealistic world; we have to cope with the challenges that nature pitches our way. Two of these obstacles are food-related allergies and intolerances.

This chapter helps you understand allergies and intolerances (and the difference between them), tells you about the signs and symptoms to watch for, and provides a handful of recipes that avoid the common allergy and intolerance triggers — so even if your child hasn't been diagnosed with one of these food-related challenges, you should still read this chapter so you know what to watch for. To help you pay close attention to the reactions to foods, flip ahead to Appendix B, where we provide a blank food log where you can chart new foods that you serve and track any reactions that your child has to those foods. If your little one experiences some food challenges, remember to consult his pediatrician so she can confirm a diagnosis and formulate a treatment plan.

The Temporary Nuisances: Food Allergies

It's not unusual for a child to have a food allergy of some kind. The FDA reports that 6 percent of all children under the age of 4 have some kind of food allergy. However, only 1.5 percent of adults have an actual food allergy. So the good news is that your child will likely outgrow it.

Breastfeeding can greatly reduce the possibility of food allergies in children, because both colostrum and breast milk naturally contain antibodies, which provide a baby with the benefit of the mother's immune system until the baby develops his own functional immune system at about 6 months of age. See Chapter 4 for more information on breastfeeding or read *Breastfeeding For Dummies* by Sharon Perkins, RN, and Carol Vannais, RN (Wiley).

So what exactly is a food allergy? Technically speaking, an allergy results when the body reacts against a food, usually a protein from the food that is absorbed into the blood. The process looks like this:

1. **Protein from food is absorbed into the bloodstream.**

2. **The body releases histamine and other antibodies to combat the perceived threat.**

   Histamine is a chemical that is held in certain cells of the body. When an allergy is triggered, the body naturally releases histamine as a defense.

3. **The histamine causes typical food allergy symptoms**

   - Sneezing

   - Runny nose

   - Hives

   - Difficulty breathing (in severe cases)

   - Anaphylactic shock (in really severe cases)

Anaphylactic shock affects breathing and blood pressure, and can be fatal. If your child has trouble breathing after eating, call 911 immediately.

A food allergy doesn't mean that something is wrong with your child. Your baby has an immature digestive and immune system, and children sometimes overreact to foods.

Common allergy triggers

Some certain foods tend to trigger food allergies in children and can even be dangerous. Don't get carried away and feed new foods too quickly or feed foods that are known allergens until your baby reaches age 1. Feeding foods too soon doesn't cause food allergies; rather, the immature immune system of a baby is just more likely to react.

Food allergies tend to be from the same collection of foods. In other words, your child is unlikely to have random food allergies, but some groups of foods trigger the histamine in the body.

Because the following foods typically cause problems with children less than 1 year of age, wait until your kid is older than 1 year old to consider trying any of these items.

These allergens are common, so introduce them with caution:

- ✔ **Cow's milk:** Many children have allergy problems with cow's milk. If you discover an allergy with cow's milk, try a soymilk substitute because the protein in the two milks is different.

- ✔ **Eggs:** If eggs present an allergy, you'll simply need to avoid them, but you can use egg substitutes that are on your grocery store shelf.

- ✔ **Gluten:** Gluten is a protein found in grains, especially wheat. Unfortunately, gluten is the cause for mostly all wheat allergies and gluten can also be found in other wheat-based products. Children that have gluten allergies must also avoid all products with wheat as well.

- ✔ **Peanuts:** Peanuts aren't true nuts — they're actually legumes from the pea and bean family. Children with allergies to peanuts can be very sensitive to foods with even tiny amounts of peanuts in them. Avoid *all* foods with peanuts. *Note:* Children who are allergic to peanuts can often eat tree nuts, such as walnuts or pecans because they're from separate plant families. Because peanuts are a common allergen, we recommend that you wait until your child is 2 years of age before introducing peanuts.

- ✔ **Shellfish:** We prefer that you wait until the age of 2 before you try serving shellfish, because shellfish often causes reactions on the more severe end of symptoms: difficulty breathing and anaphylactic shock.

- ✔ **Wheat:** Of all grains, wheat is the most likely to cause problems with allergies. Avoid all wheat and products with gluten, which is the predominant protein in wheat.

Other less common but known allergies in children that you should avoid serving during baby's first year of life are

- ✔ **Artificial additives:** *Food additives* (chemicals often used as binders and preservatives) or dyes that contain sulfites are the most common problem components of this food allergy.

- ✔ **Citrus fruit:** Some children have allergies to citrus fruit (but most outgrow it). Stick to noncitrus items, such as apples, pears, and bananas, during baby's first year of life.

- ✔ **Meats, especially beef:** You often see this allergy in children that are allergic to other food items. However, children that are allergic to one meat item may not be allergic to another (for example, you can substitute ground turkey for beef).

- ✔ **Soy:** Soy is often used as a replacement for children with allergies to cow's milk, but some children are allergic to soy, too. If your child is allergic to both cows' milk and soy, consult a pediatrician to formulate a milk replacement plan with other products.

- ✔ **Tree nuts:** Peanuts are the most common "nut" allergy, but some children are also allergic to tree nuts, such as pecans, walnuts, and almonds.

Symptoms of allergies

Unfortunately, the symptoms of food allergies are similar to other problems, such as a virus or even a cold, so it's not unusual for parents to miss the allergy at first, and in truth, a pediatrician should be the final authority on whether your child has a food allergy.

The trick with food allergy symptoms is when they occur. Typically, a reaction to food will occur within 30 minutes of eating the food. Carefully monitor what your toddler eats, and any time that any of the following symptoms occur soon after eating, consider whether any new foods were in the meal:

- ✔ **Rashes and hives:** Especially around the mouth and throat area. Sudden rashes or hives are often the most recognizable signs of a food allergy.

- ✔ **Wheezing or difficulty breathing:** This is another symptom that can become severe. Don't hesitate to call 911 if your child is having trouble breathing.

- ✔ **Nausea, abdominal pain, and diarrhea:** Digestive problems that occur soon after eating a certain food are often a sign of a food intolerance (and in some cases, an allergy).

In many cases, a certain food will give a person an upset stomach or gas, but this is not necessarily a food allergy. Rather, digestive problems like these are called food intolerances and aren't the result of an allergy (food intolerances are covered in the next section). Also, a runny nose without other symptoms is typically not a sign of a food allergy either.

Getting a diagnosis

The first tactic in diagnosing a food allergy is to introduce new foods the right way. In Chapter 5, we tell you all about introducing foods, but the key point to remember is to wait about five days after introducing a new food before introducing another. This procedure gives you plenty of opportunity to observe your child and see if she's having problems with certain foods. If you introduce several foods at the same time, you won't be able to figure out which food is causing the problem.

Be careful when you assume a food allergy, especially when digestive problems are the symptom. Just because your child seems to have a possible digestive reaction one time doesn't mean she will again. Also, food allergies can be tricky to track down depending on what foods you're feeding. For example, is the allergy really the French fry or the peanut oil it's fried in?

In most cases, parents tend to ignore the first reactive episode, but if your child's symptoms appear again with the food in question, you'll need to see a pediatrician who can make a proper diagnosis.

Although you can do some of the legwork yourself to identify potential allergies, be sure to talk with a pediatrician about food allergy concerns so you can get an accurate diagnosis. Identifying a food allergy requires a health history, physical exam, and diagnostic tests. (An allergy can only be truly diagnosed by testing for antibodies because even symptoms exactly like those of an allergy may not be caused by one.) If your child has several apparent allergies, his pediatrician or allergist will perform either a skin test or a blood test to see if specific food allergies can be found.

Dealing with an allergy (or allergies)

In the case of one or two allergies, you can simply avoid the problematic food and substitute another food with similar nutritional value. For example, it's not unusual for children to react to strawberries with some kind of facial or body rash. The solution is simply not to offer strawberries until your child gets older. Try to reintroduce those foods as your baby gets older, normally waiting about one year. Your child is most likely to develop tolerance to different foods if you identify the food that's causing problems and eliminate it from the diet for at least a year or two.

If your child has severe reactions to foods, such as trouble breathing, his pediatrician may also prescribe an epinephrine autoinjection device (such as the EpiPen or EpiPen JR) and ask that your child wear a medical alert bracelet to notify others of his allergy. Naturally, these steps aren't necessary unless an allergy is life threatening.

An allergy to a certain food also involves everything that food might be in. You need to avoid not only the food itself, but any dish that contains it. This typically isn't too much of a problem, unless your child is allergic to something like wheat, which is found in many dishes, or peanuts or peanut derivatives (such as peanut oil, which is used to fry many foods).

After baby has been diagnosed with a food allergy, be sure to follow the instructions of the pediatrician. If your little one is allergic to a common ingredient, such as wheat, you'll have to get in the habit of reading the package contents on any prepackaged food that you want to serve.

When in doubt, most manufacturers have a toll-free number that you can call and ask about the ingredients in the food. If you're eating out, ask for an ingredients list. Unfortunately, you have no simple workaround if your youngster is allergic to common food ingredients, but you need to be proactive about your child's eating habits to prevent reactions.

In for the Long Haul: Food Intolerances

Although children may outgrow allergies, food intolerance is a problem that may hang around for years, and in some cases, a lifetime. (For more on the differences between the two, see the corresponding sidebar later in this chapter.) Much confusion surrounds allergies and intolerances, and the two are commonly used interchangeably.

In reality, people generally have food intolerance to four specific groupings:

- ✔ Fructose (a type of sugar)
- ✔ Gluten
- ✔ Lactose
- ✔ Wheat

Food intolerances are much more common than food allergies in both children and adults, so it's important to understand the issue of food intolerances. In this section, we discuss the two most common ones.

Lactose intolerance

Lactose is a natural sugar that is found in dairy products and other foods as well as breads, cereals, cake mixes, and salad dressings. In a normal case, the body breaks down the lactose into two simple sugars: glucose and galactose, which are then absorbed by the bloodstream. When a person is *lactose intolerant,* the body isn't able to digest this sugar easily.

Lactose intolerance is caused by a lack of the lactase enzyme in the body that breaks the lactose into simple sugars. When more lactose is eaten than the available lactase can digest, lactose molecules remain in the intestine undigested, attracting water and causing the characteristic bloating, abdominal discomfort, and diarrhea. The undigested lactose becomes food for intestinal bacteria, which multiply and produce gas.

Lactose intolerance is a rather common problem in young children, and in fact, it's also a common problem in many adults. Actually, lactase function is highest immediately after birth, but in the majority of people, lactase activity declines dramatically during childhood and adolescence. Only a small percentage of people retain enough lactase to digest and absorb lactose efficiently throughout their adult life. It's pretty rare for an infant to be born with a deficiency.

Symptoms of lactose intolerance

The result of lactose digestion problems is that when the affected person eats or drinks any dairy product that contains lactose, she ends up with a number of bad symptoms:

✔ Diarrhea

✔ Bloating

✔ Nausea

✔ Abdominal pain

✔ Very bad breath (no kidding!)

The preceding symptoms may appear from 30 minutes to 2 hours after ingesting lactose.

Can you be allergic to milk and not be lactose intolerant? Yes — they're very different. A milk allergy is an immunologic response to a protein, and lactose intolerance is an enzyme deficiency. Sometimes intolerances to foods can be diagnosed as allergies, but they aren't. Adverse reactions to foods that involve symptoms but no antibody/histamine production are considered intolerances. And, of course, the most common intolerance is that of lactose.

It's also important to note that in some cases, babies can have lactose intolerance problems even when they breastfeed. Although rare, it's a known condition and one that your doctor can help you diagnose. The key to these issues is remembering the symptoms — if your child seems to have the symptoms mentioned in the previous list and is generally cranky, often after eating, get your doctor involved so that he or she can confirm a diagnosis and provide guidance.

You say allergy; I say intolerance

The terms *allergy* and *intolerance* are often used interchangeably, and sometimes food intolerances are diagnosed as an allergy. So how can you cut through the confusion? Keep reading to see the difference.

Food allergy:

✔ A rather fast response by the body's immune system to a perceived invader.

✔ Signs or symptoms are typically immediate, dramatic, and visible: coughing, sneezing, vomiting, migraines, watering eyes, rashes, swelling tissue, hives, or in severe cases, anaphylactic shock, which requires emergency intervention.

Food intolerance:

✔ The body's inability to digest some foods properly.

✔ The gastrointestinal tract is unable to produce appropriate enzymes for normal chemical breakdown. The food passes through unprocessed and causes intestinal problems.

✔ Symptoms such as nausea, vomiting, and diarrhea can be delayed for hours.

Treatment for lactose intolerance

If your child has a lactose problem, it's likely that he'll have to contend with it for a long time. There is good news though: Several over-the-counter products exist that can help with lactose intolerance.

Many adults and children have problems digesting lactose, and there are a couple of commercial products for you to choose from:

✔ **Prepared milk products:** Products that have been treated with an enzyme that breaks down the lactose.

✔ **Enzyme replacement:** You can purchase enzyme tablets or drops that can be added to milk. This product is often sold near the antacids in your local supermarket. However, child use should be supervise by your doctor.

Milk products that are labeled *lactose free* still have the same nutrition and can be given to children who have lactose problems. Fortunately for lactose intolerant folks, these products can greatly help manage problems without having to avoid dairy altogether.

Tolerance to lactose varies widely. Many people with intolerance can consume foods and drinks with up to 6 grams of lactose (½ cup of milk) without symptoms. The best strategies would be to begin with small portions and increase the portion size until mild symptoms appear; eat or drink with other foods in a meal; and spread out intake throughout the day. Total elimination of milk products is usually not necessary.

As with all childhood problems, you should discuss the issue with your pediatrician and follow her advice. If your child has severe problems with lactose intolerance, your pediatrician may recommend a milk replacement product. Visit www.brightbeginnings.com to see a good example of a milk replacement product that uses soy. Some other foods that don't cause as many problems related to lactose intolerance are

- ✔ **Yogurt:** A great source for calcium intake. Active cultures in most types of yogurt provide their own enzyme to digest lactose; look for *active culture* on the label.

- ✔ **Cheese:** Some cheeses don't cause symptoms because most of the lactose is removed during processing. Try serving aged, hard cheeses such as cheddar, Swiss, or Parmesan.

- ✔ **Cottage cheese:** This product has a lower lactose level due to the reduction during processing.

Gluten intolerance

Gluten is a protein found commonly in wheat and in lesser degrees in rye and barley, giving dough its elastic nature and enhancing the texture and taste of bread. Children who have gluten intolerance (as opposed to a gluten allergy) have a greater challenge because there aren't many substitute products for gluten. Before jumping the gun and assuming that your child has gluten intolerance, be sure to see a doctor first. Check out *Living Gluten-Free For Dummies* (Wiley) by Danna Korn.

Avoiding gluten requires avoiding wheat and other related grain products that contain gluten. Wheat is used in all kinds of products, including breads, cereals, and crackers. In fact, the following common items all contain wheat and gluten:

- ✔ Bran
- ✔ Breadcrumbs
- ✔ Cereal extract (used in crackers)
- ✔ Couscous
- ✔ Cracker meal
- ✔ Enriched flour
- ✔ Gelatinized starch
- ✔ Gluten
- ✔ High-gluten flour

- High-protein flour
- Hydrolyzed vegetable protein
- Modified food starch
- Modified starch
- Natural flavoring
- Semolina wheat
- Soy sauce
- Starch
- Vegetable gum
- Vegetable starch
- Vital gluten
- Wheat bran, germ, gluten, malt, and starch
- Whole-wheat flour

True gluten intolerance is called Celiac Disease. *Celiac Disease* is a permanent intolerance to gluten that results in damage to the small intestine. The only way to prevent it is by avoiding gluten entirely.

Symptoms of gluten intolerance

The symptoms of Celiac Disease can vary. They generally consist of severe gas, bloating, diarrhea, and abdominal pain. If these effects are left untreated, your child may experience malnutrition.

Symptoms don't always involve the digestive system. Other indicators include irritability, depression, muscle cramps, joint pain, and fatigue. Reactions to ingestion of gluten can be immediate, or delayed for weeks or even months.

Because gluten intolerance can be difficult to diagnose, you should see a pediatrician if your little one experiences persistent symptoms described in this section. Try to give the doctor as much information as possible about your child's eating habits.

Treatment for gluten intolerance

The only real treatment for gluten intolerance requires a lifetime adherence to a strict diet that avoids all products containing gluten. A gluten-free diet can prevent almost all complications caused by the disease.

Follow these tips to help you avoid gluten:

✔ **Read food labels.** Gluten is often used as a thickener. Check canned soups, ketchups, mustards, soy sauce, and other condiments — many contain gluten.

✔ **Watch out for other grains.** Wheat isn't the only problem. Rye, oats, barley, and other multigrain products contain gluten.

✔ **Look for the *wheat-free* label.** But don't be fooled. Remember that products labeled *wheat free* aren't necessarily gluten free.

✔ **Locate other key words.** Watch out for the following items:

- Caramel coloring
- Cereal
- Distilled vinegar
- Durum
- Emulsifiers
- Enriched flour
- Farina
- Flour
- Malt flavoring or extracts
- Modified food starch
- MSG
- Semolina
- Stabilizers
- Triticale

Spitting Up (Or, Technically Speaking, Reflux)

Reflux is a condition where much of the stomach contents are pushed back up into the esophagus and out through the mouth or nose, which typically occurs shortly after eating. In truth, everyone experiences reflux to a minor degree every day and isn't aware of it.

Reflux in babies and children occurs because of an uncoordinated upper digestive system. A ring of muscle at the bottom of the esophagus opens and closes to allow food to enter the stomach. This ring is called the lower esophageal sphincter (LES). Reflux can occur when the LES opens, allowing stomach contents and acid to come back up into the esophagus. As your child's digestive system develops and becomes more mature, the LES stops opening when it's not supposed to, and the reflux problems typically pass. In fact, 90 percent of all babies and children who suffer from reflux simply outgrow it by 6 months old.

Watching out for common symptoms

Babies naturally spit up a lot, so regular spit up is nothing to be concerned about. However, as your baby grows to month six, you should notice an outgrowing of this behavior, and you shouldn't be overly concerned unless your child seems to spit up most of what he's eating and you see the following symptoms along with it:

- ✔ Frequent vomiting (more than once or twice daily)
- ✔ Poor weight gain
- ✔ Recurrent pneumonias
- ✔ Eating discomfort
    - Refuses to eat
    - Stiffens up
    - Arches back
    - Tries to push away from the bottle
- ✔ Persistent hiccups
- ✔ Persistent cough
- ✔ Chronic nasal and/or sinus congestion (from aspiration)
- ✔ Frequent choking episodes
- ✔ Sour breath
- ✔ Burning pain in the chest area (for children 2 years and up)
- ✔ Complaint that eating hurts (for children 2 years and up)

Chronic reflux can result in Esophagitis. This condition is caused by erosion of the esophagus from the acid in the vomit. Signs can range from pain during feedings to blood in the vomit. If this continues for a long period of time, it can cause scarring on the esophagus and, rarely, it can lead to Barretts Esophagus (a condition in which the color and composition of the cells lining your lower esophagus change because of repeated exposure to stomach acid) or even esophageal cancer.

These conditions only happen if chronic reflux is ignored and the condition continues over time. This is why detection and treatment should be considered for children who seem to have excessive problems with reflux.

Diagnosing and treating reflux

Reflux may be diagnosed based on the description of the child's behavior and a combination of the symptoms as described in the previous section. Often the doctor will order various tests to confirm the diagnosis.

Reflux is an important problem to address, but it's also important not to over-diagnose Baby's normal spitting up behavior. If the problem seems persistent, talk to a pediatrician, who can order definitive tests to confirm a diagnosis. As with most childhood problems, it's important to be proactive but not overly reactive.

If your tot suffers from reflux, see a pediatrician for treatment options, which depend on the severity of the condition. As with any problem, your pediatrician can evaluate your child's particular situation and recommend the best course of action. Your pediatrician may recommend the following treatments:

- ✔ **Thicken the formula.** Thicker formula helps keep the food in the stomach.

- ✔ **Start with rice cereal.** Rice is often easier to digest. Your doctor may recommend moving to oatmeal because it's thicker. Ultimately, follow your doctor's advice.

- ✔ **Allow naps in an infant seat or bouncy chair.** Gravity helps with the digestive process because of the upright position.

- ✔ **Sit your child upright during eating and for about 30 minutes afterward.** This often greatly reduces reflux because gravity helps keep the food in the stomach.

In more severe cases, your pediatrician may prescribe a medication to help reduce the amount of stomach acid, which will reduce the symptoms of reflux.

Helpful Recipes

The following recipes address some common allergy and lactose issues that children often experience. These recipes are all "starter" recipes in that they'll give you some foods you can make for your children and hopefully point in the right direction for making more.

Gluten-free recipes

Here are a few recipes to get you started in the right direction if your child has a gluten allergy or intolerance.

⟳ Homemade Gluten-Free Flour

If your child has an allergy to gluten, you'll find yourself in a jam because most bread contains gluten, including typical flour you would use to make a wide assortment of recipes. Begin by making this gluten-free flour substitute, which you can then use in other recipes that call for flour. You may be able to find some of the ingredients at your local supermarket, but you may also have to trek to a health-food store.

Preparation time: *5 minutes*

Yield: *About 3½ quarts*

8 cups rice flour

5 cups potato starch flour

2½ cups tapioca flour

Mix all the ingredients together and store in a flour container.

Tip: *You can easily make more or less by simply adjusting the measurements in this recipe. The recipe without measurements is 1 part rice flour, ⅔ part potato starch flour, and ⅓ part tapioca flour.*

⟳ Rice Sponge Cake

For a light sponge cake that is flour free and gluten free, try this rice version. This recipe is a lot like angel food cake, so it works well with fruit toppings, especially strawberries. **Note:** If you haven't the foggiest idea how to separate an egg, check out Figure 13-1.

Preparation time: *15 minutes*

Cooking time: *45 minutes*

Tools: *9-inch tube pan*

Yield: *20 servings*

¾ cup rice flour

½ cup sugar

8 egg yolks

9 egg whites

Nonstick cooking spray

1 Preheat the oven to 350 degrees.

2 Mix rice flour and sugar in a medium bowl and sift together 4 to 5 times by using a flour sifter.

3 In a separate bowl, beat the egg yolks with an electric mixer until fluffy. Pour the eggs into the flour-and-sugar mixture and stir well.

4 In yet another bowl, beat the egg whites with an electric mixer until fluffy.

5 Lightly spray a 9-inch tube pan with cooking spray.

6 Fold the egg whites into the mixture with a wooden spoon.

7 Pour the mixture in the tube pan and bake for 45 minutes, or until a fork inserted into the cake comes out clean. Cool the cake before cutting. Cut into equal pieces and serve.

How to Separate an Egg

Figure 13-1:
Separating an egg is as simple as 1-2-3-4-5.

1. Hold the egg in one hand over two small bowls.

2. Crack the shell on the side of one bowl.

3. Let the white fall into one of the bowls.

4. Pass the yolk back & forth, each time releasing more white.

5. When all the white is in the bowl, drop yolk in the other bowl.

Allergen-Free Teething Biscuits

Finding teething biscuits for your allergic youngster can be nearly impossible. And when you have a screaming child whose teeth hurt, you'll want something quick to soothe his pain. With this quick recipe, you make your own biscuits, but note that they tend to be harder than the store-bought variety.

Preparation time: *15 minutes*

Cooking time: *30 minutes*

Yield: *15 servings*

1 cup rice cereal	*1 cup apple juice*
1 cup millet flour	*Butter or oil for baking*

1 Preheat the oven to 350 degrees.

2 Mix all the ingredients in a large bowl with a wooden spoon to form the dough.

3 Lightly butter or oil a bread pan and place the dough in the pan.

4 Bake the dough for 30 minutes. Let the bread cool for a few hours, and then bake again for another 15 minutes to make it harder. This will make the biscuits firmer and more useful as a teething biscuit.

5 Remove the loaf from the oven and cut it into small biscuits, about 1½ inches wide by 1½ inches long; allow the biscuits to cool completely before serving. We suggest putting them in the refrigerator so they're cold when you serve them — the cold will also ease your child's teething pain.

Other Allergy / Intolerance Recipes

Here's a collection of different recipes that can be helpful if your child has an allergy or intolerance to certain foods. All the recipes in this section are naturally lactose free as well. These will get you started, and you can find out more about children and allergies at `http://kidswithfoodallergies.org/index.php`.

☺ Milk- and Egg-Free Bread

This recipe allows you to make and serve bread to your little one. "But bread contains milk and egg!" you say. Not this recipe. We've removed the two most common allergens. Enjoy the great texture and use the loaf to replace regular bread.

Preparation time: 15 minutes; allow 45 minutes for bread to rise

Cooking time: 1 to 1¼ hours

Tools: 10-inch springform pan

Yield: 8 servings

⅓ ounce yeast (about 1 packet)	2 cups white rice flour
1 teaspoon sugar	½ cup potato starch
2 cups lukewarm water	¼ cup tapioca flour
2 tablespoons olive oil	½ cup corn flour
½ tablespoon vinegar	2 teaspoons carob powder
Cooking spray	1 teaspoon salt

1 In a 2-cup glass measuring container, mix the yeast and sugar. Add 1 cup of lukewarm water and add oil and vinegar. Mix well, and add another cup of lukewarm water and mix again.

2 Mix the remaining ingredients in a separate bowl.

3 Coat a springform pan (10 inches in diameter) or bread pan with cooking spray and dust it with the dry mix.

4 Pour the wet mixture into the bowl with the dry ingredients and mix with a wooden spoon. You can add a bit more water as necessary to make the dough smooth.

5 Put the dough in the springform or bread pan and place it in the microwave to rise for 45 minutes.

6 Preheat the oven to 400 degrees during the last 15 minutes that the bread is rising. Place the bread in the oven and bake for 1 to 1¼ hours.

7 Allow the bread to cool, then slice and serve.

☺ Allergy-Free Breakfast Crumble

Make this breakfast crumble in advance to have on hand when you need a breakfast idea in a jiffy.

Preparation time: *15 minutes*

Cooking time: *30 minutes*

Yield: *Six 1-cup servings*

2 cups rolled oats, uncooked

1½ cups ground oats (use a food processor and grind them to a powder)

1 cup raisins

1 cup orange or apple juice

¼ cup sugar

½ teaspoon cinnamon

½ teaspoon salt

½ cup vegetable oil

¼ cup sesame seeds or sunflower seeds

Additional oil to grease pan

1 Preheat the oven to 375 degrees.

2 Combine all the ingredients in a large bowl and mix well. You should be able to form a ball with the dough.

3 Grease a 9-x-13-inch pan with the vegetable oil.

4 Place the mixture evenly in the pan and bake for 30 minutes.

5 Remove the pan from the oven and scoop the servings onto plates. Because this recipe is a "crumble" (which it does!), serve with a fork.

⟳ *Rice Milk*

Many children, and well, adults too, may not be able to tolerate milk. If you need a milk alternative for cooking, try this recipe. The process of making rice milk is easy. The final product may turn out a little bland, so we add a bit of vanilla to give it some flair. Rice milk also works as a good substitute for regular milk in recipes. Naturally, you can buy rice milk already prepared, but if you'd rather make your own, use this handy recipe. You can also freeze the extra for later use.

If your child has a cow's milk allergy, this rice milk isn't a good substitute because it doesn't contain the calcium and other nutrients found in milk. You should feed your child a comparable milk substitute, such as soymilk.

Preparation time: *2½ hours*

Tools: *Cheesecloth*

Yield: *10 cups*

2 cups rice	*Salt or vanilla extract to taste*
12 cups water (you may need a bit more)	

1 Bring the water to a boil in a large saucepan. Put rice in another large saucepan and pour boiling water over the rice. Soak for 2 hours.

2 Using a blender, blend 1 cup of soaked rice with 2½ cups of water. The blended mixture should be a bit chunky, not a smooth liquid.

3 Pour the mixture into a clean, large, pot and repeat the process in Step 2 with the rest of the rice, blending one cup at the time with 2½ cups of water.

4 After that process is finished, bring the rice liquid to a boil, reduce heat, and simmer for 20 minutes.

5 Line a colander with a few layers of cheesecloth, and pour the rice liquid through the colander into a large, clean pot. You can also add another cup of water into the colander to get more milk to seep through after you complete this process.

6 Add a bit of salt or vanilla extract to the milk to enhance the taste. Refrigerate the milk or freeze the extra.

☕ Basic Smoothie

Children love smoothies and will often drink a smoothie when they refuse to eat anything else. That is why parents often rely on smoothies to provide some solid nutrition. This basic smoothie recipe avoids cow's milk and can be adapted to any kind of fruit you desire. If your child has severe milk allergies, consider trying a soy yogurt.

Preparation time: *10 minutes*

Chill time: *15 minutes*

Yield: *Three 1-cup servings*

2 cups plain, full-fat yogurt

2 tablespoons honey (omit if your child is less than 1 year old)

1 cup water

1 teaspoon lemon juice

1 cup fruit, crushed and drained

Pour all the ingredients in a blender and blend until smooth. Chill for 15 minutes and serve cold.

Simple Allergy-Free Turkey Meatballs

Beef sometimes causes allergies in children, especially to those who're prone to other allergy problems with food. This simple turkey meatball recipe contains only ground turkey and applesauce. You can multiply the ingredients in this recipe and make the meatballs and freeze the extras for easy use later.

Preparation time: *40 minutes*

Cook time: *20 minutes*

Yield: *6 servings (3 meatballs per serving)*

1 pound ground turkey (make sure that you buy ground turkey with no additives or flavorings)

1 cup pure applesauce

Salt to taste if desired

Cooking oil for baking

1 Preheat the oven to 350 degrees.

2 In a large bowl, mix the ground turkey and applesauce with a wooden spoon. Add a bit of salt if desired.

3 Form ½-inch meatballs (or a bit larger if desired) and bake them on an oiled cookie sheet for 20 minutes, or until brown. Serve warm.

Chicken with Beans and Rice

Chicken with beans and rice is a rather standard southern dinner recipe, but this one avoids any kind of lactose. The good news is that you can adapt this recipe easily so that the adults in your family who aren't concerned about lactose can spice it up. See the Vary It icon at the end of the recipe.

Preparation time: *15 minutes*

Yield: *6 servings*

16 ounces boneless, skinless chicken breast, cooked and cut into bite-size pieces	*½ cup chopped red bell pepper*
¾ cup mild salsa	*¼ cup onion, minced*
15-ounce can black beans, drained	*2 cups cooked instant rice*

1 Mix all the ingredients together except the rice in a large skillet and simmer for 10 minutes.

2 In a large serving dish, mix the rice with the skillet ingredients and serve warm.

Vary It! *You can spice this recipe up for adults by adding another ½ cup of salsa or jalapeno slices to taste. You can also wrap this mixture in a flour tortilla for a quick burrito.*

Allergy-Free Chili

What do you think of when you think of chili? Everyone's answer may be different, but we think of cold nights and curling up to a bowl of steaming chili and having our tummies full of homemade goodness. This chili recipe contains allergy-free ingredients, so put your mind at ease as you and your family are warming your bellies.

Preparation time: *1 hour 30 minutes*

Yield: *Six 1-cup servings*

2 tablespoons olive oil or vegetable oil	1 teaspoon chili powder
1 clove garlic, diced	½ pound ground turkey, browned
1 small onion, chopped	¼ cup mild salsa
1 medium green bell pepper, chopped	15-ounce can red kidney beans, drained
6-ounce can crushed tomatoes	15-ounce can black beans, drained
6-ounce can tomato paste	

1 In a large skillet, heat the oil over medium-high heat.

2 Add the garlic and onion and cook until the onion is translucent, about 7 minutes.

3 Add the green bell pepper and sauté for a few minutes. Add the crushed tomatoes, tomato paste, chili powder, turkey, and salsa.

4 Let the mixture heat until bubbly, reduce the heat to simmer, and add the beans. Cover and simmer for at least 60 minutes, stirring occasionally. Serve warm.

Chapter 14

Tempting Dishes for a Picky Eater

. . . .

In This Chapter

▶ Understanding picky eaters and managing eating behaviors

▶ Sharing recipes and creating lunches, dinners, and side dishes

▶ Munching on snacks for picky eaters

▶ Blending up juices and smoothies

. . . .

*Y*ou know the look. It's a look of quiet disgust — and the quiet part of the look can quickly turn into complaints and even angry behavior. You see this look, in many cases, no matter what you seem to fix for lunch or dinner. It's the look of a picky eater.

Children from 2 to 5 are notorious for being diffi-cult eaters. Even if you've followed our advice in previous chapters about offering balanced meals, healthy snacks, and a variety of foods, your child still may turn into a picky eater for reasons beyond your control. Children, yes your kids too, are unpredictable, and just like the rest of their lives, they seem to go through stages where some-times they eat well, sometimes they don't seem to eat at all, and sometimes they seem to eat only one food, all the time, period.

These stages of eating and degrees of pickiness are all normal. Children differ, so don't get in the habit of comparing what your child does with your best friend's child. In terms of eating, some children are simply pickier than others. What can you do to help? A ton! In this chapter, you'll find tips to help you manage your needs and some recipes that tempt even the pickiest of eaters.

Understanding Why Kids Are Picky

Above all things, we want you to know this: Picky eaters are normal children. Any child development book that talks about eating probably mentions the issue of picky eaters. This childhood behavior, though, often pushes parents over the edge. So, the first tactic to managing your child's picky eating habits is first to understand those habits.

Picky eaters don't eat the same way adults eat. As adults, we tend to eat two to four meals a day, perhaps with some snacks in-between. In many ways, we're conditioned to eat this way, and we tend to follow that same routine every day. In fact, we often eat because it's *time* to eat, even though we're not *really* hungry.

Children, on the other hand, eat when they're hungry — plain and simple. So the result is that your child may tank up at one meal a day and tend to pick at her food the rest of the day. She may eat like a horse one day and barely touch her food for the next day or two. Or she may get stuck in a rut and only eat a couple of different things.

Whatever the case may be, there's plenty of room for individuality. The point isn't to be overly concerned or troubled by your child's picky eating behavior — in fact, the more focus you put on the eating habit, the more little Jenny resists eating and thinks negatively of food in general. Except for rare cases, your tot is fine and ends up eating like a normal adult.

So, why are children picky eaters? There are a number of explanations. Your child may lean more toward one reason or the behavior simply may be caused by a combination of events. Understanding, however, leads to easier management, so consider the following issues:

✔ **Appearance:** Children, like adults, are visually driven when it comes to food. However, children have to learn what looks good to eat and what doesn't look good to eat. The cheesy lasagne may look great to you, but it looks like a bunch of goo to your toddler. So, when your dish is rejected, don't take it personally.

✔ **Immature emotions:** Let's face it; toddlers haven't exactly mastered the management of stress and frustration. In light of this fact, don't be surprised if your child unleashes a torrent of emotions concerning food. Illogical? Yes. Childlike? Yes. But it's still important to teach what is and what isn't polite early on. Work with your youngsters concerning table manners. If your little ones don't like a food, a simple "No thank you" is enough.

Discerning whether Susie is really too choosy

To help you gauge how to handle your child at mealtime, your best bet is to keep a journal. Grab a spiral notebook, and write down everything your picky eater actually eats or drinks in a given day. Why? You may be surprised at your findings. After you recognize these patterns, you can take steps to correct them.

✔ Parents are often surprised to find that their picky eater is actually eating more than they think. Many parents have difficulty when they offer their children food because the portions are much bigger than the child can eat, and so what she eats doesn't look like much to us. If you keep an accurate record of what your child eats, you may find that your little one eats more than you think.

✔ Your child eats too much of one item, such as some kind of snack food instead of meals. Check your journal (that we know you've been keeping) to see the eating patterns and how much of any one single item you've been serving.

✔ Your child tanks up on milk or juice. Depending on the age of your kid, it's common for children to appear to be picky eaters, when in fact they're full from drinking too much milk or juice. A journal helps you identify the *liquid creep,* which may contribute to the picky eating behavior, and then you can offer other liquids such as water.

✔ **Lack of schedule:** It takes time for children to become scheduled eaters. Your child may eat a lot of one item and not eat again all day. In other words, children want to eat when they're hungry and not based on a certain time of day. That's why one of your most important jobs is ensuring mealtime consistency. Even if a child isn't hungry or doesn't eat much at a meal, you should still offer food at the same time every day, instead of asking, "Are you hungry yet?"

✔ **Smell:** Smell is a learned response. In other words, it takes time to figure out what smells good and what smells bad. Your child may immediately reject something in the kitchen based on smell, even though it smells good to you.

✔ **Texture:** Don't forget that food provides many different textures. For example, a raw carrot and a cooked carrot are very different with regards to texture. Children often like one texture and reject another, even though the food may taste like something a child would typically want. Texture takes time to get used to, and a child's taste buds have to mature.

In the end, the final reason that children are picky eaters is unknown. In fact, some researchers believe that pickiness is even "wired" into your children as a preventative measure that helps them from eating something poisonous.

Picky eating typically peaks around the time a child enters preschool (4 years old) and tends to decline after that. Again, this norm isn't a hard and fast rule that you'd be able to observe.

Either way, as the parent, you'll contend with picky eaters, and the important tactics in this chapter help you battle the cooking woes.

Tactics for Managing Your Picky Eater

If you end up with a picky eater (and 30 to 40 percent of you reading this book will), you can put to work some important tactics as you continue to feed and work with your finicky child. In fact, dealing with selective eaters can be frustrating and parents often make situations worse by letting their emotions get in the mix. Therefore, gather the information from the tactics in this chapter and put your knowledge to work in the kitchen.

Be consistent

The key tactic to managing a picky eater is being consistent. Don't give up or give in. A consistent mealtime offers your child three healthy meals a day and healthy snacks in between. Offer a variety of foods, and don't allow your little beggars to panhandle for snacks between meals, either. Also, keep the milk and juice in check, and serve water occasionally.

Your child won't starve to death. Just because she's picky, don't feel like you have to throw organization and nutrition to the wind just to get her to eat. Be consistent and firm, and don't force the issue. She'll eat when she's hungry.

Defuse the stress

Unfortunately, a finicky eater can be stressful for you and the rest of the family. Unfortunately, the stress and aggravation you feel can end up making mealtime a war zone, and your stress can actually make the problem much worse. In fact, reactions from you can make your picky eater pickier!

As you work with your kid, it's important to remember that you're not alone, and pickiness is actually common in children. With this in mind, don't take a food protest as a personal attack against your cooking. Instead of letting mealtimes stress you out, just do your best and move on — tomorrow is another day.

Parents often make mealtime stressful for their children by putting too much food on their plates. Keep portion sizes small to diffuse your child's stress — she can always have more.

Use the time in the kitchen as a teaching moment and for building positive relationships between you and your family. Get your kids involved in the kitchen and consider letting them help you cook. Because cooking with your kids contributes to positive activity on many levels (such as math skills, language skills, and organizational skills), we've included an entire chapter dedicated to whipping up meals together. This tactic will also help your child be more interested in food and improve her desire to try new foods that she's helped prepare. Flip back to Chapter 11 to find out more about preparing meals with your little one.

Mix it up

As you're working with your picky eater, you may fall into the routine of letting your child eat whatever he'll eat for the sake of simplicity and your sanity. In the end, though, this form of nourishment isn't a good tactic. This behavior produces an older child that automatically rejects any new foods and continues to be picky. Avoid planning meals based on what your picky child eats. This tactic decreases variety and the rest of the family ends up resenting having to eat only what the picky one eats.

Keep mixing up the meals and encouraging good eating behavior. We always encourage our kids to try new things. Sure, sometimes they complain, and sometimes they gag, but our children are comfortable with trying new foods. And you can nurture adventurous kids too! Our 9-year-old tries anything — if she doesn't like it, no big deal. You don't want to end up with children who only eat five things.

Mix it up with the following recipes that we've designed especially for your picky eaters. These easy, friendly recipes stimulate the eye, which helps encourage your child to try them.

Serve meals away from the table

If eating is a problem, then your child may associate the kitchen table with negativity. This is the time to shake things up and get away from the kitchen table:

- ✔ Plan a backyard picnic.
- ✔ Have a "tea party" (with real mealtime food) in your child's bedroom.
- ✔ Play restaurant — move the meal to another area of the house and pretend like you're eating out. Have your toddler help out as a waiter!

Use the kitchen table for activities other than cooking. Let your child work with molding clay or other craft projects. By putting this tactic to work in your home, having craft time at the same table at which you eat may lessen the opposition.

Avoid disciplining behavior

One of the worst mistakes to make is allowing the kitchen table to become a place of discipline, criticism, or arguing. As frustrating as your child's defiance to food can be, avoid using discipline, and never force-feed — this is dangerous due to the choking hazard and results in more eating problems later.

Instead of focusing on discipline, try these tips at the dinner table:

- ✔ Reinforce table manners with your behavior. Lead by example.

- ✔ Focus your child on eating, but talk about other things at the table as well. Conversation defuses the attention away from the food. Tell little Becky what foods she's eating, but don't talk about food after that. Avoid comments such as "Look, mommy likes it," or "Don't you want to be strong like daddy?" These comments only add to the stress of the situation and don't help the picky eater.

- ✔ Remove the plate if your child simply refuses to eat, but don't allow him to leave the table until everyone else is finished, and don't give him a snack within the next hour. Keep the same meal and snack schedule whether your toddler eats. Children may manipulate dinner situations if you allow them to skip meals but eat a snack afterward.

- ✔ Never, ever bribe your child to eat one food based on a reward for another food (such as something sweet). This reward pattern begins a lifelong struggle with sweets, which can lead to weight and health problems.

Lunches with Great Taste Appeal

Lunch tends to be a meal that most kids want to eat. And that's the good news! Use lunchtime as an opportunity to test out different recipes on your child. Eventually, if you have a picky eater, you'll find meals that your kids enjoy. Try these recipes to help you do just that.

☺ Grilled Apple and Cheese Sandwich

Even the pickiest of children eat apples and cheese. Put the two together with whole-grain bread and a few carrot sticks on the side to create a healthy lunch. Put this quick recipe to work in your kitchen.

Preparation time: *10 minutes*

Cooking time: *5 minutes*

Yield: *1 serving*

2 teaspoons mayonnaise or salad dressing

2 slices whole-wheat or oatmeal bread

4 slices cheddar cheese

½ small apple, cored, peeled, and thinly sliced into rings

1 tablespoon butter or margarine, softened

1 Spread one teaspoon of mayonnaise on each slice of bread.

2 Place cheese and apple slices on one slice of bread in alternating layers. Place the second piece of bread on top to make the sandwich.

3 Smear half of the butter on the outside of each piece of bread and fry the sandwich in a frying pan on medium-high heat until browned on both sides and cheese melts.

4 Remove the pan from the heat, and place the sandwich on a plate. Cut the sandwich in quarters, and serve with a pickle slice or carrot sticks.

Vary It! *Leave off the mayonnaise if your child doesn't like it.*

Bacon, Cheese, and Tomato Sandwich

You're probably familiar with the typical bacon, lettuce, and tomato sandwich, but this version uses cheese instead of lettuce, making the sandwich tastier (in your child's mind). It's quick and easy to make and works great as a lunchtime meal with some fresh veggies and ranch dip on the side.

Preparation time: *10 minutes*

Cooking time: *5 minutes*

Yield: *1 serving*

1 slice American cheese	2 strips cooked bacon, chopped into small pieces
2 slices whole-wheat or oatmeal bread	
2 teaspoons mayonnaise or salad dressing	2 thin slices tomato

Place the cheese on one slice of the bread and put in the microwave for 20 seconds or so until cheese melts. Create the sandwich, adding the other items as desired. Cut the sandwich into quarters. Serve with raw vegetables and a dip.

Vary It! *For a healthier version, try using turkey bacon instead of pork.*

Simply Hearty Beef Stew

On those cold winter days, nothing quite compares to the home-cooked taste of beef stew. This recipe is simple, uses a slow cooker, and doesn't contain a lot of fancy ingredients. It's perfect for your picky child!

Preparation time: *15 minutes*

Cooking time: *9 hours*

Yield: *Ten 1-cup servings*

½-pound beef stew meat	10½-ounce can cream of celery soup
10½-ounce can condensed cream of mushroom soup	

Pour all the ingredients into a slow cooker and cook on low for 9 hours. Occasionally add a bit of water and stir the soup so it doesn't stick to the bottom of the slow cooker. Serve the stew.

Vary It! *Consider serving this stew on a bed of brown rice, or if your child loves mashed potatoes, he can enjoy Simply Hearty Beef Stew with mashed potatoes instead.*

Cheeseburger Macaroni

Macaroni dishes don't have to come in a box — you can make this cheeseburger macaroni in no time from scratch. This dish is picky-kid friendly and doesn't contain extra ingredients that hard-to-please kids tend to reject.

Preparation time: *15 minutes*

Cooking time: *30 minutes*

Yield: *Eight 1-cup servings*

Medium onion, chopped	*1 pound mild cheddar cheese, grated and divided*
1 pound ground beef	
16-ounce package large elbow macaroni, cooked according to package directions and drained	*14-ounce can cream of mushroom soup*
	28-ounce can tomato sauce
	½ cup water

1 Preheat the oven to 450 degrees.

2 Sauté the onion. Add the ground beef and brown. Remove the pan from the heat, drain off any excess fat, and set aside.

3 In a 9-x-13-inch ungreased glass baking dish, mix the meat mixture, macaroni, cheese (reserve 1 cup), soup, and tomato sauce. Pour the water over the mixture.

4 Top with the remaining cup of cheese and bake for 30 minutes or until the cheese melts and is bubbly. Cool before serving.

Tempting Chicken Tacos

Many picky eaters enjoy tacos because of the crunch. This recipe uses pieces of chopped chicken breast and a zippy Italian dressing for a bit of a different taste from the standard beef tacos.

Preparation time: *30 minutes*

Yield: *2 servings*

4 tablespoons finely chopped cooked chicken breast	½ cup chopped lettuce
2 taco shells	½ cup chopped tomatoes
2 teaspoons Italian dressing	½ cup grated cheddar cheese

1 Evenly place 2 tablespoons of chicken in each taco shell.

2 Sprinkle the meat with 1 teaspoon of Italian dressing for each taco.

3 Add lettuce, tomatoes, and cheese as desired, and serve.

Ham and Corkscrew Pasta

For the picky eater, sometimes a simple lunch like this one can break the cycle of finicky eating. The cheddar cheese is the tempting factor here.

Preparation time: *20 minutes*

Yield: *Two 1-cup servings*

1 cup cooked rotini pasta	2 heaping tablespoons finely chopped ham
½ cup shredded cheddar cheese	Salt to taste
1 tablespoon butter, optional	

1 Cook the pasta according to the package directions. Drain the water and stir in the cheese. Add a teaspoon of butter to make the pasta and cheese smoother.

2 Add the ham and stir, adding salt to taste. Serve with fresh fruit and milk.

All the ham that's fit to please

Trying to get your kids to eat ham? Here's a quick and easy recipe that often works for picky eaters. Buy a regular sized "picnic" ham. Place the ham in your slow cooker and pour 2 cups of apple juice over the ham. Cook on high for about an hour, then on low for about 7 hours. You'll end up with an apple taste and very tender meat. A combination even the pickiest of children have trouble passing up!

Irresistible Dinners and Sides

One of the greatest problems with a picky eater tends to be main meals. You may be able to get your child to eat a snack or side item, but chowing down on a main meal seems like a distant dream. The dishes in this section may help your finicky eater be more interested in taking a bite out of his picky eating.

Sautéed Hamburger with Zucchini and Squash

We love any sautéed food and for good reason. Sautéed foods simply have a different flavor than foods cooked in other ways. If you can introduce your selective eater to sautéed veggies, he's more likely to eat them once he acquires the taste. This simple hamburger and veggie mix is one that you may have luck getting your kids to eat.

Preparation time: *30 minutes*

Yield: *Seven ½-cup servings*

1 pound hamburger meat	1 medium yellow squash, finely sliced
1 teaspoon garlic	Medium zucchini, finely sliced
2 teaspoons Italian seasoning	Salt to taste
Olive oil	

1 In a medium saucepan, brown the hamburger meat. When the meat is near completion, add garlic and Italian seasoning. Stir well. Set aside.

2 Lightly oil the bottom of a frying pan with olive oil. Heat the oil in a medium skillet over medium-high heat, and sauté the squash and zucchini until slightly brown.

3 In a serving dish, mix the meat with the veggies. Add 1 teaspoon of olive oil and toss well. Salt to taste and serve.

Picky Eater Spaghetti

Kids often eat pasta dishes even when they reject every other food. So, as the parent of a picky eater, you can take advantage of that fact with this spaghetti. This recipe is easy to make and makes a lot of food, but it freezes well so you can easily keep it on hand.

Preparation time: *30 minutes*

Yield: *Seven 1-cup servings*

1 pound ground beef	*1 carrot, thinly sliced*
1 tablespoon garlic salt	*1 small zucchini, thinly sliced*
1 tablespoon Italian seasoning	*26-ounce jar plain spaghetti sauce*
Olive oil	*1-pound box spaghetti, any variety, cooked*
4-ounce can mushrooms, sliced	

1 In a medium saucepan, brown the hamburger meat. Drain the excess fat. Add the garlic and Italian seasoning. Stir well and set aside.

2 Lightly coat the bottom of a large frying pan with olive oil. Sauté the mushrooms, carrot, and zucchini together until they turn slightly brown, about 7 minutes.

3 Add the spaghetti sauce to the frying pan and stir. Add the hamburger meat. Stir well, and after the mixture is hot and bubbly, remove from the heat.

4 In a large bowl, stir together the sauce mixture and the pasta. Serve.

Chicken Whips

This recipe combines chicken pieces, veggies, and mushroom soup in mashed potatoes for a delicious "pie." Consider having your child help make this dish. Chicken Whips freeze well for later use.

Preparation time: *15 minutes*

Cooking time: *20 minutes*

Tools: *Custard cups*

Yield: *7 servings*

Cooking spray	*¼ pound shredded American cheese (about ½ cup)*
16-ounce package frozen mixed vegetables	
2 cups cooked chicken breast, cubed	*2½ cups prepared mashed potatoes (can be instant)*
10½-ounce can condensed cream of mushroom soup	

1 Preheat the oven to 350 degrees.

2 Spray the custard cups with nonstick cooking spray and place on a cookie sheet.

3 Prepare the mixed vegetables according to the package directions. Mix the veggies, chicken, soup, and cheese in a large bowl.

4 Spoon the mixture evenly into custard cups (about ¾ cup per custard cup) and top with mashed potatoes (about ½ cup per custard cup).

5 Place the cookie sheet in the oven and bake for 20 minutes. Serve warm.

Homemade Fish Sticks

Picky eaters often reduce themselves to eating only a few items, and fish sticks tend to be one of those items. You can replace the store-bought frozen box of fish sticks with this homemade, healthy version and feel good about your child's fixation on them. (You can also freeze your healthy sticks for a quick meal later.)

Preparation time: *20 minutes*

Cooking time: *8 to 10 minutes*

Yield: *5 servings (2 fish sticks per serving)*

1⅓ pound fresh cod	*½ cup dry breadcrumbs*
⅓ cup whole milk	*¼ teaspoon salt*
½ cup cornflakes	*Olive oil for cooking*

1 Preheat oven to 425 degrees.

2 Cut the cod into strips, roughly 4 inches long by ½ inch thick. Soak the strips in the milk.

3 In a food processor, mix the cornflakes, breadcrumbs, and salt. Dump the processed mixture in a bowl, and roll the fish strips in the mixture.

4 Place strips on a lightly oiled cookie sheet and bake for 8 to 10 minutes or until crispy and firm.

☞ Hidden Treasure Mac and Cheese

Vegetables are one of the biggest problems with picky children — they tend to avoid those veggies like the plague! However, even the pickier children typically eat mac and cheese — and this recipe hides the veggies. Shhhh! Don't tell!

Preparation time: *20 minutes*

Yield: *Six ½-cup servings*

7¼-ounce box macaroni and cheese,   1 cup frozen mixed vegetables
any variety

1 Cook the mac and cheese according to the package directions.

2 While the mac and cheese is cooking, cook the mixed vegetables on the stovetop or in the microwave. Be careful not to overcook.

3 Stir mac and cheese and vegetables together and serve warm.

☞ Breadsticks and Homemade Pizza Sauce

Children often like meals where they can dip their food. This quick recipe is sure to be a hit. You may also use this recipe to serve as a side dish to go along with any Italian meal.

Preparation time: *10 minutes*

Yield: *Breadsticks: About 7 servings (2 sticks per serving); Sauce: Eight ¼-cup servings*

6-ounce can tomato paste   ½ teaspoon garlic salt

8-ounce can tomato sauce   ¼ cup grated, fresh Parmesan cheese

¼ teaspoon dried oregano   ¼ teaspoon minced fresh parsley

¼ teaspoon brown sugar   3 tablespoons butter

1 teaspoon minced garlic   1 loaf French bread

1 In a large saucepan, mix tomato paste, tomato sauce, oregano, brown sugar, minced garlic, garlic salt, Parmesan cheese, and parsley. Heat the mixture on the stove until it's warm. Set aside and serve as dip.

2 Melt the butter and brush it on the bread. Place the bread on a baking tray, and brown the French bread in a toaster oven. After the bread has browned, slice it into sticks.

Munchies That'll Groove You

Snacks are an important part of any child's diet. After all, your kids not only need three healthy meals a day, but also two healthy snacks in between meals. This schedule keeps their motors running and ensures the nutrition they need for a healthy and active lifestyle. If your child tends to be a picky eater, you'll enjoy putting these recipes to work.

 Smiley Apple

This munchie has visual appeal, which helps your child want to eat it. Children can even help make this recipe, which will hopefully encourage them to eat it as well. Smiley Apples are quick and fun to make.

Preparation time: *10 minutes*

Yield: *1 serving*

1 apple, any variety	*About 10 raisins*
1 teaspoon peanut butter, crunchy or smooth	

1 Cut a full slice of apple so it's a flat round shape. Make this slice as thick as possible but still flat on both sides.

2 Carve out the core of the slice and spread the peanut butter over one side of the apple.

3 Use the raisins to form eyes, nose, and a mouth. Serve.

> ***Vary It!*** *You can use miniature marshmallows for this recipe instead of raisins, but we prefer raisins because they're healthier. You can also use regular green grapes instead of the raisins. Just make sure you supervise because anything with grapes can be a choking hazard.*

☺ Hatching Chicks

This recipe gives you the taste of deviled eggs and some fun with its appearance. Kids love the look of these "hatching" deviled eggs. Have your toddler help you with this recipe. You'll both get some giggles out of the finished product. For a visual of what each egg should generally look like as you go through the steps, see Figure 14-1.

Preparation time: *25 minutes*

Yield: *6 servings*

6 hard boiled eggs, peeled	*1 teaspoon yellow mustard*
3 tablespoons mayonnaise or salad dressing	*12 green stuffed olive slices*
2 tablespoons dill or sweet relish	*Pepper to taste*

1 Cut the eggs in half lengthwise. Remove the yolks and place them in a medium bowl.

2 Mash the yolks with a fork and add the remaining ingredients, except the olive slices. Pepper to taste.

3 Carefully mound the mixture into 6 of the egg white halves.

4 Take one of the empty egg whites and cut slivers out of one side to give the egg white the appearance of being broken, as if a chick is breaking through.

5 Carefully place the empty egg white on top of a stuffed half, leaving a ¼-inch crack so the yellow appears. You're essentially tilting the top portion so you can see the yellow yolk inside through the opening, surrounded by the notches that you cut earlier.

6 Take two olive slices and put them in the crack so they'll resemble eyes. The idea is to make the chick appear to be looking out of the crack, as if it is about to hatch.

7 Repeat this process for the other eggs.

Figure 14-1:
An egg's metamorph-osis into a hatching chick.

☺ *Peanut Butter and Apple Toast*

This healthy snack (shown in the color section of this book) contains whole grain bread, peanut butter, and apple slices. The different shapes entice children and help your picky eater devour this wholesome snack.

Preparation time: *15 minutes*

Tools: *Various cookie cutters*

Yield: *3 servings*

3 pieces of whole-wheat bread	*2 tablespoons peanut butter, smooth*
Butter for spreading	*Finely sliced apple pieces*

1 Toast the bread in a toaster or toaster oven until lightly brown.

2 Using a cookie cutter, gently press the cutter into each piece of toast to cut the desired shape. Discard the extra pieces of bread.

3 Place each toast shape on a plate, lightly butter, and spread with 1 tablespoon of peanut butter over each piece of buttered toast. Place the apple slices as desired on top of the peanut butter and serve.

Tip: *If you don't want to throw out the extra bread trimmings, save them in a plastic bag and take your kids to a local pond to feed the ducks — yet another activity to do with your little ones.*

⏁ Cheese Bites

If you've ever tried toasted cheese bites (in the cracker aisle of your supermarket), you know how yummy they can be. Here's a homemade version your picky eater will love.

Preparation time: *15 minutes*

Chill time: *1 hour*

Cooking time: *20 minutes*

Yield: *4 servings (5 snacks per serving)*

2 cups flour	*16-ounce package shredded cheddar cheese*
1-ounce envelope of dry onion soup mix	*1 cup melted butter*

1 Combine all ingredients in a bowl. Mix together with your hands, then remove from the bowl and knead all the ingredients together on a floured counter until the mixture forms a stiff dough. (If you're not sure how to knead dough, check out Chapter 11 to find out.)

2 Divide the dough equally, and shape both parts into logs that are about ¾ inch in diameter.

3 Wrap each log in wax paper and chill the logs for 1 hour in the refrigerator until firm.

4 Preheat oven to 350 degrees.

5 Take the logs out of the refrigerator, and remove the wax paper. Cut the dough into ¼-inch slices. Bake slices on an ungreased cookie sheet for 20 minutes or until golden brown. Serve.

Sippable Sweets: Yummy Smoothies

Nutrition comes from many sources. You don't just have to feed your child solid foods. Many smoothies are fun to make and even more delicious to drink. If your son or daughter eats the same thing all the time, and varied nutrition worries you, consider the drink recipes in this section.

Summer Sun Smoothie

This smoothie recipe provides a heaping portion of vitamin C, and Summer Sun Smoothie tastes great — especially on hot summer days. To find out more about vitamin C and nutrition for kids, see Chapter 2.

Preparation time: *5 minutes*

Yield: *Two 1-cup servings*

1 cup orange juice	*½ cup vanilla yogurt*
½ cup grapefruit juice	*½ teaspoon vanilla extract*
Medium banana, ripe	

Place all the ingredients in a blender and blend until smooth. Serve immediately.

Carrot Pineapple Smoothie

This smoothie, which is delicious when served very cold, has the tangy zip of pineapple, but you get to add a veggie serving as well — possibly without your child even realizing it. It's perfect for a hot summer day, and it works as an alternative dessert after a meal.

Preparation time: *15 minutes*

Yield: *Two 1-cup servings*

¾ cup finely shredded carrot or pure carrot juice	*8-ounce can crushed pineapple, in its own juice*
1 cup water	*1 cup ice cubes*

1 Place the shredded carrot and water in a blender and blend for about a minute. If you're using carrot juice, pour into a blender and move to Step 3.

2 Strain mixture through a sieve or even a clean kitchen towel, collecting juice in a bowl. Return strained juice to the blender.

3 Add the pineapple and its juice along with the ice, and blend until smooth. Serve immediately.

Blueberry Banana Smoothie

This cold treat tempts the pickiest of eaters (as well as everyone else in your house). We love the blueberry-banana taste, and you'll be happy as a parent because you're providing two servings of fruit, plus a milk serving, all in one delicious smoothie.

Preparation time: 5 minutes

Yield: Two 1-cup servings

Medium banana, ripe	¾ cup whole milk
¾ cup fresh or frozen blueberries	Pinch of cinnamon
¼ cup full-fat vanilla yogurt	½ cup crushed ice

Place all the ingredients in a blender and blend until smooth. Serve cold.

Watermelon Strawberry Smoothie

There is something about watermelon and strawberries that just sounds like a treat on a hot summer day. Our family loves these smoothies out by the pool, but you'll find them perfect for just about any time of the year.

Preparation time: 10 minutes

Yield: Two 1-cup servings

4 cups ½-inch cubes seeded watermelon	1 cup fresh strawberries, cut into small pieces
½ pint strawberry sorbet	

Place all the ingredients in a blender and blend until smooth. Serve cold.

Chapter 15

Eating Away from Home

In This Chapter
▶ Making a plan
▶ Packing up your meals: Tips for transporting food
▶ Dealing with fast food
▶ Whipping up travel-friendly recipes

Ah, life on the run. Not that your life wasn't busy enough before kids, but now you move at lighting speed. You head out the door and think, "We'll grab something to eat on the way." That *something* almost always ends up as fast food, typically something fried. Sure, you have good intentions, but unless you're eating a healthy meal at Grandma's house, eating away from home will get you into nutritional trouble every time. Your life seems as though you're constantly rushing from one place to another, so how can you ever juggle your life and healthy meals successfully?

Great news! Armed with the right information and the recipes in this chapter, you'll make better decisions for your kids when you're running out the front door, because these recipes give you the ability to take healthy foods with you. Naturally, it's best if you eat at home as a family as much as possible, because doing so provides structure and a good learning environment for children. If activities or travels have you scrambling, though, you don't have to fall into the fast-food pit.

Best of all, you'll feel much better as a parent if you give your children healthy meals and snacks, even when an active schedule causes you a bit more work and planning. So if you've decided to go the extra mile, give yourself a nice pat on the back.

Planning Ahead

The greatest key to eating healthy outside your dining room is getting pre-pared ahead of time. After all, as you march through your daily routine, healthy meals and snacks won't fall into place without your careful attention and planning (and they certainly won't fall from the sky). The meals and snacks in this chapter all work well for eating while you're out and about, but they require that you prepare and package them beforehand, which you can easily do with just a bit of organization.

At the beginning of every week, sit down with a calendar and look at your schedule for that week. Think about work, school, and all the extracurricular activities. Identify your routine for each and then think in terms of your youngster's meals. Try to anticipate moments where you may need to be flex-ible with mealtime and meal options. If your schedule looks really busy, you may need to make a priority list and determine which activities are really important and which ones you can lose so that you have more time for family meals at home.

Fortunately, you can prepare some meals and snacks in advance of the day you need them, so it's helpful to plan out a menu for the week. In fact, every-one in your family is much more likely to eat healthy if you do so.

As you're organizing and planning meals, consider what meals need to be kept cool. Think carefully about your routine and decide whether a cold meal is convenient for you to transport.

Keeping Foods Cool or Warm en Route

You possibly grew up carrying your lunch to school, so the concept of trans-porting food may be nothing new to you. Plenty of resources exist today that can help you transport food for your children, and we discuss a handful of them in this section. Before we divulge the packaging details, though, we pro-vide some information to remember as you plan and pack Jimmy's meals.

Keep the following facts tucked in your memory when sending your child off with packed cold snacks or meals:

- ✔ Cold foods must be kept cold or they'll spoil — ideally, you should keep them at 40 degrees or less.

- ✔ Spoiled food can lead to salmonella poisoning and can even land your child in the hospital.

✔ Products with eggs and mayonnaise are particularly susceptible to spoiling if they don't stay cold.

✔ Cold foods can be moved to room temperature for 2 hours before you need to throw them away, and only 1 hour if the temperature is over 90 degrees.

What is the best way to transport meals and snacks so that they stay safe and cool? Check out these products and ideas, and you can find more information about different types of containers in Chapter 3:

✔ **Insulated, soft-sided lunch boxes or bags:** These items are the best for keeping food and snacks cold.

- Include a frozen gel pack or two to keep the temperature at a safe level.

- If you make the cold meal the night before, make sure that you keep it refrigerated. This step helps cool the bag down more quickly because the food is already cold.

- If you're sending along a juice box with other cold items, freeze the juice box the night before. The juice box then becomes another frozen item that will help keep the rest of the food cold and will thaw for drinking after a few hours.

✔ **Standard lunch boxes, bags, and thermoses:** These products work well for keeping nonperishable food items in a safe place, and you'll find plenty of options at your local department store or superstore.

✔ **Hard plastic containers:** Some foods can easily get crushed and ruined or may even leak.

✔ **Child-size thermos:** If you're taking along hot soup or a hot drink, a good child-size thermos with a cup is an excellent choice so your little one has something to drink out of.

As you're planning, remember to keep foods as simple as possible — now isn't the time to try that new casserole and bring it along. Also, as you prepare, don't forget about condiments, napkins, forks, and spoons!

When You Can't Avoid Fast Food

Fast food is just that — fast, and that's about it. The fast-food industry has managed to package a cheap and ever-present source of temptation for both kids and parents. After all, if you can just grab something from a fast-food restaurant, you save time.

However, giving in to this temptation all the time is the worst behavior you can follow in terms of your child's nutritional health. Now, we're not health-food nuts, and we let our children eat fast food from time to time, but all too often, fast food becomes a way of life in many families. Follow this rule: If you or your children eat fast food at least once every week, that's too often. Fast food should be a treat, not a main part of your child's diet routine.

Typical fast food contains high levels of saturated fat, over-processed carbo-hydrates, sugar, and sodium. It also tends to be calorie dense with little nutri-tional value. All things considered, nothing is good about fast food, except the taste (and that's how they reel you in).

Sometimes, though, you need to or choose to eat fast food, and if you find yourself in that situation, you should know how you can make better fast-food choices for your kids.

Consider the following tips:

- **Skip the drinks.** Fast-food restaurants often report that they make most of their money from soft drinks. Although most people love soft drinks, they're calorie dense, sugar laden, and provide no nutritional content at all. On top of that, the carbonation is bad for your teeth. Ask for water or milk instead.

- **Avoid chicken nuggets.** Have you ever thought, "I'll get little Suzie some chicken nuggets — at least they're healthier than other options"? It's a common trap because we know that chicken is a leaner meat. Yet, chicken nuggets from fast-food restaurants are deep-fried, which cancels out the fact that the meat hidden inside all the breading and grease is lean. (Keep in mind, too, that most chicken nuggets contain processed meat, which isn't nearly as good for you.)

- **Pass on the fries.** Yes, French fries taste great — thanks to grease and salt. In most cases, fast-food French fries contain little amounts of pota-toes, and in the end, you're essentially eating grease and salt with virtu-ally no nutritional value. In fact, French fries aren't a good meal option at home, either, because they're fried. Many fast-food restaurants provide substitutes, such as fruit cups, yogurt, side salads, and so on. Choose one of these options instead, but realize that even these items are often high in saturated fat due to dressings, nuts, and so forth, so be sure to pluck out the unhealthy parts and opt for lowfat dressings.

- **Look for grilled options.** If you stop for fast food, try to look for menu options that are lean and grilled. Some fast-food restaurants offer grilled lean chicken sandwiches and salads. Take advantage of these "adult" meals by taking an extra minute and cutting the grilled chicken into bite-size pieces. Fried chicken breasts or fried fish sandwiches aren't healthy meal options.

✔ **Make your burgers better.** Hamburgers aren't bad, but you can greatly improve the nutritional content of a burger with a couple of quick changes. First, order the burger with no mayonnaise (this cuts the fat content). Ask for extra veggies, such as lettuce and tomato, which balances the meal a bit. Be wary of special sauces and other condiments, which tend to add a lot of empty calories. Avoid burgers with bacon and/or more than one meat patty.

✔ **Watch portion sizes.** Everyone has a tendency to eat more at a restaurant or while traveling than at home. After all, when you walk into any restaurant, the plethora of choices is really tempting. When you're hungry, these choices can put you over the edge, not to mention the fact that you're paying a chunk of change, so you want to get your money's worth. So while you dine out, remember to think about portion sizes, and take home a doggy bag if you want. Like you, your child doesn't need to eat more at a fast-food restaurant than he eats at home, so order wisely.

✔ **Choose fast-food restaurants with more healthy options than their competitors.** You don't have to be a victim to what's on the menu. If you know you'll be eating more fast food than you should, spend a little time on the Internet and look at the menu options from the various fast-food restaurants in your area. Most of them give you nutritional information at their respective Web sites on the foods they serve. Choose the restaurants that give you the most flexibility and healthy options — a smart move for both you and your child.

Wholesome Snacks

In many cases, you need healthy snacks on hand that you can grab and then run. Even if you don't plan on eating a *meal* out, you still need to provide your child with a healthy snack midmorning or midafternoon. If you're planning to be away from home, use the quick and handy recipes in this section to prepare nutritious, portable snacks in advance.

Many of these recipes contain honey and nuts. Remember that children less than 1 year old shouldn't eat honey, and due to potential allergies and choking hazards, we recommend that children be at least 2 years old before eating peanuts.

☜ Grape and Nut Mix

This quick snack takes only moments to prepare and travels well, so it's perfect for road trips. This recipe yields only 1 cup, but you can easily increase the amount. However, keep in mind that grapes don't last very long, so don't mix up more than you need for any given outing.

Warning: Because this recipe contains nuts and grapes, it isn't appropriate for children under 2 years old. Carefully supervise older toddlers as they eat this snack to avoid a choking hazard.

Preparation time: *5 minutes*

Yield: *Two ½-cup servings*

¼ cup green seedless grapes

¼ cup purple seedless grapes

¼ cup mixed nuts

⅛ cup raisins

⅛ cup hulled sunflower seeds, unsalted

1 tablespoon honey

Wash and dry the grapes. Mix all the ingredients in a plastic storage container.

☜ Healthy, Nutty Snack Mix

This road-trip snack mix is a good snack for your child. Full of fiber and calories, it's healthy and filling. However, the recipe contains both popcorn and nuts, so it's a potential choking hazard. We recommend this snack mix for children near the age of 3 or older, and to minimize the danger of choking, we recommend that you stop off at the rest area of your choosing so your child can eat.

Preparation time: *5 minutes*

Yield: *Six ½-cup servings*

1 cup popped popcorn

½ cup O-shaped cereal

½ cup Grape-Nuts cereal

¼ cup raisins

½ cup mixed nuts

½ mini pretzels

½ teaspoon cinnamon

1 teaspoon sugar

Put all the ingredients in a large plastic storage bag, and then shake the bag well to blend the cinnamon and sugar with the rest of the ingredients.

⏱ Stuffed Logs

You may be familiar with the celery and peanut butter snack that you probably had as a kid growing up. This snack is a variation of that recipe with more dense calories and nutrition. As such, it works great as a heavy snack that your kids can take along with them when they're on the move, because it'll keep them full for a longer period of time!

Yield: 6 servings (½ celery stalk per serving)

3 celery stalks

¼ cup granola or Grape-Nuts cereal

6 tablespoons lowfat cream cheese

2 tablespoons raisins or hulled sunflower seeds (or a combination of both)

1 Wash and dry the celery stalks and cut each one in half widthwise.

2 Mix all the ingredients except the celery in a large bowl with a wooden spoon until well blended. Spoon the mixture into each celery stalk half. Serve.

⏱ Peanut Butter Cup and Apples

This lunch alternative is often met with a smile and it's a healthy and portable meal. Keep in mind that peanut butter can be a choking hazard, so offer this snack to older toddlers when you can supervise.

Preparation time: 10 minutes

Yield: Two ½-cup servings

½ cup peanut butter

1 tablespoon lowfat cream cheese

½ ripe banana, thinly sliced

1 apple, sliced in wedges

In a transportable, resealable plastic cup, combine the peanut butter, cream cheese, and banana. Mix well. Serve with the apple wedges, and you may want to include some celery sticks as well.

⌣ Nutty Veggie Dip

Children often like fresh veggies with dip because it gives them something to do with their hands. You can take this delicious nutty dip on the road, but make sure that you serve it at a rest stop, or you just might have dip on the back of your seat, on the inside of the window, and all over your child!

Preparation time: *15 minutes*

Yield: *Two ½-cup servings*

½ cup mayonnaise

½ cup sour cream

½ envelope zesty Italian seasoning

2 tablespoons ground pecans

1 In a small bowl, blend all the ingredients together until smooth.

2 Put the dip in a resealable travel bowl. Serve it with mixed raw veggies such as celery, carrots, broccoli, and cauliflower. You can also serve this dip in individual portions by using smaller storage cups.

Pickle Wraps

Although this lunch wrap may sound odd, kids often love the tangy taste of pickles mixed with smooth cream cheese.

Preparation time: *10 minutes*

Yield: *2 servings*

2 whole kosher dill pickles

1 tablespoon lowfat cream cheese, divided

2 thin slices deli-style turkey breast

Dry the pickles completely with a paper towel, and then spread ½ tablespoon of cream cheese all over each pickle. Depending on the size of the pickles, you may need a bit more cream cheese. You can also spread the cream cheese on the turkey slice instead of the pickle, if you find that approach easier. Wrap each pickle in a slice of turkey breast. Keep cool until serving.

Wrapped Hard-Boiled Egg

This quick-to-prepare food functions well as a heavy snack or a full meal when you're on the road, because it's easy to transport.

Preparation time: *15 minutes*

Yield: *1 serving*

1 hard-boiled egg	*1 slice whole-wheat bread*
1 tablespoon chopped ham	*1 tablespoon honey*
1 teaspoon slivered almonds	

1 Slice the hardboiled egg in half widthwise. In each egg half, scoop out about half the yolk and discard it.

2 Fill each side of the egg with the ham and almonds.

3 Smear the bread with honey on one side.

4 Press the egg back together and place it on the bread, quickly wrapping the bread around the egg. You can use a long toothpick to hold the snack together until serving, or wrap it tightly with plastic wrap. If you use a toothpick, make sure that you remove it prior to serving.

Sandwiches and Other Tummy Fillers

Sandwiches are a natural option when you're moving about because they're so portable. Sure, you can serve the standard PB&J, but these sandwiches and other portable meals give you some different, tasty options.

Ham and Pear Sandwiches

The crunchy taste of the pear keeps this sandwich from being anything but ordinary. We've found that the sweet taste of the pear mixes well with the ham, and your child is bound to like it.

Preparation time: *10 minutes*

Yield: *2 servings*

1 tablespoon lowfat cream cheese	*2 slices ripe pear*
2 slices sandwich bread (try oatmeal bread)	*2 slices deli-style ham*

1 Spread the cream cheese on both pieces of bread.

2 Add the pear and ham slices, and then put the two pieces of bread together to form the sandwich. Cut the sandwich into squares or other shapes as desired.

Tip: Gather your favorite cookie cutters and cut this sandwich into different shapes. Your children will love sandwiches the visual appeal.

Avocado Chicken Sandwiches

This sandwich is one of our kids' favorites, and it's very healthy. We love using avocados because they're easy to digest, they taste great, and they're vitamin dense. Combine avocado with lean chicken and you'll feel great that you're giving your child plenty of protein and vitamins in this quick and easy sandwich.

Preparation time: *10 minutes*

Yield: *2 servings*

1 tablespoon mayonnaise or mustard	*2 thin slices ripe avocado*
2 slices whole-wheat bread	*1 thin slice tomato*
2 thin slices cooked chicken breast	

1 Evenly spread the mayonnaise or mustard over both slices of bread.

2 Stack the chicken, avocado, and tomato on one slice of bread, top it with the other slice, and cut into squares or other shapes as desired.

Stuffed Croissant

Croissants are always a great choice because they're a bit different from your ordinary square bread and work great for any mixture that you want to stuff inside to make a sandwich. The turkey and cream cheese mixture tastes like a combo from a specialty deli — but you can make it quickly in your kitchen. You may want to make an extra one for yourself!

Preparation time: *10 minutes*

Yield: *1 serving*

2 deli-style slices turkey breast	*1 croissant roll*
1 tablespoon lowfat cream cheese	*1 tablespoon finely chopped tomato*
1 teaspoon finely chopped almonds	*2 thick slices ripe avocado*

1 On one piece of turkey breast, spread the cream cheese and sprinkle the almonds.

2 Place the second slice of turkey breast on top and roll it up.

3 Cut a lengthwise slit down one side of the croissant.

4 Put the turkey roll, tomato, and avocado inside the croissant and press down a bit to close the croissant.

Turkey Roll-Ups

These roll-ups provide the nutrition of an entire meal, not just a snack. All the ingredients are healthy. In fact, these roll-ups are a great snack for adults as well, so pack a few extras for yourself.

Preparation time: *15 minutes*

Yield: *2 servings (2 roll-ups per serving)*

8-ounce package lowfat cream cheese

4 10-inch flour or whole-wheat tortillas

4 slices deli-style turkey

⅓ head lettuce, any variety

½ cup shredded carrots, divided

1 cup shredded cheddar cheese, divided

1 Spread the cream cheese evenly over one side of each tortilla, and then tear the turkey slices into bite-size pieces.

2 Line the tortillas with lettuce, and then sprinkle the turkey pieces, carrots, and cheese evenly over each tortilla. Roll up the tortillas and keep them cool until serving.

Peanut Butter and Banana Wraps

This very filling on-the-go lunch is a favorite with kids and parents as well — and it's a cinch to prepare. Remember that peanut butter is a choking risk, so supervise your child as he eats this snack.

Preparation time: *10 minutes*

Yield: *2 servings*

4 tablespoons smooth peanut butter

2 tablespoons lowfat cream cheese

2 flour or whole-wheat tortillas

1 large banana, thinly sliced

1 Spread the peanut butter and cream cheese evenly over each tortilla.

2 Add the thin banana slices.

3 Roll up each tortilla tightly. You can cut the tortillas into pieces for easier transporting.

⏱ Bagel Pizzas

This lunch "pizza" is a healthy alternative to your typical Italian fare. This recipe uses nuts, which you may remove if you want to feed this meal to a younger child. However, bagels, as with any dense bread, can be a choking hazard for younger children, so use caution and supervise your child when she eats this wholesome meal.

Preparation time: *10 minutes*

Yield: *2 servings*

1 bagel (any kind, but plain typically works best)

2 tablespoons cream cheese

¼ cup finely chopped veggies

1 tablespoon chopped pecans

1 Cut the bagel in half and evenly spread the cream cheese on each half.

2 Sprinkle the chopped veggies over each half and add the pecans. Wrap individually in foil for easy transport.

Not Your Average Salads

Salads are a great on-the-run option because you can contain them in a bowl and avoid the mess that you get with some meals. In this section, we provide salads with balanced nutrition that are not only delicious but also filling. In fact, you'll enjoy many of them, so make extra for yourself!

Grilled Chicken and Pasta Salad

This cold salad is perfect when you're out on the town. Grilled chicken and pasta always make a good combination, and you can feel good about the protein, healthy carbs, and vitamins your child gets from this easy-to-make salad.

Preparation time: *20 minutes*

Yield: *Two 1¼-cup servings*

½ grilled chicken breast, cut in small chunks

2 cups cooked corkscrew pasta, drained

2 tablespoons Italian dressing

2 tablespoons shredded mozzarella cheese

1 tablespoon chopped walnuts

Toss all the ingredients in a resealable plastic travel bowl. You may add a bit more Italian dressing if desired. Keep this salad cool until serving.

Bow-Tie Chicken Salad

We love this cold salad during the summertime, and so do our kids. The mandarin oranges provide an extra zing, making this salad quite refreshing.

Preparation time: *10 minutes*

Yield: *Three 1-cup servings*

½ skinless, boneless chicken breast, grilled and cut in small pieces

2 cups cooked bow-tie pasta, drained

¼ cup mandarin oranges, drained

2 tablespoons balsamic salad dressing

2 tablespoons shredded mozzarella cheese

¼ cup chopped tomato

Toss all the ingredients in a resealable plastic travel bowl and keep it cool until serving. You may add a bit more dressing if desired.

☺ Fruit Pasta Salad

This cold salad with fruit is perfect for any lunch. The salty nuts and the fruit make a surprisingly good combination, and your child will love this salad as a meal or even as a side dish or snack.

Preparation time: 10 minutes

Yield: Three 1-cup servings

2 cups cooked corkscrew pasta, drained

2 tablespoons raspberry or strawberry salad dressing

1 cup mixed fruit chunks, such as orange, apple, strawberry, and kiwi

1 tablespoon chopped peanuts

Toss all the ingredients in a resealable plastic travel bowl and keep it cool until serving. You may add a bit more dressing if desired.

Sweet Sides for Sweetie Pies

Yes, we love sweets, and there's nothing wrong with them in moderation. And the great news is that you can prepare sweet treats for travel and still keep them healthy. We provide a balance of both in this section, and we think your kids will eat them up (in both senses of the word).

Fruit Bowl

Fruit is often a good snack because it satisfies a sweet tooth and is a healthy alternative to snack cakes and other sweets.

Preparation time: 15 minutes

Yield: Two 1-cup servings

10 seedless grapes, cut in half

½ orange, peeled and cut in small wedges

½ apple, cored and cut in small wedges

¼ cup pineapple chunks

2 tablespoons apple juice

Mix all the ingredients in a large plastic bowl. If you want smaller servings, transfer contents to individual, sealable serving dishes. Keep the fruit cool until serving.

Peanut Butter Balls

This recipe is rather common; you often see it during the holiday season. The coconut adds a boost to the flavor (and helps keep the balls together). Because this dessert is in a ball shape, it's a choking hazard for young children. We recommend that you reserve this dessert for children 3 years and older, but still supervise their eating even for this age.

This recipe makes 3 dozen Peanut Butter Balls, so freeze the extras for quick use when you're in a hurry.

Preparation time: *15 minutes*

Chill time: *15 minutes*

Yield: *12 servings (3 treats per serving)*

1 cup creamy peanut butter	*1 cup shredded coconut*
2 sticks butter, softened	*¼ cup chopped pecans*
16-ounce box confectioners' sugar	*¼ cup crushed graham crackers*

1 In a microwavable bowl, melt the peanut butter and butter until you can stir them together. Set aside.

2 In a large bowl, mix the remaining ingredients with a wooden spoon until the mixture is well blended. Pour the peanut butter and butter mixture on top and stir until well mixed.

3 Form the mixture into 1-inch balls and place them on a cookie sheet lined with wax paper.

4 Refrigerate until cold and the snacks set up, about 15 minutes. Individually wrap each ball in plastic wrap so the snacks don't stick together, and keep the balls cold until serving.

Apricot Fruit Chews

Fruit chews are a good option for traveling because they're easy to transport. We love this homemade variety because they have a tangy taste, which your kids will undoubtedly love. Although these treats are perfect for dessert, they also work well as a snack any time.

Preparation time: *15 minutes*

Chill time: *15 minutes*

Yield: *10 servings (2 treats per serving)*

1 cup dried apricots	*¼ cup honey*
⅓ cup wheat-flake cereal	*Nonstick cooking spray*
½ ounce unsweetened chocolate, melted	*½ cup chopped pecans*

1 In a medium pot, place the apricots in 4 cups of boiling water. Remove the pot from heat and let it stand for 5 minutes.

2 Remove the apricots from the pot, drain the water, and place the fruit in a food processor. Add the cereal and puree until the mixture is coarse.

3 In a small bowl, mix the apricot and cereal mixture with the chocolate and honey.

4 Spray your hands lightly with the nonstick cooking spray and shape the mixture into 1-inch balls. Roll each ball in the pecans and place them on a cookie sheet lined with wax paper. Chill in the refrigerator until cold, about 15 minutes, and keep cold until serving.

Part VI
The Part of Tens

The 5th Wave   By Rich Tennant

"Actually, it's not party ice, it's homemade baby food I keep in ice trays. Why?"

In this part . . .

Every *For Dummies* book has a Part of Tens — a section with quick and helpful lists arranged in, what do you know, groups of ten (or so). Our Part of Tens is no exception to that rule, so in Part VI, we impart our top ten timesaving tips for busy parents and ten ways to get your child to try new foods.

Chapter 16

Ten Timesavers and Tips for Busy Parents

- -

- -

*W*e know what you're thinking: "I've read this book and the information is great, but how do I juggle cooking, my job, and taking care of my baby, my house, my car, my other children . . ." and the list goes on. We understand; after all, we're working parents as well.

Cooking your child's meals can be a time-consuming task, but with a few tips and tactics tucked in your hat, you'll be able to cook healthy meals without it becoming a huge time problem.

Cook in Advance

Cooking for family and for a child requires one simple task — planning. If you plan your meals, you'll also organize your time, and you'll find that cooking for your child as well as any other family members doesn't have to be a mountainous chore.

You may notice that throughout this book we've included many recipes that freeze well, and time is the main reason. Your time is precious. Follow these steps to help make your meal planning successful:

✔ Get a calendar with a lot of writing space.

- Purchase one.

- Print some pages off the Internet.

- Make a calendar from your desktop publishing software.

✔ Make a family meal outline for the week.
  • Plan every day and every meal if possible.
  • Find a certain day or evening that serves as your "cook" time.

With a just a couple of hours, you can cook most of the meals for the week and simply freeze them. If you can find a large block of time to cook and prepare future meals, then you can simply reheat your food and serve it without much fuss. This way, your entire week is planned out and your meals are ready at once with no more asking yourself, "What in the world will I cook tonight?"

Cook Multiple Portions

More is less (in this case at least). Many of the recipes in this book cook more than one serving. That's great, because if the recipe can be frozen, you can automatically gain a meal here and there just by cooking a recipe that feeds multiple people. A few extra ingredients to multiply a batch will save you time because you're making more food and creating less work for yourself later in the days, weeks, and months to come.

Combine Easy and More Difficult

Some of the recipes in this book are a real snap — they'll only take a few minutes to complete. Some are more complicated and will take a bit longer. When we cook, we try to combine easy recipes with difficult recipes. For example, if the meat recipe is more involved, we try to fix easy sides. Or, if we cook a more difficult side, we try and make sure the meat recipe is quick and easy. This way, you're cooking good food, but you aren't overwhelming yourself with three or four complicated recipes at each cooking session. In every meal, always try to combine easy and more difficult recipes to save some time for you to relax after the kids have gone to bed.

Plan One-Dish Recipe Night

Because you're cooking for your child (and probably other family members), it's a good idea to plan a "one-dish recipe night" each week. This simply means that the dish for the night is something that has both meat and vegetables cooked together so you can avoid having any side dishes. This method cuts down on the amount of work as well as the amount of freezer space required to store meals. One-dish recipes also cut down on the amount of dishes for cleanup.

Keep in mind that this suggestion only works with older toddlers who've started sharing meals with the family.

Keep Lunch Quick and Easy

Try to keep lunch healthy and simple, preferably something that can be easily heated in the microwave. Keep in mind that you shouldn't strive to cook overly complicated lunches every day — they simply take up too much time. That's why most of the lunch recipes in this book are rather easy. Reserve lunchtime, at least a few days a week, as a quick and easy affair.

Limit Shopping to Once a Week

Many cooks have a bad habit of running to the grocery store three or more times a week. The back and forth costs you extra money and certainly time. A better method is to get organized and know what you'll need for the week, and then buy everything in one trip. This way, you're much more likely to have what you really need, avoiding extra time-eating trips and impulse buys. Develop a list throughout the week as you plan meals and notice that you've run out of certain staple items.

If something is on sale that you use often and you have the storage space, stock up! Don't forget to clip coupons — we save money on groceries every time we shop just by spending a few minutes clipping coupons each week. Take advantage of the savings!

Don't go to the grocery store hungry. If you're stocking up to feed the family for the week, an extra item here and there may not seem too bad. But those impulse items you pull off the shelf, especially when you're hungry, can add up to big bucks spent at the checkout. Try to stick to your list and eat at least a snack before going to the store.

Be Mindful of Appliances

When you cook for your child, be mindful what appliances you'll need. When your baby is little, you'll need a food processor frequently, but as your child grows and the recipes become more involved, you'll need a variety of appliances. As you're planning your menu, try to think about what appliances and even cookware you'll need and make sure they're varied. In other words, if you're trying to cook several recipes at once, you want to make sure that you don't need to use the same appliance over and over because this will slow you down — you'll need to wait and wash the appliance several times. Again, plan carefully! See Chapter 3 for help and information about kitchen appliances.

Get Ready Before You Cook

Before you start cooking a meal or multiple meals, get your kitchen ready.

- ✔ Make sure that you have ample time to prepare the recipes that you want to cook.
- ✔ Make sure that you have everything you'll need.
- ✔ Check your recipes against the ingredients you have, and don't forget to check the cookware and cooking tools you'll need to make sure you have them.

 Regularly ensure that simple things like emptying the dishwasher and cleaning up the kitchen happen at your house. This habit ensures that everything is in order before you start so you don't have to stop cooking to do other tasks.

Clean as You Go

It's always tempting to focus on cooking and not on cleaning (after all, cooking is more fun). However, you'll save time if you clean up as you go. Don't get in the habit of cooking entire meals and letting the pots and pans stack up to the ceiling. Once you get behind on the dishes, it feels like it takes forever to catch up. This wastes time that you may not necessarily have, so get in the habit of cooking and cleaning as you work. You'll end up with wonderful meals and a clean kitchen at the same time — and that's good news for everyone.

 Cleanup is typically easier when you measure out all the ingredients and then put them away. This technique prevents clutter, which causes a mess, and also allows things, such as milk, to go back in the fridge (to prevent spoiling). Also, if your child is old enough to help you, give your child a task; it will speed things along and help you keep things clean as you cook.

Team Up

You don't have to go it alone! If you have a friend or neighbor who's also cooking for a child the same age as yours, consider teaming up. You and your friend can get together and cook meals, making the event a social time, or you can consider trading foods each week. Try to plan your weekly meals together, and then share the cooking responsibilities and food. It can save you a lot of time and it can be a lot of fun! Your kids can also play together and keep each other occupied so you don't have to worry about whether your child is bored while you're creating a week's worth of meals in the kitchen.

Chapter 17

Ten Tips to Get Your Child to Try New Foods

*N*aturally, as a parent, you want to make sure that your child gets the nutrition that he needs, so you try to introduce new and healthy foods. However, what do you do when your child reaches that age where he refuses to try anything new? Let's face it: Many children are picky at certain times when it comes to food. It's important to keep in mind that your little tyke may be resistant to new and different foods, and some kids box themselves into a place where they only want to eat one or two food items. This behavior is often frustrating for parents, but it's important to keep in mind that the behavior is normal. In fact, most children go through various stages of pickiness with their food. You can help overcome this hurdle with the tips in this chapter. So, before you pull your hair out, relax, take a deep breath, grab a cup of tea, and read this chapter.

Choose the Right Time

Half the battle of getting your child to try a new food is knowing when to introduce that new food. If you're trying to expand your child's food repertoire or just trying to get your child to eat more than two or three food items at any given meal, make sure that you introduce the new foods or try to expand your child's diet at the right time of day. This time is often at lunch or dinner.

Lunch or dinner is often the best time to try and introduce a new food because your child is the hungriest after hours of playtime. At either meal, use this naturally hungry time to push beyond the pickiness barriers.

It's important to avoid any snacks or drinks other than water for at least an hour before lunch or dinner, and strive to make lunch and dinner sit-down meals — not something you do while watching television or performing some other activity. Gathering around the kitchen table gives you the best option to offer new foods when your child is naturally hungry. Also, make sure that you offer some familiar foods along with the new food. This process helps make the meals easier for your child.

Control the "Fill Factor"

Do you ever think of your child as a panhandler? Think again! One mistake parents often make with a picker eater is they end up letting the child control in-between mealtime snacks and drinks. Your child needs healthy snacks in between meals (and we've provided lots of recipes for them in this book). However, your child also manipulates the "fill factor" with milk and juice.

The scenario goes something like this: Your child picks at lunch. Forty-five minutes later, your child asks for a glass of milk or juice. You provide it. Your child nibbles at his snack, but asks for more milk or juice half an hour later. What is happening is that your child is tanking up on milk and juice instead of having to eat food. And you're letting him! This isn't what you want because your child isn't getting balanced nutrition.

Take a firm stand and offer only water in between meals and snacks. We recommend milk with snacks. You actually want your child to be hungry when it's time to eat.

Mix Old Foods with New Foods

One helpful tactic to try and introduce new foods into your kid's diet is to make certain that you serve your child foods that she likes when you're introducing the new foods. In other words, never try to get your child to eat several new or different foods at the same time during a picky eating phase because the newness can be overwhelming to your child, and she may resist you the entire way.

The best approach is to give your child a few foods that she likes and a new or different food. Place bites of the familiar food with the new food on the highchair tray as your child eats. Many times, children discover that they like the new food if you can just get them to actually try and taste it.

Remember, pickiness is more about a mental attitude than anything else. At this age, your child is managing the world around her. Naturally, food can become a source of control. As parents, it's important to keep your cool, relax, and remember that this behavior is normal. As your child discovers new foods and has the option of trying them with foods she already likes, she'll be less likely to resist.

Incorporate Condiments

Have you ever watched small children eat French fries when you're out at a restaurant? They methodically dip each fry in a glop of ketchup and lick the ketchup off the fry and go back in for another dip. They may not eat the fry until the ketchup is gone. If your child likes condiments, such as ketchup or even mustard, by all means take advantage of this preference when you introduce new foods. Don't add a huge pile of ketchup, but instead, place a small dollop of the condiment on the plate and show your child how to dip the new food in it. Naturally, condiments don't necessarily go with every food that you may want to introduce, but if you can, use a condiment to help your child be creative and adventurous with his meals.

Watch Out for Texture

When your child is in a picky eating phase, she may be overly sensitive to different food textures. As adults, we tend to think about food in terms of taste, but in fact, the texture of food has a lot to do with our likes and dislikes. As a child, many textures may take some getting used to. Many children like things that go "crunch," but tend to be wary of dishes that seem slimy, saucy, or overly complicated in terms of different textures. So as you introduce foods, take note of how your child reacts. If the food is rejected at first, feed a familiar food; then go back to the new textured food later. If your child rejects the food all together, you may need to hold off on serving that particular item for a few more weeks.

You can help with this issue by slowly adding foods with differing textures, at least during this picky eating phase. It may seem odd, at least it was to us, but our youngest child wouldn't eat most bread, unless the bread was well toasted. There was something about the texture of soft bread that she didn't like. She eventually decided that she liked untoasted French bread, however, and once she accepted it, she finally moved on to other breads as well.

Realize that all kids are different and this "texture issue phase" will pass with time. Just keep offering foods with different textures and allow your child to experiment with them.

Create a Visual Sensation

Like adults, children weigh the visual impact of food pretty heavily. Children resist trying new foods that don't look appetizing, and if we're honest, adults are much the same way — why do you think those expensive gourmet meals are presented in such cool designs?

You don't have to spend all day trying to come up with something new, but as the opportunity arises, put some creativity into your child's meals. To entice your tot, try these suggestions:

- ✔ Create shapes with veggies and other foods.
- ✔ Arrange the food on the plate in a creative fashion.
- ✔ Use fruit and cheese to make a smiley face on a plate or even make a cat or dog face. Our kids loved this approach and we've used it to sneak in new foods.

Take every advantage to make your child's meals have a fun, creative impact. If your child is old enough to help prepare the meal and creatively display it, let him — he may be more open to eating the food in the meal.

Liven Up the Plates and Spoons

Here's a helpful tactic: Get your child a plate, spoon, and fork that he really likes. In fact, let him pick it out. When you're kid is eating a new food, be sure to use his favorite plate and utensils. Once again, picky eating is more of a mental block than any real issue concerning the food (see Chapter 14 for more on that topic), and in many cases, a favorite plate, spoon, and fork help your child be more positive about the eating experience. In fact, this is empowering for your child.

You'll find plenty of fun and festive plates, bowls, forks, and spoons at most department stores or at your local superstore. Look for your child's favorite cartoon characters and even movie figures; have your child help pick out his plate, bowl, and utensils and explain that he'll be using these to eat his meals.

Invent Mealtime Games

You're probably familiar with the game parents play with their young children to help them eat: the airplane. You know, you make airplane noises and fly the spoon around until it reaches your child's mouth, and your kid sits there with his mouth closed and looks at you like you're the idiot (the airplane usually only works on infants just starting to eat). As your child ages, you can continue to put simple games to work if your child is having a tough time with a picky phase.

As your child learns how to count, have your child count bites (but not to reach a goal of a particular number of bites) with you and practice verbal skills with the names of the different foods. These tactics often help distract your child from his position of not eating and get him a bit more interested in trying something new. Keep everything positive and keep mealtime a good time. Here are a few examples to get you started:

- ✔ **Name the food:** Play a game where your child tries to name every food being served (and this gives you a chance to teach new foods). For combination dishes, see if he can name some of the individual ingredients. After your toddler starts learning the names, you can also teach him what food group the food belongs to.

- ✔ **Counting games:** Try to use various counting games. Have your child count the number of beans on his plate, or count the number of bites he's taken. The idea is to get his mind off the concept of eating and over to the concept of counting.

- ✔ **Round robin storytelling:** You'll need everyone in your family to play along. This game starts with the parent. The parent gives a starting line for a made up story, such as "Once upon a time there was an alligator." The parent then takes a bite of food. Next, your child has to add a sentence to the story, "And the alligator lived in a swamp." Then your child has to take a bite. This game can go around and around the table. Everyone plays, but most importantly, everyone eats while they're playing!

Make a Food Chart

You may not realize it, but children are meticulous by nature. They often like to organize and count, and they tend to see life in "black and white," concrete terms. Put this developmental behavior to work with a chart of foods.

Create a chart on a piece of poster board with listings of the foods in MyPyramid for Kids (in fact, make the chart to look like a pyramid). You can spice up this chart by using pictures of the various foods. Then, pick up some adhesive gold stars and simply star the foods that your child has already tried. Then, as your child tries a new food, place a star on the chart next to the food.

As your child looks at the poster, he may not like the fact that some stars are missing. So, when you want to introduce a new food, you can talk about how your child will get a star. Filling the poster with stars appeals to your child's meticulous nature and it will help expand his range of food options. We know of several people who've tried this approach with picky eaters and have ended up with kids who are much more open to trying something new.

Model Positive Behavior

It's always helpful to model good behavior for your child. When your family makes a meal, have everyone (including older siblings — young children often want to do what their older siblings do) eat the same foods that your little ones are eating. You may even want to talk about the ingredients in the meal. Try to pique your youngster's interest. This modeling behavior helps your child to be more open to trying foods, thus reducing the pickiness factor. However, don't use this time as a "sales conference" to try and get your child to eat. Model eating behavior, but don't try to convince your child to try it just because you're eating it.

Part VII
Appendixes

The 5th Wave   By Rich Tennant

"You've either lost the lid to the blender, or you're introducing solid food to the baby."

In this part . . .

When it comes to their kids, all parents can use extra help and guidance from time to time — if you're part of that club, you've come to the right place. In this part, you find three helpful appendixes that make your baby-food-making journey easier. In Appendix A, we provide a measurement conversion chart that shows you how to convert teaspoons, tablespoons, cups, and so forth, to different measurements. In Appendix B, we give you a handy collection of food logs where you can track new foods that you feed your child, when you feed them, your child's reaction (to watch for possible allergies or intolerances), and his or her likes and dislikes. To help you organize your baby's meals for a week, in Appendix C, we cap off the book by laying out some suggested menus, divided by age, that use the recipes in this book.

Appendix A

Metric Conversion Guide

· ·

*N*ote: The recipes in this cookbook weren't developed or tested using metric measures. There may be some variation in quality when converting to metric units.

Common Abbreviations

Abbreviation(s)	What It Stands For
C, c	cup
g	gram
kg	kilogram
L, l	liter
lb	pound
mL, ml	milliliter
oz	ounce
pt	pint
t, tsp	teaspoon
T, TB, Tbl, Tbsp	tablespoon

Volume

U.S. Units	Canadian Metric	Australian Metric
¼ teaspoon	1 milliliter	1 milliliter
½ teaspoon	2 milliliters	2 milliliters
1 teaspoon	5 milliliters	5 milliliters
1 tablespoon	15 milliliters	20 milliliters

(continued)

Volume *(continued)*

U.S. Units	Canadian Metric	Australian Metric
¼ cup	50 milliliters	60 milliliters
⅓ cup	75 milliliters	80 milliliters
½ cup	125 milliliters	125 milliliters
⅔ cup	150 milliliters	170 milliliters
¾ cup	175 milliliters	190 milliliters
1 cup	250 milliliters	250 milliliters
1 quart	1 liter	1 liter
1½ quarts	1.5 liters	1.5 liters
2 quarts	2 liters	2 liters
2½ quarts	2.5 liters	2.5 liters
3 quarts	3 liters	3 liters
4 quarts	4 liters	4 liters

Weight

U.S. Units	Canadian Metric	Australian Metric
1 ounce	30 grams	30 grams
2 ounces	55 grams	60 grams
3 ounces	85 grams	90 grams
4 ounces (¼ pound)	115 grams	125 grams
8 ounces (½ pound)	225 grams	225 grams
16 ounces (1 pound)	455 grams	500 grams
1 pound	455 grams	½ kilogram

Measurements

Inches	Centimeters
½	1.5
1	2.5

Inches	Centimeters
2	5.0
3	7.5
4	10.0
5	12.5
6	15.0
7	17.5
8	20.5
9	23.0
10	25.5
11	28.0
12	30.5
13	33.0

Temperature (Degrees)

Fahrenheit	Celsius
32	0
212	100
250	120
275	140
300	150
325	160
350	180
375	190
400	200
425	220
450	230
475	240
500	260

Appendix B

Food Logs

*T*hroughout this book, we talk a lot about introducing new foods. After all, as your child grows, you increasingly expand his food options and choices, and variety is important. You don't want him to get bored with your cooking (and you want to emphasize healthy choices, of course). Naturally, you'll need to watch out for food allergies or intolerances as you serve your latest creations, and the handy charts you find in this appendix give you a quick and easy way to log what foods your child tries, and any reactions and preferences to certain foods. (Head to Chapter 13 for an in-depth look at the most common childhood allergies and intolerances.)

We've organized this appendix into five different logs — one for each of the different USDA food categories — so you can easily keep track of each food group. As your baby grows, you'll introduce new foods. Record the food in the appropriate food category log as a way to track your baby's new foods. Each food log contains the following categories:

- ✔ **Food:** Write down the name of the new food your child eats. Be specific. For example, in the log for Grains, don't just write "bread." Write down the specific kind. The specifics track the new food exactly.

- ✔ **Dates offered to child:** Include the initial date when you offered the food and jot down subsequent dates as well for the first few feedings.

- ✔ **Reaction? What type? Possible food allergy or intolerance:** After you offer a new food, watch closely for signs of allergies or intolerances. Record your findings in this column. In the event that an allergy or intolerance occurs, you'll have a detailed log to take to the doctor. Remember that you should offer a food for at least five consecutive days to rule out possible allergies or intolerances.

- ✔ **Like or dislike? Other foods preferred with:** Write down your child's preferences and note other foods served that made the new food acceptable. Children may need to try a new food several times in a row (some dieticians say ten times or more) before they take a liking to it.

- ✔ **Other observations:** Write down additional observations that you make.

Keep in mind that some foods are known problems for younger children. Never give a child under 1 year old honey because of the risk of botulism. Also, nuts, peanuts, peanut butter, and shellfish are all known allergens, and these should be avoided until age 2. See Chapter 2 for more about foods and potential allergen-causing foods.

Grains

Grain	Dates Offered to Child	Reaction? What Type? Possible Food Allergy or Intolerance?	Like or Dislike? Other Foods Preferred with?	Other Observations

Veggies

Vegetable	Dates Offered to Child	Reaction? What Type? Possible Food Allergy or Intolerance?	Like or Dislike? Other Foods Preferred with?	Other Observations

Fruits

Fruit	Dates Offered to Child	Reaction? What Type? Possible Food Allergy or Intolerance?	Like or Dislike? Other Foods Preferred with?	Other Observations

Milk Products

Milk Product	Dates Offered to Child	Reaction? What Type? Possible Food Allergy or Intolerance?	Like or Dislike? Other Foods Preferred with?	Other Observations

Meat and Beans

Meat or Bean	Dates Offered to Child	Reaction? What Type? Possible Food Allergy or Intolerance?	Like or Dislike? Other Foods Preferred with?	Other Observations

Appendix C

Sample Menus

• •

*T*his book contains a lot of delightful recipes that you can prepare for your young one. In case you're having a tough time getting started or want to ensure that your child gets a balanced diet, in this appendix we've included some helpful, seven-day menus built around the recipes and age brackets that you find in this book.

Remember to refer to the chapters where the recipes are pulled from for important information regarding food combining and introducing new foods. You can quickly locate the page a particular recipe is on by checking out the Recipes at a Glance section in the very front of this book. The Recipes at a Glance section lists every recipe in this book and the chapters they're in.

Meal Plans for 5- to 6-Month-Olds

During the 4- to 6-month age range, you begin serving cereals and introducing purees. Keep in mind that you should introduce new foods slowly because of allergy issues (see respective recipe chapters for more information), but after your child begins building a good repertoire of foods, around the age of 6 months, you can use this handy menu.

Keep in mind that during this age range, you should still feed breast milk or formula on demand — you don't want to create a completely structured meal plan for children this age. Their main nutritional component is breast milk or formula, so keep that in mind as you plan.

Day	Breakfast	Lunch	Dinner	Snacks
1	Milk; Rice Cereal	Milk; Green Bean Puree	Milk; Rice Cereal	N/A
2	Milk; Oatmeal Cereal	Milk; Summer Squash Puree	Milk; Oatmeal Cereal	N/A

(continued)

Day	Breakfast	Lunch	Dinner	Snacks
3	Milk; Barley Cereal	Milk; Fresh Carrot Puree	Milk; Barley Cereal	N/A
4	Milk; Mixed-Grain Cereal	Milk; Fresh Sweet Potato Puree	Milk; Mixed-Grain Cereal	N/A
5	Milk; Rice Cereal	Milk; Oatmeal and Potato Puree	Milk; Rice Cereal	N/A
6	Milk; Barley Cereal	Milk; Mixed Greens Puree; Creamy Corn Puree	Milk; Barley Cereal	N/A
7	Milk; Oatmeal Cereal	Milk; Potato Puree; Winter Squash Puree	Milk; Oatmeal Cereal	N/A

Meal Plans for 6- to 12-Month-Olds

When your infant passes the 6-month mark, you continue to introduce new foods with the ones that you're currently serving, but you also realize that your baby eats more with each passing day. This trend continues until your child is about 12 months old. This eating pattern makes your menu selections more important (so you balance nutrition at mealtime) and even complex (trying to please your baby) at times.

It's important to realize that this menu includes combination meals that can be served in a more chunky fashion when children are in the 10- to 12-month age range. So, if you're looking at this menu and your baby is still 6 months old, you'll need to make sure that you first slowly introduce some of these dishes and graduate up to some of the ones that are chunkier in nature.

Keep in mind that "milk" as shown in the menu refers to breast milk or formula. Children should not be given cow's milk until after 1 year of age. Remember that breast milk and formula are still a primary part of your child's diet. You can also serve water in a sippy cup.

Day	Breakfast	Lunch	Dinner	Snacks
1	Milk; Rice Cereal	Milk; Avocado and Squash Puree; Banana Peach Puree	Milk; Blueberry Steak Puree; Rice and Peach Puree	Yogurt
2	Milk; Oatmeal Cereal	Milk; Turkey and Peas; Cinnamon Pear Puree	Milk; Meat and Potato Puree; Green Bean Puree	Yogurt or fresh peaches
3	Milk; Barley Cereal	Milk; Apple Chicken and Veggies; Summer Squash Puree	Milk; Cod and Veggie Puree; Dried Apricot Puree	Cheese slice or yogurt
4	Milk; Mixed Grain Cereal	Milk; Chicken and Peaches; Fresh Sweet Potato Puree	Milk; Cheesy Alphabet Pasta; Broccoli and Cauliflower Puree; Yogurt Banana Puree	Any fruit puree
5	Milk; Rice Cereal	Milk; Ham and Veggie Casserole for Little Ones; Banana Peach Puree	Milk; Apple Chicken and Veggies; Sweet Potato Puree	Yogurt
6	Milk; Barley Cereal	Milk; Fish and Greens; Rice and Peaches	Milk; Blueberry Steak Puree; Avocado and Squash Puree	Cheese slice or yogurt
7	Milk; Oatmeal Cereal	Milk; Blueberry Steak Puree; Broccoli and Cauliflower Puree	Milk; Ham and Veggie Casserole for Little Ones; Cinnamon Pear Puree	Any fruit puree

Meal Plans for 12- to 18-Month-Olds

Your baby enjoys many different foods and recipes at this stage of growth. Use the following menu options to get your week off to the right start!

During this age range, your child transitions from breast milk or formula to whole cow's milk. You should give cow's milk, juice, or water in a sippy cup by this age. Limit juice to about 8 ounces daily, and don't offer too much in between meals because it will fill your child up and keep her from eating well. Instead, serve water if your little one is thirsty.

Day	Breakfast	Lunch	Dinner	Snack
1	Milk; Any hot cereal or Carrot Muffins	Milk; Corn and Chicken Soup; Veggie puree of choice	Milk; Apple-and-Turkey Meatballs; Veggie of choice; Fruit of choice	Ants on a Log
2	Milk; Any hot cereal or Banana Parfait	Milk; Avocado Turkey Sandwich; Yogurt Banana Puree	Milk; Tofu and Pasta Dinner; Veggie of choice; Fruit of choice	Muffin and Applesauce
3	Milk; Any hot cereal and yogurt	Milk; English Muffin Pizza; Veggie of choice	Milk; Red Beans and Rice; Veggie of choice	Orange Banana Smoothie
4	Milk; Any hot cereal or Breakfast Pizza	Milk; Cheesy Apple Toast; Avocado slices	Milk; Corn and Chicken Soup; Veggie of choice	Banana slices; Yogurt
5	Milk; Any hot cereal or Banana Parfait	Milk; Grilled Cheese with Tomato; Carrot Muffins	Milk; Bow-Tie Pasta with the Works; Veggie Fritters	Carrot Muffins
6	Milk; Any hot cereal or Carrot Muffins	Milk; Cheesy Orzo and Veggies; Veggie of choice	Milk; English Muffin Pizza; Veggie of choice; Fruit of choice	Yogurt; Cheese and crackers

Day	Breakfast	Lunch	Dinner	Snack
7	Milk; Any hot cereal or Breakfast Pizza	Milk; Bow-Tie Pasta with the Works; Veggie Fritters	Milk; Apple Chicken and Veggies; Fruit of choice	Yogurt; Fruit of choice

Meal Plans for 18-Month- to 2-Year-Olds

By this age, flexibility is your friend when you feed your toddler. Your tyke shows an interest in a wide variety of foods, but may experience picky spells as well.

Be careful of items that present choking hazards during this stage of the game, such as hard candy or whole grapes. Make sure that foods are cut into small, bite-size pieces. This sample menu helps give your child a varied and healthy diet.

Day	Breakfast	Lunch	Dinner	Snack
1	Milk; Cereal of choice; Fruit of choice	Milk; Chicken Quesadilla Triangles; Two veggies of choice	Milk; Mushroom Chicken; Two veggies of choice	Sweet Potato Cookies
2	Milk; Smiling Toast; Fruit of choice	Milk; Cornflake Chicken Bites; Two veggies of choice	Milk; Quick Fish Fillets; Stuffed Potatoes; Vanilla Apricot Squares	Fresh veggies with ranch dip
3	Milk; Zucchini Pear Pancakes; Sausage or ham	Milk; Fruit Salad; Green veggie of choice	Milk; Quick and Easy Turkey Chili; Two veggies of choice; Yogurt	Yogurt with fruit chunks

(continued)

Day	Breakfast	Lunch	Dinner	Snack
4	Milk; Cereal of choice; Fruit of choice	Milk; Vegetable Rounds; Lean meat of choice; Yogurt	Milk; Cheesy Rice and Broccoli; Lean meat of choice; Gummy Worm Mud	Cheese sticks; Crackers; Veggie of choice
5	Milk; Yogurt Delight; Toast	Milk; Cheesy Orzo and Veggies; Fruit of choice	Milk; Apple Chicken and Veggies; Fruit of choice	Yogurt; Fruit of choice
6	Milk; Smiling French Toast; Fruit of choice	Milk; Avocado Turkey Sandwich; Banana slices; Yogurt	Milk; Bow-Tie Pasta with the Works; Veggie Fritters	Fresh veggies with ranch dip
7	Milk; Toast; Fruit of choice	Milk; Corn and Chicken Soup; Carrot and celery sticks with ranch dip	Milk; Simple Mini-Meatballs; Veggie of choice; Fruit of choice	Ham and pickle slices

Meal Plans for 2-Year-Olds

When your kid reaches the age of 2, his menu options grow again. You can serve many foods from any of the previous menus, including most of the foods your family eats. Continue to watch out for choking hazards, and it's a good idea to reduce whole milk to 2 percent in order to lower the fat intake. Use this sample menu as a guide to give your child a balanced diet and to combat the picky eating behaviors that can exist during this age.

Day	Breakfast	Lunch	Dinner	Snack
1	Milk; Piggy in a Blanket; Fruit of choice	Tex-Mex Roll-ups; Veggie of choice	Cheesy Ham and Peas; Fruit of choice	Any shake or yogurt smoothie
2	Milk; Fruity Toast Sticks; Lean ham slices	Cheeseburger Tator Tot Bake; Veggie of choice	Crab Patties; Two veggies of choice (one green); Fruit of choice	Milk; Fresh veggies with ranch dip

Day	Breakfast	Lunch	Dinner	Snack
3	Milk; Cereal of choice; Fruit of choice	Stuffed Apple; Green veggie of choice	Corn Chowder with Beef; Fruit of choice; Yogurt	Milk; Stuffed Celery
4	Milk; Cheesy Eggs and Toast	Cheesy Orzo and Veggies; Veggie of choice	Pizza Meatloaf; Banana Split	Milk; Yogurt; Fruit of choice
5	Milk; Zucchini Pear Cakes; Sausage or ham	Quesadilla Triangles; Two veggies of choice	Mushroom Chicken; Two veggies of choice	Fruity Shake
6	Milk; Yogurt Delight; Toast	Pasta Veggie Casserole; Meat of choice; Fruit of choice	Apple-and-Turkey Meatballs; Veggie of choice; Fruit of choice	Milk; Frozen Peanut Butter Bananas on a Stick
7	Milk; Smiling Toast; Fruit of choice	Avocado Turkey Sandwich; Banana slices; Yogurt	Quick and Easy Turkey Chili; Two veggies of choice; Yogurt	Milk; Sweet Potato Cookies

Meal Plans for 3- to 5-Year-Olds

By age 3, you can essentially try a wide variety of recipe options. Your toddler will be eating with your family, and you can use the menu provided here as a guide, but also realize that you shouldn't fix an entirely different meal for your child.

Keep in mind that even at this age, toddlers will still need healthy snacks each day, possibly more than one, but you can use the menu here as a guide.

Day	Breakfast	Lunch	Dinner	Snack
1	Milk; Peanut Butter and Jelly Waffles	Southwestern Tortilla Roll-ups; Veggie of choice; Fruit of choice	Cheesy Ham and Peas; Fruit of choice	Milk; Fresh veggies with ranch dip

(continued)

Day	Breakfast	Lunch	Dinner	Snack
2	Peaches and Cheese Sandwich; Juice	Cheeseburger Soup; Veggie of choice	Meat and Veggie Kebabs; Two veggies of choice (one green); Fruit of choice	Milk; Stuffed Celery
3	Milk; Fruity Toast Sticks; Lean ham slices	Cheeseburger Tator Tot Bake; Veggie of choice	Cheesy Ham and Peas; Fruit of choice	Milk; Stuffed Apple
4	Milk; Cheesy Eggs and Toast	Tex-Mex Roll-ups; Veggie of choice	Chicken Lo Mein; Double Chocolate Éclair Pie	Any shake or yogurt smoothie
5	Milk; Zucchini Pear Pancakes; Sausage or ham	Veggie Burritos; Fruit of choice	Vegetable Chow Mein; Fruit of choice; Cupcake Family	Milk; Frozen Peanut Butter Bananas on a Stick
6	Milk; Blueberry Whole-Wheat Waffles; Lean sausage	Homemade Stuffed Corn Dogs; Veggie of choice	Hearty Meatballs; Veggie of choice; Fruit of choice	Milk; Sweet Potato Cookies
7	Milk; Zucchini Pear Pancakes; Sausage or ham	Pasta Veggie Casserole; Turkey breast; Fruit of choice	Vegetable Primavera; Green veggie of choice; Fruit of choice	Milk; Cheese sticks; Baby carrots

Meal Plans for Families with 3-Year-Olds and Up

This menu option includes a variety of recipes from this book, including meals for the family. This healthy and varied menu plan can help get you on the right track to feeding your toddler with your entire family.

Your toddler, at this age, can eat anything that the rest of the family is enjoying. You may just need to cut up the food into smaller pieces. Also, you'll see a snack suggestion in each menu. Keep in mind that your child needs healthy snacks each day, likely more than one, but you can use the menu suggestions to get you started.

Day	Breakfast	Lunch	Dinner	Snack
1	Milk; Sausage and Egg Casserole; Fruit of choice	Turkey Soft Tacos; Veggie of choice	Veggie and Chicken Calzone; Fruit of choice	Milk; Fruit Kebabs
2	Milk; Smiley Face Omelets	Chicken Apple Salad Sandwiches; Fruit of choice	Honey-Lime Grilled Chicken; Two veggies of choice (one green); Orange Dreamsicle	Milk; Fresh veggies with ranch dip
3	Milk; Cereal of choice; Fruit of choice	Cheesy Beef and Noodles; Green veggie of choice	Stuffed Burgers; Fruit of choice; Yogurt	Milk; Stuffed Celery
4	Milk; Smiling Toast; Fruit of choice	Cheesy Orzo and Veggies; Veggie of choice	Baked Ham; Two veggies of choice; Banana Cake	Milk; Yogurt Pineapple Pops
5	Milk; Snowflake Pancakes; Ham	Watercress and Carrot Burgers; Fresh veggies with ranch dip	Fresh Vegetable Soup; Fruit of choice; Blonde Brownies	Counting Fruit Salad
6	Yogurt Delight; Toast	Hearty Meatballs; Fruit of choice	Baked Ziti; Veggie of choice; Fruit of choice	Milk; Frozen Peanut Butter Bananas on a Stick
7	Milk; Holiday French Toast; Sausage or Ham	Pesto Veggie Soup; Banana slices; Yogurt	Surprise Family Meatloaf; Two veggies of choice	Milk; Crispy Rice and Peanut Butter Logs

Index

• *D* •

• E •

• F •

• N •

• O •

• P •

• T •

• U •

INESS, CAREERS & PERSONAL FINANCE

0-7645-5307-0

0-7645-5331-3 *†

Also available:

- Accounting For Dummies †
  0-7645-5314-3
- Business Plans Kit For Dummies †
  0-7645-5365-8
- Cover Letters For Dummies
  0-7645-5224-4
- Frugal Living For Dummies
  0-7645-5403-4
- Leadership For Dummies
  0-7645-5176-0
- Managing For Dummies
  0-7645-1771-6

- Marketing For Dummies
  0-7645-5600-2
- Personal Finance For Dummies *
  0-7645-2590-5
- Project Management For Dummies
  0-7645-5283-X
- Resumes For Dummies †
  0-7645-5471-9
- Selling For Dummies
  0-7645-5363-1
- Small Business Kit For Dummies *†
  0-7645-5093-4

ME & BUSINESS COMPUTER BASICS

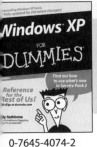

0-7645-4074-2

0-7645-3758-X

Also available:

- ACT! 6 For Dummies
  0-7645-2645-6
- iLife '04 All-in-One Desk Reference
  For Dummies
  0-7645-7347-0
- iPAQ For Dummies
  0-7645-6769-1
- Mac OS X Panther Timesaving
  Techniques For Dummies
  0-7645-5812-9
- Macs For Dummies
  0-7645-5656-8

- Microsoft Money 2004 For Dummies
  0-7645-4195-1
- Office 2003 All-in-One Desk Reference
  For Dummies
  0-7645-3883-7
- Outlook 2003 For Dummies
  0-7645-3759-8
- PCs For Dummies
  0-7645-4074-2
- TiVo For Dummies
  0-7645-6923-6
- Upgrading and Fixing PCs For Dummies
  0-7645-1665-5
- Windows XP Timesaving Techniques
  For Dummies
  0-7645-3748-2

OD, HOME, GARDEN, HOBBIES, MUSIC & PETS

0-7645-5295-3

0-7645-5232-5

Also available:

- Bass Guitar For Dummies
  0-7645-2487-9
- Diabetes Cookbook For Dummies
  0-7645-5230-9
- Gardening For Dummies *
  0-7645-5130-2
- Guitar For Dummies
  0-7645-5106-X
- Holiday Decorating For Dummies
  0-7645-2570-0
- Home Improvement All-in-One
  For Dummies
  0-7645-5680-0

- Knitting For Dummies
  0-7645-5395-X
- Piano For Dummies
  0-7645-5105-1
- Puppies For Dummies
  0-7645-5255-4
- Scrapbooking For Dummies
  0-7645-7208-3
- Senior Dogs For Dummies
  0-7645-5818-8
- Singing For Dummies
  0-7645-2475-5
- 30-Minute Meals For Dummies
  0-7645-2589-1

TERNET & DIGITAL MEDIA

0-7645-1664-7

0-7645-6924-4

Also available:

- 2005 Online Shopping Directory
  For Dummies
  0-7645-7495-7
- CD & DVD Recording For Dummies
  0-7645-5956-7
- eBay For Dummies
  0-7645-5654-1
- Fighting Spam For Dummies
  0-7645-5965-6
- Genealogy Online For Dummies
  0-7645-5964-8
- Google For Dummies
  0-7645-4420-9

- Home Recording For Musicians
  For Dummies
  0-7645-1634-5
- The Internet For Dummies
  0-7645-4173-0
- iPod & iTunes For Dummies
  0-7645-7772-7
- Preventing Identity Theft For Dummies
  0-7645-7336-5
- Pro Tools All-in-One Desk Reference
  For Dummies
  0-7645-5714-9
- Roxio Easy Media Creator For Dummies
  0-7645-7131-1

parate Canadian edition also available
parate U.K. edition also available

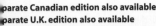

able wherever books are sold. For more information or to order direct: U.S. customers visit www.dummies.com or call 1-877-762-2974.
customers visit www.wileyeurope.com or call 0800 243407. Canadian customers visit www.wiley.ca or call 1-800-567-4797.

WILEY

SPORTS, FITNESS, PARENTING, RELIGION & SPIRITUALITY

0-7645-5146-9

0-7645-5418-2

Also available:
- Adoption For Dummies
  0-7645-5488-3
- Basketball For Dummies
  0-7645-5248-1
- The Bible For Dummies
  0-7645-5296-1
- Buddhism For Dummies
  0-7645-5359-3
- Catholicism For Dummies
  0-7645-5391-7
- Hockey For Dummies
  0-7645-5228-7

- Judaism For Dummies
  0-7645-5299-6
- Martial Arts For Dummies
  0-7645-5358-5
- Pilates For Dummies
  0-7645-5397-6
- Religion For Dummies
  0-7645-5264-3
- Teaching Kids to Read For Dummie
  0-7645-4043-2
- Weight Training For Dummies
  0-7645-5168-X
- Yoga For Dummies
  0-7645-5117-5

TRAVEL

0-7645-5438-7

0-7645-5453-0

Also available:
- Alaska For Dummies
  0-7645-1761-9
- Arizona For Dummies
  0-7645-6938-4
- Cancún and the Yucatán For Dummies
  0-7645-2437-2
- Cruise Vacations For Dummies
  0-7645-6941-4
- Europe For Dummies
  0-7645-5456-5
- Ireland For Dummies
  0-7645-5455-7

- Las Vegas For Dummies
  0-7645-5448-4
- London For Dummies
  0-7645-4277-X
- New York City For Dummies
  0-7645-6945-7
- Paris For Dummies
  0-7645-5494-8
- RV Vacations For Dummies
  0-7645-5443-3
- Walt Disney World & Orlando For Dumr
  0-7645-6943-0

GRAPHICS, DESIGN & WEB DEVELOPMENT

0-7645-4345-8

0-7645-5589-8

Also available:
- Adobe Acrobat 6 PDF For Dummies
  0-7645-3760-1
- Building a Web Site For Dummies
  0-7645-7144-3
- Dreamweaver MX 2004 For Dummies
  0-7645-4342-3
- FrontPage 2003 For Dummies
  0-7645-3882-9
- HTML 4 For Dummies
  0-7645-1995-6
- Illustrator CS For Dummies
  0-7645-4084-X

- Macromedia Flash MX 2004 For Dumr
  0-7645-4358-X
- Photoshop 7 All-in-One Desk
  Reference For Dummies
  0-7645-1667-1
- Photoshop CS Timesaving Techniqu
  For Dummies
  0-7645-6782-9
- PHP 5 For Dummies
  0-7645-4166-8
- PowerPoint 2003 For Dummies
  0-7645-3908-6
- QuarkXPress 6 For Dummies
  0-7645-2593-X

NETWORKING, SECURITY, PROGRAMMING & DATABASES

0-7645-6852-3

0-7645-5784-X

Also available:
- A+ Certification For Dummies
  0-7645-4187-0
- Access 2003 All-in-One Desk
  Reference For Dummies
  0-7645-3988-4
- Beginning Programming For Dummies
  0-7645-4997-9
- C For Dummies
  0-7645-7068-4
- Firewalls For Dummies
  0-7645-4048-3
- Home Networking For Dummies
  0-7645-42796

- Network Security For Dummies
  0-7645-1679-5
- Networking For Dummies
  0-7645-1677-9
- TCP/IP For Dummies
  0-7645-1760-0
- VBA For Dummies
  0-7645-3989-2
- Wireless All In-One Desk Reference
  For Dummies
  0-7645-7496-5
- Wireless Home Networking For Dumr
  0-7645-3910-8